# THE
# NASCENT MIND
## OF
# SHELLEY

BY

## A. M. D. HUGHES

EMERITUS PROFESSOR OF ENGLISH LITERATURE
IN THE UNIVERSITY OF BIRMINGHAM

## OXFORD
## AT THE CLARENDON PRESS

*Oxford University Press, Ely House, London W. 1*

GLASGOW NEW YORK TORONTO MELBOURNE WELLINGTON
CAPE TOWN SALISBURY IBADAN NAIROBI DAR ES SALAAM LUSAKA ADDIS ABABA
BOMBAY CALCUTTA MADRAS KARACHI LAHORE DACCA
KUALA LUMPUR SINGAPORE HONG KONG TOKYO

FIRST PUBLISHED 1947
REPRINTED LITHOGRAPHICALLY IN GREAT BRITAIN
FROM CORRECTED SHEETS OF THE FIRST EDITION
AT THE UNIVERSITY PRESS, OXFORD
BY VIVIAN RIDLER
PRINTER TO THE UNIVERSITY
1971

# PREFACE

THIS book has been written in order to demonstrate the high degree of continuity in Shelley's main ideas and the relevance to his poetry of their worth and weight. For this purpose I have given a full account of the earliest writings in prose and verse to the year 1814 and focused the argument on the 'philosophical poem' of *Queen Mab,* the garner of his cruder speculations and the first sketch of his indeterminate theology. And since in him the boy or man was extraordinarily close to the artist and the seeker for truth, it seemed necessary to tell the story of his life to the spring of 1813, when the poem was sent to the press and a period of his personal evolution distinctly ends. For I could not talk of that chapter of his thinking without some talk of him, and could not talk of him without his history. I have tried, however, to tell the tale so as to give the background of the novels, pamphlets, or poems, and to make out the moral essence, not attempting to put in all the known facts. The narrative, therefore, does not pretend to add to our historical knowledge or to rest on any research deeper than the printed sources. Much has been written lately on Shelley's life and the lives of his friends; letters and diaries, published for the first time in the last few years, have afforded us new light; and we have the advantage of the massive biographies by Professor W. E. Peck and Professor Newman Ivy White. Moreover, the discussion and interpretation of the poems and their contents has come on fuller and faster. My debts are many, and I have acknowledged them in particular as they occurred. But I do not claim to have read all the books on Shelley, and have had to content myself with the primary documents and a certain number of the commentaries and aids. One obligation anyone writing on my subject is likely to incur. The philosophical data are exhaustively assembled and thoroughly canvassed by Professor Ellsworth Barnard in *Shelley's Religion,* University of Minnesota Press, 1937. Mr. Edmund Blunden's recent biography of the poet came out after my work had gone to the press, and to my regret I have not had the use of it.

This work was pursued under the encouragement of Ernest de Sélincourt, whose generous nature and liberal and incisive

mind how many students of English Literature have had reason
to bless! My cordial thanks are due for counsel and advice to
two other of my friends and colleagues in the Department of
English at Birmingham, Mrs. Isabel Bisson and Mr. J. F.
Waterhouse; to Miss Margaret Wharam and Dr. Ernst Ruhm
for their services to me as readers; and to Mrs. Anneliese
Braun for indispensable help long and unstintedly given.
Finally, I am especially grateful to Nirna Hughes for the
unfailing kindness without which this undertaking could not
have been carried to an end.

A. M. D. H.

# CONTENTS

# I
## PARENTAGE AND HOME
### 1. Bysshe Shelley

THE Shelleys have been important people in Sussex and the neighbouring counties since they came over with the Conqueror, and some few are named in history, most of them on hard enterprises and losing sides. One was attainted 'for endeavouring to set up King Richard II'; another for his share in a Catholic conspiracy under Elizabeth; a third, Sir Richard Shelley, the last Grand Prior of the English Hospitallers, was famous for his generous ardour in the Turkish wars, and after Elizabeth's accession lived and died a Catholic exile in Venice. On the other hand Fortune dealt kindly with Sir William, the father of the Hospitaller, a strenuous judge of Common Pleas under Henry VIII. From him descended the Shelleys of Michelgrove in Sussex, and from his younger brother, Edward, the Shelleys seated originally at Worminghurst. Of these two lines William's was for more than two centuries a good deal the higher in the social scale, and attained a baronetcy when the order was created in 1611. Edward's posterity in the meantime consisted of undistinguished gentlefolks until Bysshe Shelley raised the family to its local eminence. Bysshe had been the maiden name of the wife of John Shelley, who acquired by his marriage the property of Fen Place, Worth, Sussex, and died in 1739. This John had a younger son Timothy (1700–70), who set up as a merchant in Newark, New Jersey, and married Johanna Plum, a widow of New York. His elder brothers having died, Timothy returned to England in the year 1739, and inherited his father's property, to which was added, a few years later, under the will of an uncle, the manor of Field Place in the parish of Warnham, near Horsham. He brought with him from America two sons: John, the elder, and the aforementioned Bysshe, who was born in 1731,[1] and who owed his

---

[1] Mr. Ingpen points out that he cannot have practised, as Medwin avers, in the capacity of a quack doctor in America, having left that country at the age of eight. But something about a medical practice persisted in the popular talk or legend of him; the fact being only that he advanced money to a quack doctor James Graham, famous for his 'Temple of Health', his 'earth-baths', of which Hogg supplies an amusing account (ch. xlv), and his 'celestial beds'. Graham had driven his trade at one time in America.

B

success in a large measure to a handsome presence and engaging manners. Before Bysshe was ten years old a not inconsiderable property in land and money was bequeathed to him by his grandparents; and at the age of twenty-one he abducted and married Catherine Michell, a girl of sixteen, daughter and heiress of a wealthy clergyman, Theobald Michell of Horsham. This lady died in 1760, leaving him a son, Timothy, born in 1753, and two daughters. Nine years later he again eloped with an heiress, Elizabeth Jane Sidney, a daughter of William Perry of Penshurst, and a descendant on her mother's side of a younger brother of Sir Philip Sidney. The first son of this second marriage, Sir John Shelley Sidney of Penshurst, was made a baronet in 1818. Finally, in 1790, on the death of his elder brother, the fortunate Bysshe inherited the family estates. In the following year he made over the manor of Field Place to his eldest son Timothy, upon Timothy's marriage with Elizabeth, daughter of Charles Pilfold, of Effingham in Surrey; of which union six children survived infancy, who were born at the manor house of Field Place in the order following: Percy Bysshe, on 4 August 1792; then four girls, Elizabeth, Mary, Hellen, Margaret, at intervals of some two or three years; and in 1806 a younger son, John.

The architect of fortune coveted for his family every appurtenance of a high position. He cultivated good relations with Charles, Duke of Norfolk (Duke from 1786 to 1815), who had turned Protestant and Whig, and in whom a certain interest in antiquity and art and an outspoken liberalism in opinion were some amends for his uncouth manners and his obscene profligacy. This nobleman, an 'inveterate trafficker' in political goods, procured the baronetcy for his neighbour, and received in return the unswerving subservience of Timothy Shelley in his seat in Parliament for the Rape of Bramber. One more of the marks and means of eminence the Shelleys wanted—a great house—and that too was at a vast expense provided by the erection of Goring Castle. Yet Sir Bysshe, with all his riches and his 'noble and aristocratic bearing', made no attempt at a grand career in his own person. He was perhaps too tired with laying the ground to begin upon the game, and lapsed into a solitary and a crank. Always a man ill to live with, who bullied his wives and drove his daughters from home, he spent his last twenty or thirty years attended by one servant in a small house 'where all was mean and beggarly', in the centre of Horsham, and beguiled the time by visiting 'the taproom of a low inn', not, it would seem, to drink with the company, but to 'argue on politics'. His son Timothy, at sight of whom he would swear vehemently, received day by day from some source or other a report of his health, and 'began to think his father was immortal'. When death came at last, in January 1815, bank-notes to the value of £13,000 were found in the dead man's books, in the folds of his sofa, and in the lining of his dressing-gown. There was some likeness to its builder in the empty castle at Goring, with the wilfulness of its clashing styles, its sumptuous plan unfinished, and all its chambers in decay. To his grandson, who seldom encountered him, the strange old man could be even kindly; he smiled on the juvenile verses 'by Victor and Cazire' and—it would seem—paid the printer; and he listened calmly and politely, and probably with a secret relish, to the heresies of the young enthusiast, until they were flaunted in the world's eyes. When, however, the words bore fruit in the boy's disgrace at Oxford and the freak of his first marriage, Sir Bysshe, still calm and polite, stood rigidly on authority; and an antipathy many years old surges up in a letter from Shelley to Miss Hitchener in January 1812: 'He' (Sir Bysshe), writes the author of *The Necessity of Atheism*, 'is a complete atheist, and builds all his hopes on annihilation. He is a bad man. I never had respect for him. I always regarded him as a curse upon Society.'

## 2. FATHER AND MOTHER

Timothy Shelley was nearly forty when he married. He was a handsome man, 'slight of figure, tall, very fair, with the blue Shelley eyes', but otherwise less presentable. He had studied the seigneurial accomplishments at University College, Oxford, on the Grand Tour, and in the pages of Lord Chesterfield; but his mind, when he tried to think, and his grammar, when he tried to write, were in equal disarray, and he had brought back from his travels no more than 'a smattering of French, a bad picture of Vesuvius, and a certain air, miscalled that of the old school, which he could put off and on'. He respected education as useful and decorative to a gentleman, but ideas were an alien element, into which, however, he would sometimes plunge to his sore distress. Himself an amateur theologian of a liberal tendency, he shrank from an outright scepticism as a form of depravity, and was careful to make his household go to church, and occasionally to go himself. He told his son he 'would never pardon a *mésalliance*, but would maintain for him as many natural children as he chose to get'. In short, a 'pillar of society'. As a Parliamentary candidate for Horsham he was not too good for some malpractices of the usual kind, but he caused his party at Westminster not a moment's anxiety, sensible as he was that 'the exalted mind of the Duke of Norfolk protected him with the world'. The obituary in the *Gentleman's Magazine* commended him as a 'practical agriculturist and a friend to the labouring poor'. 'The whole House of Commons', he informed Hogg over a bottle, 'respected him, and the Speaker in particular had declared they could not get on without him.' To all this must be added inconsequent loquacity, with much laughing and swearing, or scolding and the shedding of tears; a propensity to dictation; and a hasty temper, especially in the fits of his gout, when, if Medwin may be credited, he would throw the nearest thing at whoever annoyed him.

With these strident failings he is, and was, easy to misjudge. He had a poor heart, but not a bad one. It is true, as the sequel will show, that in the quarrel with his son he was stubborn, resentful, stupid, frightened, and came in the end to deal with the young man as a stranger, and harden against him living and dead. Yet his other children and his servants loved him well; and it is hard to resist Hogg's opinion that 'if he had been taken the right way'—and not sometimes a way so amazingly wrong—'things might have gone better'. He was sometimes genially simple and genuinely kind, and for several years he kept his son's affection. One of his sisters remembered Bysshe, at the age of 'about fourteen', watching with a dog-like solicitude at the door of the room where the Squire was lying ill. Four years afterwards, however, all that warm attachment was in default. 'I was required to love,' wrote Shelley to Godwin, 'because it was *my duty* to love. It is scarcely necessary to remark that coercion obviated its own intention.' It all came cumulatively, no doubt, but we learn of one occurrence that for years afterwards burned in the sufferer's memory. Shelley used to tell his friends that once, on returning home from school, he contracted a fever, and, as he learnt from one of the servants, who were all devoted to him, the Squire, alarmed by the nervous disorder, would have sent him to a madhouse, had not his friend at Windsor, the king's physician, James Lind, hastened to his side at a secret summons, and prevented the calamity. After that, as we learn from Peacock, 'the idea that his father was continually on the watch for a pretext to lock him up haunted him'; and it was some intimation of that danger—or so he would aver—that moved him from time to time to change his residence or go abroad. The story of the fever has been put down, but on insufficient grounds,[1] to ungovernable fantasy; and fantasy, whether or no it created that looming madhouse, certainly played a large part in the tragedy of father and son, for each had more than a grain of it. As time went on, each made a bogy of the other; and the younger man's bogy would sometimes take the appearance of a guy.[2]

Of Elizabeth Pilfold, by her maiden name, the record is singularly small, and she played in the drama of her son's life a minor and unavailing part. She came to Field Place a young woman—much younger than her husband—with gifts of rare beauty and lively intelligence, from a home equally pervaded by the tastes and notions of her class. 'She had been brought up', writes Medwin, 'by her aunt, Lady Ferdinand Pool, the wife of the well-known father of the turf, and owner of the celebrated "Waxy" and "Mealy".' 'A clever woman', writes one who evidently knew her, 'and though of all persons most unpoetical, possessed of strong masculine sense and a keen observation of character which might have made her a Madame de Sévigné or a Lady Wortley-Montagu, for she wrote admirable

---

[1] It is given in *Shelley Memorials*, pp. 9, 10. Peacock and Hogg are doubtful of the story of the fever and Lind's intervention, but Dowden believes it. Shelley repeated it to Polidori in the summer of 1816.

[2] Hogg relates that old Etonians, visiting Shelley at Oxford, would entreat him to 'curse his father', as he had been in the habit of doing at school; and that Shelley, after some demur, would recite a malediction of much force and fire. He explained to Hogg that he was partly imitating Sir Bysshe, who frequently discharged those expressions at his son. No more is to be gathered from this story than that the boy's artistic relish sometimes had the better of his good feeling. He once declared that memories of his own life were woven into *Rosalind and Helen*, but we must not conclude, with Medwin, that Rosalind's cruel husband is a portrait of Timothy Shelley.

letters; but judging of men and things by the narrow circle in which she moved, she was as little capable of understanding Shelley as a peasant would be of comprehending Berkeley.' But she did sometimes attain to 'liberality' in her son's eyes by bold theological heresies which she would not for the world have openly avowed. As time went on, her hard prudential mind and the fact that, not being with him, she was against him diminished his affection for her; nor had she redeeming graces on the moral side. On the contrary, he could entertain doubts —with how much reason there is no determining—on one occasion whether she were honest, and on another whether she were chaste.[1] Yet affection there had been, and on both sides, and it rode out the trouble over his 'atheism' and the worse trouble over his marriage. When Bysshe was banished from his home she kept touch, sent him necessaries and news, and once—in June 1814—received him in his father's absence at Field Place. But a few weeks after that date the breach with his first wife and the union with Mary Godwin deeply offended her[2] and, so far as is known, she never saw or wrote to him again. No doubt she acted not entirely of her free will, and still at times 'yearned for him'[3] as before. But by that time, as is most likely, his affection for her was dead or dying of inanition.

### 3. THE CHILD AT FIELD PLACE.

Shelley's home[4] was in a rolling country of woods, meadows, and cornfields in the north-west corner of the county, with Hindhead in view to the west, and the Downs faintly visible to the south. The village of Warnham lay grey and quiet about a mile north-westwards on the Horsham road, the quaintly gabled cottages grouping around the church, the square-towered church with its tombs and monuments of Shelleys and

---

[1] He told Medwin that on a later visit to Field Place she had tried 'with hypocritical caresses' to lead him into signing a legal deed the content of which she hid from him. An account is given below (pp. 110, 111) of the scandal that touched her honour as a wife, and that he believed or half believed for a time at least.

[2] Letter from Whitton to Amory, Shelley's solicitor, 5 Jan. 1815: 'His presence [at Field Place] will, as I understand, be most painful to Mrs. S.' (Ingpen, p. 449. Kegan Paul.)

[3] The expression is used of her feeling for her son in Captain Kennedy's description of Shelley's last visit to Field Place, Dowden, i. 388.

[4] See 'Notes on Shelley's Birthplace', by William Hale White, *MacMillan's Magazine*, March 1879.

Michells and Pilfolds.[1] Three miles to the south came Horsham
~~itself a~~ small market town with old multiform houses, a wide
e comely church with the tall spire, and the
wing by. Here the Shelleys were great people,
she, and later Sir Timothy and his Lady laid
it. The white Georgian mansion of Field Place,
de-fronted, with pillared portico, lay back from
an avenue leading down to it and a common in
fr̲      s flanked and backed by trees and coppices, and
___ _y lay what remained of the Forest of St. Leonard, with
s wide-flung birch and beech, the legendary home of a head-
ess spectre and a Great Snake. Peaceful and beautiful as it all
was, Shelley was rather a changeling—a happy changeling—
in that place. A wild and wonder-loving boy, a *magister ludorum*
to his attendant sisters, fond of nothing so much as to thrill
them with his fancies and tales, fond of his pony and the open
air, and welcome to high and low with his gamesomeness and
his charm, he was never like anyone else. When he grew older
his mother would send him out to learn the mystery of angling
and shooting, but he read his book, while the gamekeeper
carried on and gave in the bag as fallen to Master Bysshe. His
solitary walks under moon and stars were spied upon with much
mistrust. He might listen to the conversation of his elders on
shooting and hunting, on crops or herds or market prices, on
Petty Sessions or the Ministry or the House, but to all these
things he was lamentably cold. In his twelfth year the pulse of
the countryside beat high at the peril of a French invasion, and
men arming and drilling, and the watch along the Downs, but
the name of Nelson had no hold upon him. The land about
him was as English as it could be, warm and homely, little rivers,
little hills; but he became the poet of

> Islanded seas, blue mountains, mighty streams,
> Dim tracts and vast,

peopled by the vivid fauna of the East. The mind is its own
place, and, faced with a world not all to its desire, can build
itself another, and of the beauty set before it will take and
transfigure as much as it loves best, and a little goes a long way.

---

[1] Among them the tomb of the first Timothy Shelley, the poet's great-grand-
father, and his American wife.

Not that he had any sense of foreignness. He was not of a kind to lose the memory of a place so fair and life so boon to him. He once wrote of the 'wrecks of childhood's sunny dream' that

> Weigh on the heart like that remorse
> Which altered friendship leaves.

For he had clinging affections, unseated and uptorn though they so often were.

## II

## AT SCHOOL: THE ORDEAL

### 1. SION HOUSE, BRENTFORD

SHELLEY received his first schooling at the age of six from the Rev. Evan Edwards, the Vicar of Warnham. In 1802, at the age of ten, he was sent to Sion House at Brentford, a private seminary attended for the most part by sons of London tradesmen and by other boys who were higher in the social scale. In this large gloomy brick building some sixty pupils were half starved,[1] it would seem, and taught Latin and Greek by Dr. Greenlaw, 'a choleric Scotch divine of a sanguinary complexion', who helped his lessons on with severe castigations and salacious pleasantries. He was not a bad scholar, and Shelley profited by him in the dead languages, which he seemed to learn by intuition. It was perhaps in this period that, as Hellen Shelley remembered, 'he used at my father's bidding to repeat long Latin quotations', and in doing so 'would act, and the expression of his face and movement of his arms are distinct recollections, though the subject of his declamation was a sealed book to his infant hearers'. Moreover, the doctor was sufficiently progressive for those days to engage the popular lecturer, Adam Walker, to lecture on the wonders of Nature, and to exhibit his 'empyreal stove', his 'eidouranion, or transparent orrery', and his solar microscope.[2]

Adam Walker, a self-taught man with a lively talent for his business, was the first mover of the eager interest in natural science that went to Shelley's making, and the first intelligencer of the laws that inspired him with his radiant myth of *The Cloud*, for instance, or of the celestial concert in the ecstasy of *Prometheus Unbound*. He gave his discourses and demonstrations from time to time at Westminster and at Eton and more or less repeated them at other places. We have an account of the course in a printed syllabus of 86 pages.[3] It comprised

---

[1] So Medwin makes out. Sir John Rennie, another contemporary at the school, says in his *Autobiography* (1875) that the boys were 'well fed and taken care of by the Doctor's excellent wife'.

[2] Dowden, i. 17, 18.

[3] Besides the syllabus above referred to, from which White has quoted, Walker

Magnetism, Mechanics, Chemistry, 'Pneumatics' or 'the Principles of the Air', Fortification, Optics, the Use of the Globes,
Astronomy. It was speculative and astonishing and Shelley
was fascinated. He gazed through the microscope at 'mites in
cheese and the wing of a fly', and thrilled to the discourse on
the heavens—system after system; stars 'so distant that their
light has not reached the Earth since creation'; 30,000 stars
invisible to the naked eye; seas and hills and continents in those
heavenly bodies, and 'who can doubt that they are inhabited?'
Who could doubt, he put it to his cousin Medwin, who was at
Sion House with him, that those inhabitants 'were a higher
race than ours', and that we shall in future go through 'a series
of stages in other planets', till we become 'more Gods than men'?
But in electricity and chemistry the wonders could be operated.
Walker had a henchman who knew enough to put together
small electrical machines, and turned a pretty penny by selling
them to the auditors. Shelley purchased some of this gear in
later years at Eton; and it is likely that he did so at Brentford, and that it was in these earlier school holidays at Field
Place that the little ring of sisters would wait with a wire in their
hands and anxious hearts for the affrighting shock. It was
certainly at this time that Shelley began with his chemical
messes and mischances. He blew up the palings of the school
boundary; he blew the lid from his desk; and he poisoned
Greenlaw's pigs.[1]

There was another way to supply his hunger for marvel and

published in 1799 *A System of Familiar Philosophy in Twelve Lectures*, some 570 pages
in quarto, profusely illustrated with plans, figures, and diagrams. It covers the
same big field as the Syllabus in the same number of lectures, though some titles
are different. The presentation seems to be more sober than that of the course for
schools, though there is plenty of animation, including directions for 'entertaining
experiments' and 'magnetic amusements'. The reader is sure to come now and
then on something to remind him of a sentence or two in Shelley. 'Lewenhoeck
discovered more living animalculae in the milt of one cod-fish than there are men,
women, and children on the surface of the Earth.' Shelley speaks of love and hate
in the atom. Walker seems to regret that 'in the present order and fitness of things
an antagonist principle [repulsion] should regulate the cohesive tendency'. He
quotes Lavoisier: 'Organisation, sensation, spontaneous motion exist only in places
exposed to the light. A benevolent God, by producing light, has spread organisation, sensation, and thought over the surface of the Earth.' In these half-poetical
notes and stimulations lay the main value of the lectures or the book, if he read it,
for Shelley. Walker is a reverential deist in the Newtonian sense.

[1] White, i. 21, and note, i. 565, quoting the *Ealing Gazette* for 15 July 1922,
letter of W. H. Woolen. The poisoning was a tradition in the Greenlaw family.

mystery and power. He became an addict to the romances of
Ann Radcliffe and M. G. Lewis and their tribe, available in a
Brentford library. And among romances of a milder kind he
read the only one that in the eighteenth century could vie with
*Robinson Crusoe* and *Gulliver's Travels* in the same order of fancy—
*Peter Wilkins*, of whose author, Richard Paltock, little is known.
It is the story of a sailor who sails in a Portuguese vessel from the
coast of Africa, till a great storm wedges it in the rocks of an
unknown island, and he the sole survivor of the crew; of this
man P. W. (like the man in *Alastor*) carried in a boat on an
underground torrent to an inland lake; of winged men and
women, Glums and Gauries, inhabiting the island, and the
boys and girls 'chasing and pursuing one another, sometimes
soaring to an extravagant height, and then shooting down
again, till they even touch the trees'; of Youarkee, with injured
wings, tumbling through the roof of Peter's cave, 'a lovely
woman', as Leigh Hunt has put it, 'in front of an ethereal shell
and wafted about like a Venus', 'the sweetest creature that is
found in books'; of Peter married to Youarkee, and her economy
in the cave and her flying for the strange groceries in the ship;
of Peter welcomed by the Glums, and of his flying chair, roped
to the bodies of a team of them; and how he is declared the
promised Deliverer in their political troubles, and becomes a
dictator, a conqueror, a peace-maker, a lawgiver, instituting
arts and cultures, liberating slaves, breaking idols, and pro-
claiming the true God; and how, when Youarkee is dead, the
heartsick exile sets out on the air for England, and is taken up
at sea. First published in 1751, *Peter Wilkins* rose into fame in
the romantic era, and was dearly prized by Coleridge, by
Charles Lamb, by Leigh Hunt, and, very naturally, by Southey.
And Shelley, in or about his twelfth year, was its rapt admirer.[1]
It was the sort of thing that would grow upon him. For it compounded the simples of moral or religious reasoning, social
amendment, and wild romance, and it threw in a tender
humanity and a happy tone.

If we add to these entertainments a fervid friendship with
one of his schoolfellows unnamed,[2] that would be for Shelley
the sum of things enjoyable at Sion House. For the rest, he

[1] Medwin, revised *Life*, p. 24.
[2] Described in the *Essay on Friendship* (1821), quoted *infra*, p. 19.

found it, as Medwin tells us, 'a perfect hell', for to the vulgar herd this strange and dreamy being, unapt at sport, gentle, but under provocation 'of a violent and extremely excitable temper', 'like a girl in boy's clothes fighting with open hands', was a present from the god of fun. The only help was to remove himself in the spirit, as he paced deep in thought by the wall of the playground, or in school hours watched the clouds and birds, or 'scrawled on his school-books rude drawings of firs and cedars in memory of those on the lawn of his native home'. Here he tasted for the first time what the world is, and in the circle of his baiters or 'rolling on the floor when flogged, not from the pain but from a sense of the indignity', paid in compound suffering the scot and lot of his twice-born kind.

## 2. Eton[1]

Sydney Smith, writing on English Public Schools in the year 1809, produced an impressive list of eminent men who were not educated in those places, and ascribed the relative unfruitfulness of the public school in the higher abilities to the facts that in them the intercourse of teacher and taught went no farther than the hours in school and that the boys among themselves were all the victims or the perpetrators of cruelties and humiliations more fit for predestinated menials than for gentlemen's sons. The last of these censures certainly held good of Eton College for a long period and in a high degree. The Great Commoner once declared that he 'scarcely observed a boy who was not cowed for life at Eton', and concluded that 'a public school might suit a boy of turbulent and forward disposition, but would not do where there was any gentleness'. On the other hand, the Etonians of Shelley's day were or might have been better guided in their studies and more controlled in their daily lives than the customs in other and similar institutions, as a rule, allowed. There were then on the school list some 30 Collegers, members of the foundation, who lodged and boarded within the gate, and wore a distinctive dress, and some 470 Oppidans, so called because they lived in the town of Eton. And all Oppidans were attached at the choice of their parents

---

[1] In this section I have drawn in the main on *A History of Eton College 1440–1910*, by Sir H. C. Maxwell Lyte, 4th edition, 1911.

to one or other of the Assistant Masters, who gave them supplementary teaching in special classes—or 'private business', as it was called. A still closer contact was made possible for a few boys by a custom that came in as early as the seventeen-eighties. Till then all the Oppidans lodged and boarded in houses in the town maintained by hosts or 'domines', or hostesses or 'dames'. In 1766 there were 13 of these houses to 450 boarders. Then the tutors took to receiving a small number of their special pupils—less than ten, as a rule—in their own homes; with great advantage to the boarders, who were more strictly disciplined than in the ordinary hostels. Each had a bedroom to himself, dined on better fare in his tutor's dining-room, and 'lived as a gentleman should'.

Shelley entered the College in the autumn of 1804, and left it in the summer of 1810, more than five of these years falling in the easy headmastership of Joseph Goodall, and the last two terms in the iron reign of John Keate; and his tutor was George Bethell. At first he lived in a small house, accommodating but a few boarders, under its 'domine' Hexter, the teacher of writing and arithmetic in the Lower School. Later on the boy was received as a boarder in Bethell's own house, and might here have reaped all the benefits of the tutorial system had his tutor been worthy of him. But 'big blustering Bethell', ruddy, good-natured, ponderous, nay, dense, could only be for a nature like Shelley's null and void. Of the Assistant Masters in Shelley's time there were at least two with life and mind in them: John Bird Sumner, afterwards Archbishop of Canterbury, a pious spirit and a liberal mind, and the Bohemian Ben Drury, frequenter of theatres and prize-rings, who inspired his favourite pupils with his own love of drama, and would take them to London to see with him the great actors and the great plays. But of any kindness between Shelley and either of these there is no remembrance. Nor, until in his last year he rose to the Sixth, the *élite* of twenty in the Headmaster's especial charge, would it matter much to him, excepting the occasions of chastisement, whether the supreme authority were Goodall or Keate—Goodall, big, stately, urbane, a mild disciplinarian and a kindly nurse of taste and talent; Keate, as he lives in Kinglake's brilliant description,[1] concentrating in a body not

[1] *Eothen*, ch. xliii.

much higher than five feet 'the pluck of ten battalions', and reinforcing the terror of his rod with a truculent manner and a quacking voice, a sound and severe scholar, and a man, as the historian of the School has put it, 'thoroughly righthearted in the depth of his nature'. It did not matter much; for out of school the great personage was inaccessible, and in school was in sole charge of the Fifth, or an upper section of the Fifth, and Sixth, numbering together in Keate's last years 190 souls, so that not even he was always able to subdue the hubbub or stifle the choruses and songs, or at any time able to note and nurse the single member of the great assembly.

Shelley's worst grievance, however, was not about the authorities, and what they did or failed to do, although they loved him not and twice for unknown reasons expelled or thought of expelling him, and then relented at his father's prayer.[1] We do not hear that he nursed a memory of the whipping-post, which it is hardly possible he escaped. But he took an irrecoverable hurt from the hand of his fellows. Here were the young 'barbarians' with their 'gigs and tandems, cricket, boating, beagles, racings, rows', and their 'expeditions against bargemen'. There was poaching by night in Windsor Park. And there were amusements of the crueller kinds: 'Bull-baiting' went on with vigour in Bachelor's Acre at the time of Windsor Fair, and badger-baits, dog-fights, and cat and duck hunts were organized by the 'cads' or purveyors of the neighbourhood for the special benefit of the Eton boys. It was a good thing for the moral tone of the School when in 1829 the 'cads', the worst possible companions for the sons of gentlemen, were expelled from their daily resort in Long Walk. Worse examples of the prevailing brutality were afforded by the stand-up fights. James Milne Gaskell writes to his parents on 1 March 1824:

'A most awful and horrible warning not to fight in the playing-fields happened last night. Owing to Wood (a boy at Hawtrey's) having bullied Ashley minimus, one of Lord Shaftesbury's sons, who was above him in the school, but considerably inferior both in size and strength, the latter offered to fight him in the playing fields, a challenge which he immediately accepted, and they actually fought for two hours and a quarter. As Ashley, who fought most bravely, naturally became weak, he drank half a

[1] To Godwin, 10 Jan. 1812.

pint of brandy, which was too much for him, and after renewing the fight for some time afterwards, he fainted and died in consequence of the brandy and the blows on his temples at 10 o'clock in the evening. Wood also was very much hurt: he is now dangerously ill and was taken home this morning at half past nine.'[1]

Is it to be wondered at that Shelley ran the gauntlet? He appears in the recollections of William Henry Merle[2] as one of the three fags at Hexter's, having ceased to resist that odious servitude, if, as Mary Shelley has asserted, he at one time did. Fagging, however, was a fraction of his miseries and came to an end as soon as he had risen to the Fifth. But he never ceased to sit in the stocks. It might be thought that, as he grew older and bigger, he would be less and less brutally used, but Merle tells us he was in that respect exceptional and, while often formidable to the single assailant, continued, in his later as in his earlier days, the jest and sport of the common rout. He was innocent, excitable, recluse. He wore no hat and neglected his shoelaces. He was 'no good at games', would 'go out duck-spearing and spear his own legs', and in his fight with Sir Thomas Styles had begun with heroic snatches from Homer, and ended by taking to his heels. And his pursuits were outlandish. Fascinated a second time by the lectures of Adam Walker (a regular visitant at Eton), he threw himself, as at Sion House, into fearsome operations, and turned his room to an evil-smelling stithy. His powders and liquids, his fire-balloons, his electric battery, the solar microscope, the steam-engine, the brass cannon bought in Windsor, the exploded tree in the South Meadow, and George Bethell flung against the wall, and Hexter on one occasion, and himself on another almost blown aloft: these things fluttered the entire society. He would summon spirits by holding skulls over running water or by some ritual performed in churchyards at dead of night, night being 'his jubilee', we are told, and no building in the place from which escape was not easy. He was 'Mad Shelley', and he was 'The Atheist'; 'The Atheist' perhaps because he fell in love with Pliny's chapter *De Deo* and talked of it at large; or because the name was given conventionally, as Hogg tells us, to the arch-

---

[1] *Letters from Eton and Oxford, 1820–1830.*
[2] In a long letter contributed to *The Athenaeum* of 4 Mar. 1848, and given in full by White, ii. 489 ff.

defier of the ruling powers. The persecution was such that
once, it would seem, they sent him home almost mad. The
cloisters would ring with 'Shelley, Shelley, Shelley', as they
teased and hustled him, or he would run for it, and the hue and
cry pursued him 'up town'. 'I have seen him,' writes Merle,
'surrounded, hooted, baited like a maddened bull, and at this
distance of time I seem to hear ringing in my ear the cry which
he was wont to utter in his paroxysms of revengeful fury.' 'His
eyes would flash like a tiger's, his cheeks grow pale as death,
and his limbs quiver.'

But this picture of the School and his existence in it would be
overdrawn, were we to leave it at that. There were good minds
there and the moral ideals of a great aristocracy. As for Shelley,
he was not for ever in hot water, nor the graces of his nature
hidden. True, some of the finer spirits among his contem-
poraries—John Lonsdale, Henry Hart Milman, Edward Craven
Hawtrey—never discovered him, and few suspected what
Andrew Amos once told Merle to his great surprise, that in the
'atheist' there were 'seeds of genius to overflowing'. But there is
evidence, beside the reminiscences of Walter Halliday, that
many loved him, for his goodness, and more especially for his
'moral courage' and 'tenderness of heart'. Hogg tells us, no
doubt exaggerating, that his elders disliked, but his equals
'adored' him, and Medwin that his leaving breakfast was a
great affair. We have sight of him in the flush of social pleasure,
at the regatta, at summer picnics in the neighbouring fields,[1]
and in the fancy-dress procession *Ad Montem* in midshipman's
array. Over his chemical works, and acting his own plays with
great soulfulness to audiences intent to 'have him on', he was
in bliss. Perhaps because the houses were locked up in winter
at six and in summer at eight, he had so much peace and
privacy as to become the author of one published romance, of
another in the printer's hands, and a long poem in a publisher's
desk, to say nothing of casual effusions and broken enterprises.
And at all times the countryside and the river delighted him.[2]
He was nevertheless on the whole unhappy, his friendships few

[1] *The Boat on the Serchio*, 76–83.

[2] See quotation from Walter Halliday on his frequent walks, p. 20. Peck (i. 26)
quotes a description by Mary Shelley in *The Last Man* of a running spring and a
little wood near Salt Hill, a favourite haunt of his: 'His happiest hours were spent
here.' On his delight in boating see Medwin, revised *Life*, p. 38.

and fleeting, and his best society to 'wander alone, generally
with a book, for hours together, day after day', 'a never to be
forgotten being, who stood apart from the whole school'. In
after life he thrust his schoolfellows out of memory and the
lesion left on him by the long ordeal was never to be healed.
It was here he began to conceive himself as the herd-abandoned
deer. More than that: no influences flowed to Shelley from the
towers of Windsor or from Henry's holy shrine. The faults of
his class and generation met him at the outset in full blast, and
he left the home of the old loyalties minded only to traverse
them and to give them no room.

### 3. PERSONAL TRAITS

The boy was the image of the man. At ten or twelve years
old, he was 'tall for his age, slightly and delicately built . . .
fair and ruddy . . . with a profusion of silky brown hair that
curled naturally'. His girlish face wore the expression of
'exceeding sweetness and innocence'; but at any tale of cruelty
or wrong the blue, rather prominent eyes, dull and insensible
in the trances of his thought, would flash vividly, the voice go
shrill and harsh, and the features sharp with anger or pain.
His terrors were painful to see, and in secret the tears often
flowed. His own nature suggested to him the metaphor of the
vapour and the light for the responses of the sensitive body to
the sensitive soul;[1] and Hazlitt, had he met him in the Eton
days, might have noticed, as he did years after,[2] 'the bending
flexible form that seems to take no strong hold of things, does
not grapple with the world around him, but slides from it like
a river', and 'the fever in the blood'. But not only in lissom
evasions was he 'like a river'; he was like one also in his arrowy
will. From the beginning two natures crossed each other in
him—the shy and fugitive, not without its seasons of faltering,
'a dying lamp, a falling shower', and the 'pard-like spirit',
'tameless, and swift, and proud'.

This seemingly dual character was reflected in his imagination, and imagination was his element. He was a natural actor.
He performed with a local accent and a rustic dress so well
that the Squire of Cuckfield Park once engaged him as his

---

[1] *Hellas*, 215–17.
[2] In the essay entitled 'Paradox and Common-place' in *Table-Talk*.

gamekeeper's lad. Hellen remembered how he would regale the family with vivid fictions of where he had been and whom encountered, and how these stories were not considered reprehensible as from him. One of his waking dreams that he dreamed at Oxford is recorded by Hogg, and bears the Shelleyan mark so clearly that it is well to cite it in the present context. Hogg tells us that one day, after long walking in a bleak and bare countryside, Shelley and he took to a path in a wood, and came suddenly on the wintry anatomy of a flower garden lapped among the trees; and that on the way home Shelley discoursed with glowing inspiration of two sisters tending the flowers there, like the lady of *The Sensitive Plant*. He described them; he 'drew a lovely picture of their amiable and innocent attachment', a little daughterly on the one side, a little motherly on the other, and concluded with the excellence of sisterly love, the most spiritual instance of the passion, the fittest for that 'sweet and holy seclusion'. In that unwritten poem he was projecting one side of his nature. The desolate and forbidding environment, the sheltered paradise, the choice and gentle souls, and the communion of souls: there were his 'fear of life', his fugitiveness, and his comfort: his comfort in the hope or experience of a consummate fellowship in the gifts of the spirit and the enjoyment of beauty and good; in a word, in love, for in that sense he understood it. And when he insisted on the presence of imagination in love and love in imagination, he spoke from his own practice: for his personal devotions from childhood onwards were poetry. He touched the living person with the quality of a dream, just as he allowed to his dreams the power to move him like real life; and when he delighted in others, threw his being into theirs. A moving chapter of his history is occupied by children, with whom, as in these early years with his sisters, he was at once their attendant genius and their fellow child, by a big bit of him one of their troop and native and endued to their element. No one who has read the story will forget his rapt scrutiny of the baby snatched from its mother's arms on Magdalen Bridge, all new from the prenatal deeps, or the gipsy boy and girl whom he surprised in their search for shells and withies, and melted their shyness out of them. At one time in his boyhood at Field Place he 'had a wish to educate a child', and 'thought of purchasing one from a tumbler who came to the door to display her feats'.[1] But protectiveness had no place or play in the sovereign passion of which he became as keen a singer as any who have written verse, and which cast its shadow before it in an episode that seems to have happened at Sion House. He has himself related it:

'It is not right to say merely that friendship is exempt from the smallest alloy of sensuality, it rejects with disdain all thoughts but those of an elevated and imaginative character. I remember forming an attachment of this kind at school. . . . The object of these sentiments was a boy about my own age, of a character eminently generous, brave, and gentle . . . there was a delicacy and simplicity in his manners inexpressibly attractive—. . . . The tones of his voice were so soft and winning that every word pierced into my heart, and their pathos was so deep that, in listening to him, the tears have involuntarily gushed from my eyes. Such was the being for whom I first experienced the sacred sentiments of friendship. I remember in my simplicity writing to my Mother a long account of his admirable qualities and my own devoted attachment. I suppose she thought me out of my wits, for she returned no answer to my letter. I remember we used to walk the whole play-hours up and down by some moss-covered palings pouring out our hearts in youthful talk. We used to speak of the ladies with whom we were in love, and I remember that our usual practice was to confirm each other in the everlasting fidelity in which we had bound ourselves towards them and towards each other. I recollect thinking my friend exquisitely beautiful. Every night when we parted to go to bed, we kissed each other like children, as we still were.'[2]

There once more is the kind of love peculiar to him: the sense

---

[1] Hellen's recollections. 'A Newspaper Editor' (perhaps William Henry Merle), in his 'Reminiscences', in *Fraser's Magazine* for June 1841, states that he received a letter from Shelley about six months after his expulsion from Oxford, in which he spoke of a similar project of adopting a child, or two children. But the object then was 'to bring them up in some sequestered spot, with a view to ascertaining what impression the world produces upon the mind when veiled from human prejudice'. See Dowden, i. 124–5.

[2] Quoted by Hogg, i. 23. Shelley says, in the same passage, that all this happened when he was eleven or twelve years old, i.e. presumably at Sion House. The 'moss-grown palings' were probably those that he at some time or other blew into the air. Dowden suggests that the boy friend was one Tredcroft, who, in the *Autobiography* of Sir John Rennie (1875), another of the inmates of Sion House, is remembered as a strange and imaginative character who died at an early age.

of envelopment by the alien and the inimical, the going aside with the one or the few, and the ardour of self-bestowing.

So far the Shelley who, in retreat or hiding from the world, would have the life that is life indeed. But it is not, or seems not he who in later years 'gave his sails to the tempest' and defied all England. Of that insurgent or dynamic side of him there is enough and to spare under the long ordeal of his schooldays, and in all that we learn of his inner or imaginative life. As Browning has set forth in a famous essay, he became the poet of two cosmic principles, Love and Power, and in the beginning conceived more largely of the second than of the first. He revelled in signs and images of Life or Power at the infinite, infinite either way—in intensity or extent, in flaming evidence, or deep reserve, or incalculable possibility. The chief instance is his admiration, as boy or man or poet, of the vastness and splendour of the heavens. But the same passion looks out from the play of his fancy. He fabled to his friends or sisters of strange creatures and personages of unknown potency, at dark purposes or goings on, the Great Tortoise of Warnham Pond, or St. Leonard's Snake, or the 'alchemist old and grey' in the attics of the manor house. He preferred the Gothic romances to those of Fielding and Smollett for their bright-infernal epiphanies. The love of Power in endless career, in splendid effluence, in awful latency: this, more than the desire of knowledge, is the clue to his pyrotechnic or scientific escapades, his bonfires, and 'stoves full of flaming liquids', and dangerous batteries and retorts; and it is also a factor of his faith and hope in the boundless life of souls, his 'irrefragable proofs that Saturn is inhabited', and his belief in men advancing to godhead in that and other globes. 'Many a long and happy walk have I had with him', writes Walter Halliday, his Etonian friend. '. . . I was a delighted listener to his marvellous stories of fairyland, and apparitions, and spirits, and haunted ground, and his speculations were then of the world beyond the grave.' And here again—in this concernment with spiritual modes of being and in his solemn vagaries in vaults and churchyards—he was not more the questioner than one who would be shaken by the high experience of awe and fear.

To see the Love at one with the Power, one principle in the world around and in the heart of man, would be the Mount of

Vision. And he asked the way to it with his face thitherward. He had from the beginning the sense of the unity of things:

'Let us recollect our sensations as children. What a distinct and intense apprehension had we of the world and of ourselves. . . . We less habitually distinguished all that we saw and felt from ourselves. They seemed as it were to constitute one mass. . . . There are some persons who, in this respect, are always children. Those who are subject to the state called reverie feel as if their nature were dissolved into the surrounding universe, or as if the surrounding universe were absorbed into their being.'[1]

And if Love failed in men he could feel it pulsing in the world:

'There is no rest or respite to the heart over which it [Love] rules. Hence in solitude, or in that deserted state when we are surrounded by human beings, and yet they sympathise not with us, we love the flowers, the grass, the waters, and the sky. In the motion of the very leaves of spring, in the blue air, there is then found a secret correspondence with our heart. There is an eloquence in the tongueless wind, and a melody in the flowing brooks and the rustling of the reeds beside them, which by their inconceivable relation to something within the soul stir the spirits to a dance of breathless rapture, and bring tears of mysterious tenderness to the eyes, like the enthusiasm of patriotic success, or the voice of one beloved singing to you alone.'[2]

[1] *On Life.*        [2] *On Love.*

## III

## AT SCHOOL: THE NASCENT MIND

### 1. THE MILL AT ETON

SHELLEY left school, as Dowden judges, an 'eager and wide-ranging, if not an exact' student of the classics, with a remarkable facility in Latin verse. At that period 'there were three authors well known to Etonians, Homer, Vergil, and Horace. If a boy was in school eight or ten years, he was sure to go through the *Iliad* once and half again, the *Aeneid* twice, and of the *Odyssey* he must needs know a few hundred lines which were in the school book called *Poetae Graeci*, a book then very meagre and insufficient.'[1] This compilation and another entitled *Scriptores Graeci* in prose, and consisting of 'a lump of Lucian and scraps of Herodotus, Thucydides, Xenophon, and Plato', did not provide a real acquaintance with any Attic writer. But the narrowness of the official prescription was sometimes exceeded by Assistant Masters in 'private business', and Keate, in his lectures on Greek plays to a select number of the Sixth, 'in his quiet classroom used to give out his best knowledge, seasoned with perfect taste and free from all pedantry. It may be fairly doubted whether there was any man who was doing better work than this in English schools, except Butler of Shrewsbury.' Shelley may have heard these lectures, for he was in the Sixth in his final year, the first of Keate's headmastership. In Latin, besides Vergil, members of the Sixth Form were sure to have gone through the whole of Horace, except the *Epodes*, before leaving, and were made to read and learn by heart in the *Scriptores Romani* a great deal of Roman oratory.[2]

---

[1] These particulars of the education in Keate's time are taken mainly from Maxwell Lyte, *A History of Eton College*, 1911, pp. 382 ff. In 1834, the year of Keate's retirement, both the *Edinburgh* (vol. li, 65–80) and the *Quarterly* (vol. lii) discussed the education given at Public Schools and at Eton especially, the *Edinburgh* very critically, the *Quarterly*, on the whole, defensively. The programme of studies was fifty years old when Keate took it over, and he retained it to the end of his time.

[2] The result of these anthologies—the *Scriptores Graeci* and the *Scriptores Romani*—was, as the *Edinburgh* pointed out, that the Etonian left his school having read on the official programme 'not a single book of Herodotus, Thucydides, Xenophon, Tacitus, Livy', and (though this would not be true of the Sixth under Keate) 'not a single Greek tragedy or comedy'.

Shelley moreover read assiduously in the classics on his own account and conceived his permanent admirations for Lucretius and for Plato. His Greek was at this time weaker than his Latin, yet at Oxford, though preferring to use the versions of Plato by Madame Dacier or Floyer Sydenham, he would carry about texts of the Dialogues in Greek, as well as texts of Plutarch, Euripides, and the Septuagint, and 'read straight forward for hours'.[1]

For his strong repugnance to mathematics the school had no responsibility, for 'the study of Euclid, of algebra, and even of arithmetic was practically optional. It was publicly said at the time that some of the cleverest boys would have stood a bad chance if tried in the rule of three.' French too was an optional subject, taught by a Visiting Master three times a week; and Shelley took the chance so far that at Oxford he could read the language comfortably. Under Goodall, a scholar of the genial and liberal kind, the eagerness of the Sixth was such that they regularly prepared themselves to illustrate the classical texts as well from Italian and French as from English authors; and the interest in some quarters in modern or at any rate in English literature blossomed in 1811 into the Eton Society for the debate of historical and literary questions. Shelley in Goodall's last year was in the noisy and unmanageable Fifth, and missed his effective influence. But he caught the taste for the English poets—not in the first degree for the greatest (though Shakespeare and Milton were not neglected), but at the earliest for Gray, and afterwards for some of the artificers of the more colourful and more imitable romance—Chatterton, Scott, and Matthew Gregory Lewis. He had a more natural leaning to poetry of the order of Southey's *Thalaba* and Landor's *Gebir*. *Gebir* he frequently read and recited at Oxford, if not previously; and in 1809 he knew *Thalaba* 'almost by heart'.

One extraordinary feature of the education at Eton has much importance in the story of his mind. There was no religious instruction; Sumner found, as Assistant Master, that the system

[1] Hogg, *Life*, i. 127, 192. A useful summary of Shelley's erudition will be found in A. Droop's *Die Belesenheit P. B. Shelley's*, Jena Dissertation, 1906. At the end of 1812 (letter to Hookham, 17 Dec.) he still preferred to read the Greek classics with English or French versions on the opposite pages, but dispensed with these aids if necessary.

'practically debarred him from saying a word about God to his pupils'. It is true that at 2 o'clock on Sunday afternoons the Fifth and Sixth assembled in Upper School while the Head Master read aloud 'a short discourse in abstract morality taken from Blair's *Sermons*, from *The Spectator*, or from the works of some pagan writer like Epictetus', but as a rule on these occasions so loud was the 'yelling, booing, hissing, and scraping of feet', and so ineffectual even on the part of Keate his expedient of 'stamping and flinging his cocked hat on the desk', that the good seed fell upon the hurricane and blew away. It is also true that, beside the weekday prayers, the whole School attended Chapel twice on Sundays; but the sermons were 'mumbled and jumbled by old men [the Fellows of the College] with weak smothered voices, not one word of which could be heard, so that it was impossible to say whether they were suited to our capacity or our welfare'.[1] This pulpit style would come as a matter of course to one who from a child had sat at the feet of Mr. Edwards in Warnham Church, 'a good old man of very limited intellects', and a disconcerting Welsh accent.

With all its shortcomings Eton did more for Shelley than he acknowledged. Yet what he says in the prefatory lines to *The Revolt of Islam* is fairly true—he took the armour for his 'war among mankind' not from the official armourers. He had already formed his habit of incessant reading. In the Oxford period 'he was to be found, book in hand, at all hours, at table, in bed, and especially during a walk; not only in the quiet country and in retired paths; not only at Oxford, in the public walks and High Street, but in the most crowded thoroughfares of London'. Hogg reckons that, with his 'devouring' eyes, he often read for two-thirds of the night and the day. At Eton also there was this wind behind him, and before the end he had sailed a long way from the appointed track of thought. It is impossible to say of every instance of his first inquiries in philosophy whether it took place at school or later; but we know for certain that after he had 'read romances, and those

[1] Maxwell Lyte, p. 390. All this is confirmed with ludicrous detail in C. Allix Wilkinson's *Reminiscences of Eton (Keate's Time)*. It may be added that members of the Sixth were required to learn on Sunday, and repeat on Monday morning, fifteen verses of the New Testament in the Greek; but these repetitions were 'heard without interruption or comment'. Some reading of Tomlin on the Thirty-nine Articles was likewise expected of them, and likewise unassisted.

the most marvellous ones, unremittingly',[1] and 'pored over the reveries of Albertus Magnus and Paracelsus', his 'fondness for natural magic and ghosts abated', a passion for metaphysics and kindred studies set in, and before he left school one of his primary inspirations had fallen on him from the *Political Justice* of William Godwin. He had also discovered and translated— always a sign of his enthralment—a part of the *Historia Naturalis* of the elder Pliny, including the chapter *De Deo*, and in all probability had read the *Symposium* of Plato, and looked into the philosphers who, besides Plato, engaged him in the first degree at Oxford—Locke and Hume. And before or after reading Godwin, he was on the search for speculations of a similar kind, and took some toll of Franklin and Condorcet. How much he had of a smattering in two or three sciences it is impossible to decide. Besides what he is likely to have learnt from the publications of Adam Walker,[2] he may have heard the latest word in chemistry and electricity which Humphry Davy was in those years popularizing to large and fashionable audiences at the Royal Institution.[3] But if 'his science, like his philosophy, was thirty years late'[4] he had not dabbled unprofitably. He had risen to some conception of the harmony of Nature, and of some of her greater laws and their majestic instances, to feed his imagination and to mould his thought thenceforward.[5]

[1] Letter to T. Tisdall, 10 Jan. 1808: 'I read novels and romances all day' (at Field Place). See Julian Shelley, vii. 289. The date of this letter has been disputed, and the year 1809 preferred (*The Times*, 2 and 5 Sept. 1928).

[2] See note on pp. 9, 10 above, and A. Koszul, *La Jeunesse de Shelley*, Paris, 1910, pp. 17, 18.

[3] Dampier-Whetham, *A History of Science*, Cambridge, 1929, p. 234.

[4] Koszul, loc. cit.

[5] Shelley, in a letter to Godwin of 3 June 1812, gives an account of his studies up to the date of his first marriage. That he read *Political Justice* at Eton appears from a statement of his in a letter to Godwin of 10 Jan. 1812, in which he says: 'It is now a period of more than two years since first I saw your inestimable book.' The fact is also attested by Hogg, ii. 69: 'He saw himself at his dame's with *Political Justice*, which he had lately borrowed from Dr. Lind.' Medwin supposes (but does not affirm) that he read the *Symposium* with Dr. Lind, on the ground that Lind is represented in the Zonoras of *Prince Athanase*, and Zonoras read it with his pupil (ii. 219–29). According to Medwin again (*Life*, revised, p. 50) Shelley would quote Franklin, 'whom he swore by', and read aloud from Condorcet, on the indefinite prolongation of human life, at Christmas 1809. Godwin adduces both those authors on the same point in a footnote in *Political Justice*, ed. 1798, ii. 520.

## 2. DR. LIND

When astronomers are perplexed by the behaviour of a star, they assume that some other body, not previously reckoned with, is acting on it. They work out the sum, turn their telescopes to the proper place, and find the disturber. The extraordinary behaviour of Shelley's mind at school implies another mind impelling it, and this was undoubtedly James Lind's.

Lind was born in Scotland in 1736,[1] and studied medicine at Edinburgh. At thirty years of age he went as a ship's surgeon to the East, and collected curiosities, not without a monstrous vandalism; for once, in company with 'a large party of Englishmen and some sixty carpenters and masons', he visited the great sanctuary of the rock temples in the island of Elephanta, near Bombay, with their colossal figures of Brahma, Vishnu, and Siva, and other personages of the Siva legend; 'but after all their toilings in this wonderful excavation, they found the rock so impenetrable, and the pillars and idols so stupendous that they could only bring away an odd head or two and a few limbs'. On his return Lind proceeded M.D. with a treatise on an outbreak of fever in Bengal, and in 1769, on the ground of his 'skill in botany and natural history', was recommended to the Royal Society for their expedition to the north to observe the transit of Venus. He did not join, however, but observed the transit from near Edinburgh, and sent a report of it to the Society, of which he afterwards became a Fellow. Three years later he accompanied Sir Joseph Banks on his voyage to Iceland and invented on this occasion a portable wind-gauge. He settled in Windsor about 1777, where he became physician to the Royal Household. We can imagine him, as he appeared in 1810, by the aid of Shelley's recorded words and the earlier notices of Mrs. Delany and Madame d'Arblay—a man full of oddity and charm, kind, courtly, humorous, brimming with outlandish curiosities, tall and vigorous, 'as thin as a lath', white-haired and eager-eyed. Miss Burney, having inspected his Eastern collection, mentions 'a curious book representing every part of a Chinese monastery—buildings, utensils, gods, priests, and idols; it is very neatly and most elaborately

---

[1] For the known facts of his life see article in the *Dictionary of National Biography*.

executed, and the colours are uncommonly vivid'.[1] One
entry of Mrs. Delany's betrays the sympathies that afterwards
engaged the Doctor for the rebel Shelley. Dr. Lind at dinner
'told us many particulars of the rebellion at Eton, some laugh-
able anecdotes of the boys destroying the whipping-post and
then selling it to one another. The Marquis of Huntly bought
a piece which he showed Dr. Lind in great triumph.' After
dinner the Doctor 'brought some shells and fossils. . . . Conversation air-balloons. Dr. Lind made a drawing of one of the
first great meteors which he saw from the terrace at Windsor.'
'Singular relations of the customs and manners of the Chinese,
particularly of the animals they kill for food,' is another note of
his talk. With his 'taste for tricks, conundrums, and queer
things'—his invention, for instance, of 'Lindian Ogham',
strange wooden types with which he printed little books—he
seems to have frightened the good folk of Windsor, who were
shy of calling him in and 'thought him a better conjuror than
physician'. We learn from Hogg that he was interested in
demonology; and that may explain Hogg's extraordinary tale
that in Shelley's time Lind had come to bear a grudge against
George the Third, and used to curse the King with a commina-
tory ritual; and this was the ritual used by Shelley to curse his
father. Hogg says that Shelley told him all this, and that the
poet used to descant indignantly on the wrongs (whatever he
said they were) which Lind had suffered from the King. Possibly the old scholar had a relish for maledictory formulas, as
his pupil had for all sorts of cabalistic words; and this was the
bottom of the story. We know, however, from Miss Burney that
in her time Lind and the King were on affectionate terms,[2] and
there are credible indications[3] that Hogg intended to withdraw
the statement at the earliest opportunity.

[1] See *Diary*, 10 Dec. 1785. The Witch of Atlas, walking the Earth by night, sees
                    Princes couched under the glow
          Of sun-like gems; and round each temple court
          In dormitories ranged, row after row,
          She saw the priests asleep—all of one sort—
          For all were educated to be so.
Chinamen, I believe, are all alike.

[1] See 23 July 1799, the King's jesting with Lind. Also 30 Nov. 1785, Lind's
admiration for the King and Queen.

[3] See Dowden, i. 32, and a letter to Dowden from R. Garnett in *Letters about
Shelley* (1917), p. 132. Garnett cites a manuscript note in a copy of Hogg's *Life*:

Loyal as he certainly was to his Master, the Doctor appears to have watched the Revolution with an academic sympathy. Professor Koszul has noted[1] that in the Bodleian copy of *Essays on Several Subjects*, issued in 1769, there is a manuscript note ascribing the book to Lind. If the ascription is true, he may be called, in a mild sense, a forerunner of the liberal movement. A cautious plea for political equality and natural rights, coupled with the thesis that 'religion is the proper support of all morality', the book might well be regarded, from the conservative point of view, as carrying its disinfectants with it. But the Revolution, when it came, did not move the cheerful man from his trust in the tenor of things. The Zonoras in *Prince Athanase* and the Hermit in *Laon and Cythna*, in whom he is known to be represented, are among those few of the 'friends of man' who nurse their lamps of faith in the increasing darkness.

When Shelley first made friends with him, and when it was that, in keen distress, he called him over to Field Place[2] we do not know; but in course of time the old man ardent was sainted in his pupil's eyes: 'I owe that man,' he once said, 'more, ah! far more, than I owe to my father. He was exactly what an old man ought to be, free, calm-spirited, full of benevolence, and even of youthful ardour. . . . He loved me, and I shall never forget our long talks, when he breathed the spirit of the kindest tolerance and the purest wisdom.' Of his intellectual debt to him only a few particulars can be guessed or gleaned. There would be much encouragement to the scientific studies, and a little, perhaps, to the demonology. It was assuredly to him that Shelley owed his early interest in the mind and life of the East, and more than probably his first encounter with the *Symposium* and with *Political Justice*.[3] Lind had the old idea of the comity of scholars, so that, whosoever word he wanted on a point of truth, he would accost him straightway by the post; and with this example the young enthusiast, not always fortunately, fell in. And above these items other of his interests, such as that in Condorcet, may be put with a likelihood to the same account. Lind, indeed, performed for him to some extent the function

'Dr. Lind was an ultra-loyalist and devotedly attached to George III; he was too a man of such remarkable sweetness and gentleness of disposition that he was never known to make an unkind remark of any human being.'

[1] *La Jeunesse de Shelley*, p. 26.        [2] See p. 5.
[3] See footnote on p. 25.

of a University. To some extent; for, looking at Shelley as he was then and afterwards, so much in need of a real philosopher at his side, we may wish that he had found a tutor, not of a higher character, but of a weightier ability. No authority would have kept him from adventure or made him less intrepid in his cause; but a Master with more than a playful mind and a scant philosophy would have saved him a good deal of the waste in his poetry and the waste in his life. It may be significant that Prince Athanase in the poem outmatches his teacher and teaches him in turn.[1] Lind, to all appearance, was like a geographer in the time of the voyages who had more than a little, but much less than all, of the available knowledge, and with some promiscuity filled his shelves with charts of the new lands, some good, and others featured with imaginary localities and 'Here is Ambergris' or 'Here is Gold'. Shelley was the wistful sailor, who delighted in the charts, and sailed out in reliance on them to fine discoveries and to futile quests.

### 3. 'DISTEMPERED VISIONS'

Before Shelley left Eton, his addiction to 'Dutch sublimity' had borne fruit in two romances in prose and one in verse. The first of the fictions in prose—*Zastrozzi, a Romance, by P. B. S.*— was published at the end of March 1810[2] by G. Wilkie and J. Robinson of Paternoster Row; the second—*St. Irvyne, or The Rosicrucian, by a Gentleman of the University of Oxford*—by J. J. Stockdale in the ensuing December. It appears that the first was written in 1809, before and during the summer term; and the second, though unfinished, was offered to Robinson in the spring, and to Stockdale in the November of 1810.[3] In the

---

[1] *Prince Athanase*, ii. 174 f. When Shelley told Godwin (16 Jan. 1812) that 'I have known no tutor or adviser from whose lessons and suggestions I have not recoiled with disgust', and that 'the knowledge which I have has been acquired by my unassisted efforts', he forgot Dr. Lind—and others. But it is significant that he should have done so. Nor is there anything to show that they ever communicated from the day when Shelley left Eton to the day when Lind died in 1813.

[2] In the entry of 28 Mar. in her Journal Harriet Groves records her receipt of it.

[3] On 16 Jan. 1812 Shelley informed Godwin that his two romances had been written 'prior to my acquaintance with your writings', excepting *St. Leon*; and on the 10th of the same month that he had first read *Political Justice* 'more than two years previously'. Shelley, however, was often inexact. The date assigned in the text to the composition of *Zastrozzi* is proved by the letter to Longman of 7 May 1809. On 1 Apr. 1810 he wrote from Eton to Edward Graham in London, directing

Christmas holidays of 1809–10 he wrote, perhaps with slight assistance from Medwin, a metrical romance which should eke out the legend of *The Wandering Jew* with a love tragedy. It was not printed until the *Edinburgh Literary Journal* published a part of it in June and July 1829, and *Fraser's Magazine* the whole of an earlier and shorter version in the July number of 1831.[1]

Elizabeth Barrett, after reading *St. Irvyne*, 'could never believe Shelley capable of such a book'. 'It *is* by Shelley,' answered Robert Browning, 'if you will have the truth, proof being that Leigh Hunt told me he unearthed it in Shelley's own library at Marlow once, to the writer's horror and shame. He snatched it out of my hands, said H.' Nevertheless the early romances are not without importance for the history of his mind.

The romance of mystery and terror approached the level of fine art perhaps in Ann Radcliffe's *The Mysteries of Udolpho* in 1794, or in *The Italian* in 1797, and undoubtedly in Maturin's *Melmoth the Wanderer* in 1820; but it easily descended to the

---

him to 'pouch' the reviewers, the venal villains; and added that, if the publisher Robinson 'will not give me a devil of a price for my Poem [*The Wandering Jew*] and at least £60 for my new Romance in three Volumes, the dog shall not have them'. The 'new romance' was certainly *St. Irvyne*, and we may infer that as much of it, or nearly, was then written as Shelley managed to write, and before or after the date of the letter went to Robinson in vain. It was never completed as at first designed; for when it went to Stockdale some time before 14 Nov. 1810, with its hasty and huddled conclusion, the measure of 'three volumes' was far from being filled.

[1] This poem was first offered to the Ballantynes, and by them declined, in a letter dated 24 Sept. 1810, as offensive to the orthodox reader. On 28 Sept. Shelley asked Stockdale to publish it, acquainting him with the scruples of the Ballantynes, and professing to see no ground for them. Stockdale, having waited for nearly two months for the manuscript from Edinburgh, and having then received another copy from Shelley, declined in his turn to be instrumental. In Jan. 1811, having recovered one of his manuscripts from Stockdale's hands, Shelley added a preface, a dedication to Sir Francis Burdett, and the alternative title of *The Victim of the Eternal Avenger*; and in this month or subsequently revised and amplified the entire text. This manuscript he took with him to Edinburgh in the following August, and left it with 'a literary gentleman', who gave it to the *Journal*. Professor White (i. 580) gives evidence that the gentleman was James Ballantyne, who must have seen the poem twice over and in both its forms. The reprint in the *Journal* in 1829 consisted of large sections of the amplified text. In 1831 the whole four cantos appeared in *Fraser* in the first or shorter version. See Introduction to the Shelley Society's edition by Bertram Dobell. In the *Shelley Papers* of 1833 and the *Life* of 1847 Medwin claimed to have written large portions of the romance. But his accounts are at variance, and the echoes between the romance and Shelley's earliest poems as good as prove the single authorship.

commonness of style and tediousness of horror in Lewis's once famous *Ambrosio, or The Monk*, which appeared in 1795. At that date Mrs. Radcliffe had not yet tired the public of her regular excitements—her ancient castle or abbey, with its secret passages, dungeons, and stairways, and its cloud of mystery and crime; her gentle heroine in peril of the tyrannous guardian and the vile lover; the moving accidents of her flight; the magic of the southern cities, and the grandeur of Apennines or Alps. Lewis, however, brought in a new variety of this literature—the tremendous; for among his materials in *The Monk* were the Holy Inquisition, a demon in a woman's shape, the Arch-fiend in person, and the sale and perdition of a soul. Incited, perhaps, by her rival's success, Mrs. Radcliffe darkened her colours in *The Italian*, and added to the Gothic repertory the silent and majestic monk, Schedoni, the compeller of events, with his lined face, piercing eyes, and superhuman air. Later again—in 1799—William Godwin's *St. Leon* threw in an element of history, and moral and social theory, and also the *elixir vitae*, which the hero purchases by the infernal pact, and thereafter searches the wide world for one who will receive at his hands and in his stead the curse of the unfading prime. By now the mere imitators or copyists in this kind had plenty to choose from, and among those who shuffled and eked out the articles in stock was Mrs. Byrne, alias Charlotte Dacre, alias Rosa Matilda. She wrote a romance called *The Nun of St. Omer's*, and another in four volumes called *The Passions*; and in 1805 two volumes of verse in Lewis's vein, entitled *Hours of Solitude*. According to the portrait prefixed to these poems, and the poems themselves, she was at that time a young lady. In 1806 she published through Longman *Zofloya, or The Moor*,[1] *a Romance of the Fifteenth Century*, in three volumes; and Shelley derives all the main incident and character in both *Zastrozzi* and *St. Irvyne* from this wild story, which, as Medwin tells us, 'quite enraptured' him. So far as the events go, if we except a few additions from *The Monk*, *The Italian*, *St. Leon*, and elsewhere,

---

[1] Shelley's indebtedness for his Gothic stories was discussed by A. H. Koszul in the *Revue germanique*, Mar. 1905; by the present writer in the *Modern Language Review*, Jan. 1912; and by W. E. Peck in *Shelley, his Life and Work*. Among the minor sources discovered by Professor Koszul is a romance entitled *La Caverne de Strozzi*, by J. J. Regnault-Warin (Paris, 1798). Shelley named *St. Leon* to Stockdale as one of his originals (19 Nov. 1810).

he has taken the cards from the hand of Mrs. Byrne, and has dealt them out again.

Shelley found a person called Strozzi in *Zofloya*, added a syllable, and spelt his hero's name in the first romance with three Z's, a letter very dear to the Gothic writers for a whiff of uncanniness about it. The tall and terrible Zastrozzi is a high-wayman who, for a wrong inflicted on his mother, pursues a relentless vengeance on Verezzi, the wrongdoer's son. Verezzi is loved by Matilda di Laurentini, a fierce and shameless woman, but himself loves the heavenly Countess Julia; and Zastrozzi, masterful designer, who is in Matilda's trust, determines that the young man shall succumb to the bad woman, forswear his angel, and lose his soul. To part him from Julia, he seizes and immures him in a cave; the cave is riven by lightning; but, after an interval of freedom, the victim is again discovered, and induced to live unwillingly in Matilda's house. In her mansion at Passau, or her castle near Venice, deep within forest and mountain, he holds out against her wiles and entreaties and her affected melancholy and shame. She brings him false news that Julia is dead; he faints, and waking with his head on her bosom, recoils as from a scorpion. She nurses him in a fever, for all his loathing of her presence and his truth, incessantly protested, to Julia's memory. Zastrozzi meanwhile is lurking near by in the forest, his majestic figure swathed in gloom or licked by lightnings. By pre-arrangement with Matilda he attacks Verezzi with a dagger; she, rushing to the rescue, is slightly wounded; and the thankful youth relents and marries her. But she is not happy while Julia lives; Zastrozzi must kill Julia or help to kill her. He, however, will preserve her rather, that his victim, seeing her living whom he thought dead, and all his untruth to her, may suffer pangs unspeakable. He therefore inveigles the pair to Venice, where they see Julia in a passing gondola. Returning home, Matilda vainly attempts to rouse her husband from his stupor of grief, when Julia enters the room, and dies under a thousand strokes of her rival's dagger, but not before Verezzi with the same instrument has dispatched himself. In the prison of the Inquisition, by whose sentence she dies, the murderess perceives the falsity of the atheistical arguments in which Zastrozzi has schooled her, and, repenting, is assured by an angel in a dream that the divine mercy is infinite. But Zastrozzi confronts his judges with disdainful composure, exults in his atheism, and dies unflinching by extreme tortures.

It speaks much for the vendibility of the Gothic stories that Shelley received £40 for *Zastrozzi*, and Stockdale, his second publisher, printed *St. Irvyne, or The Rosicrucian* though he could not see, and the author could not tell him, what really happened in it. It was, however, very Satanic. Mrs. Byrne had borrowed and bettered the supernatural element of *The Monk*. Her Zofloya, apparently the Moorish servant of a Venetian grandee, but in truth Satan himself, Protean in form and limitless in power, leads the heroine through a long course of adultery and murder to the surrender of her soul, and appears to her at the last in all his terrors. Then there was the man with the elixir in *St. Leon*. Shelley might use up the supernatural in *Zofloya*, which in *Zastrozzi* he had left aside, and add the elixir,[1] and having made his first romance in the mould of Mrs. Radcliffe, might cast his second in that of Lewis. The hero he seems to have thought might be amphibian, at once an infernal agent pursuing a woman's soul, and a man, who, having obtained the rejuvenating liquid at his own soul's cost, and cursing his immortality, will never rest till someone relieves him of the potion and its dread effect. *St. Irvyne* divides, therefore, into two trains of incident, the hero playing separate parts in the one capacity and the other; but though the lines of action should in time converge, they never do, nor can the reader more than surmise that the Ginotti in the one is the Nempere in the other. Thus: (*a*) Ginotti, as a young student, denied God, devoted himself to the Devil, discovered and drank the elixir. Under the terror of his immortality, he determines to victimize the young nobleman, Wolfstein, and induce him to take and drink the liquor and thus take over the attendant curse. Haunting and completely mastering him, knowing and governing his thoughts, he plunges him into pleasure and crime, so as to destroy his conscience; then cajoles him into accepting the elixir. At an appointed hour, at midnight, by the ruined Abbey near St. Irvyne, Wolfstein takes the unholy draught, whereupon his tempter exhorts him to deny the being

[1] The sub-title, *The Rosicrucian*, is a designation of the elixir, as Shelley informed Stockdale on 19 Nov. 1810.

of God; but Wolfstein is still redeemable, and refuses to blaspheme. The Devil appears, and tempter and tempted fall down dead as by a blast of fire. Shelley, however, informed Stockdale (14 Nov. 1810) that they perished by the elixir and not really by fire; and, this being so, the tale must read as follows: the drink does not confer the unfading prime without the blasphemy; without that it kills. Wolfstein escapes with his death, and Hell, the text informs us, is cheated of his soul. Ginotti, having transferred the potion, may now die of it; die, that is, in the body; but his soul goes down to the infernal torment. (b) In the opening chapter (VII) of the second plot the maiden Eloise, daughter of the Lady of the Castle at St. Irvyne, leaves her home for Genoa, in company with her mother, who is dying. In five years' time, as the reader is told, she returns to St. Irvyne outcast and destitute to the bosom of a beloved sister. As the tale stands, however, we leave her in England, happily married. What happened to her between this stage and her final undoing has not been told. On the journey to Genoa she meets the mysterious and fascinating bandit Nempere, whose figure haunts her dreams and thoughts, and who, after her mother's death, makes her his mistress, and then sells her to an English nobleman, Mountford. Mountford, however, treats her with respect; and at his house she meets Fitzeustace, a beautiful soul, and marries him. Nempere—in an incident briefly reported and not described—is killed by Mountfort in a duel, and the Englishman flees to London, whither the lovers follow him to a life of assured happiness.

At this point the book ends with a curt intimation: 'Ginotti is Nempere; Eloise is the sister of Wolfstein.' But Ginotti or Nempere, if he be human, cannot die twice—by the elixir and by the sword of Mountfort; and human he ought to be, as the man from *St. Leon*. In both actions he carries with him infernal properties—an uncanny beauty, Tartarean glances, the power of haunting and flitting and an ineluctable power over minds and wills. He is a fiend, then. But if he is, why should the elixir be a burden to him? And if he is human, we must take it with the ingenious Stockdale that he died by the potion, and that Mountfort only thought he killed him.[1] Had Shelley brought

[1] Apparently Stockdale suggested this solution to Shelley, who answered, most unhelpfully, that he *did* kill him (19 Nov. 1810).

his book to an end, he would not have left us, presumably, to wander in this fog.

Much above the measure represented by these summaries he rifles the pages of his predecessors for heart-shaking things; and he raises Pelion upon Ossa.

> Tremble, Ambrosio! . . . Hark! 't was the shriek of your better angel; he flees, and leaves you for ever.

So Lewis had written; but Shelley overtopped him:

> But hush! What was that scream that was heard by the ear of listening enthusiasm? It was the shriek of the fair Eloise's better genius. It screamed to see the foe of the innocent girl so near—it is fled fast to Geneva. There, Eloise, will we meet again, me-thought it whispered, whilst a low hollow tone, hoarse from the dank vapours of the grave, seemed lowly to howl in the ear of rapt Fancy—'We meet again likewise'.

*His* prisoner in a cavern goes mad, and the cavern teems with reptiles. Similarly, he has twice borrowed from Mrs. Byrne the case of a lover who surprises his mistress while murmuring of her love for him, and the case of a woman who comes upon her lover in a rival's arms, and overwhelms him with her silence. Schedoni about to poniard his sleeping daughter in *The Italian* suffers not so exquisitely as Wolfstein contemplating the lovely Olympia before he shall murder sleep. In the description of the castles, the streets of Venice, the courts of the Inquisition, he is weak and scanty; but, though his mountains and forests in storm or moonlight cannot vie with Mrs. Radcliffe's,[1] a touch of detail here or there promises the especial vision of his nature poetry—the moon that 'like the spirit of the spotless ether, which shrinks from the obtrusive gaze of man, hung behind a leaden-coloured cloud', or the arid grasses in castle walls[2] or the lone scathed pine in the glacier's track,[3] symbols of

---

[1] Cf. the moonlit scene in *Zastrozzi*, ch. x, with *The Mysteries of Udolpho*, ch. iv; the storm in the beginning of *St. Irvyne* with *Udolpho*, ch. i, and *St. Leon*, ch. vii, where the lightning that 'dances on the tops of the mountains' was noted and purloined. The figure in *St. Irvyne*, ch. i, of the storm as the 'long-protracted war echoing from cavern to cavern' remained in his memory to be splendidly rendered in *Prince Athanase*, 69–72.

[2] Perhaps a memory of a passage in *The Mysteries of Udolpho*, ch. xix. Cf. *Rosalind and Helen*, 823, *Julian and Maddalo*, 224.

[3] Cf. *Revolt of Islam*, VI. x.

a quenchless life and will. It is especially in the emotional passages, however, that he elaborates his models; scantier than they in the action and description, in the passion he is more profuse and far more hectic.

But, above all, the titanic malefactors attracted him. That laws exist for the weak, and God and conscience for the simple-minded, that passion of whatever kind is the grand virtue, that the free and sovereign soul will bend to no pain or fear in heaven or earth is the true faith of Zastrozzi and his forerunners; and the writers of this family make amends for their zest in the wickedness and the heresy by frequently rebuking it and invoking on it the divine mercy or wrath. Moreover, an inward need in the man of iniquity to associate with himself and subdue to his element some other soul attaches him like a vampire to his chosen prey, and the spoil of innocence is another of the Gothic themes.[1]

All this matter Shelley has handled with a touch of his own; the titanic philosophy is taller than ever, and again and again his piety exclaims. He has not spared, as the occasion may be, to imprecate the anger of God or declare his mercies, though without one instance of the Christian note; and there are hints of his later faith in a heart or citadel of the soul that cannot be taken by any evil power.[2] But his imagination drew by instinct to the desolate grandeur intended in the Gothic giants, and they and bits of their histories lay in his memory till he should touch them to far finer issues in the after years.[3]

He came on the figure of the Wandering Jew in *Ambrosio, or The Monk*, in a German author whom he has cited but not named,[4] and probably in other books as well, for in that heyday

---

[1] Mrs. Radcliffe's Schedoni acts upon this motive, and Wordsworth's Oswald in *The Borderers* is in the same tradition.

[2] See the conversation between Eloise and Fitzeustace in *St. Irvyne*, ch. xii.

[3] John Cordy Jeaffreson, in *The Real Shelley*, i. 119 ff., has noted many echoes from *Zastrozzi*, ch. i and ii (where Verezzi is imprisoned in a cavern), in the account of Laon carried by his captors along an underground passage and up a stairway to the summit of the hill-crowning column, and there bound in chains, and maddened with heat and thirst, till the old hermit ministers to him (*Revolt of Islam*, Canto III). There is another echo in the earthquake that rends the sea-cave entombing Cythna in Canto VII. The family connexion of Zastrozzi and Cenci has often been remarked.

[4] At i. 764 he quotes in a footnote a translated passage from this unidentified author on the outcast seeking death in volcanoes and seas; not the passage from Schubart's prose poem, *Der Ewige Jude*, which he or Medwin picked up one day in Lincoln's Inn Fields in a 'torn and dirty' fragment of *La Belle Assemblée*, or *Bell's*

of romance the Wanderer was a popular person.[1] Shelley's
Jew has a novel part to play. He snatches the novice Rosa
from the altar where under duress she is taking the veil, and
lives with her in a mountain castle. Here he tells her his story
—the scene at the Crucifixion, the journey through the ages,
and the soliciting of death—and uncovers the fiery cross in his
brow. But his friend Victorio, a nobleman of proud lineage,
falls in love with Rosa, and obtains from a demon witch by
rites and incantations in a cave, Satan himself attending, a
philtre to subdue her heart;[2] of the result of which the reader
can make out only that Rosa dies, and the Jew, bereft of her
pity, is summoned by a demon to go on with his miserable life.
Tempests, earthquakes, demons, ghosts, and fustian all the way,
as in the prose romances. But the thing has a certain fire, and
to the historian of the author's mind a certain value. For it
fails, or rather hesitates, to allow to the Wanderer that appeal
with which he comes henceforward into Shelley's pages from
time to time. He appears in *Queen Mab*, in *The Assassins*, and
in *Hellas*; and on each occasion as the victim of a false God of
mastery and wrath, as the bearer of the curse and prophet of
the blessedness of man. Not much more, perhaps, than a year
later, in the fragment entitled *The Wandering Jew's Soliloquy*,[3]
Shelley rose on the wings of this theme to his earliest flight of
indubitable poetry:

> Tyrant of Earth! pale Misery's jackal Thou!
> Are there no stores of vengeful violent fate
> Within the magazines of thy fierce hate?
> No poison in the clouds to bathe a brow
> That lowers on Thee with desperate contempt?
> Where is the noonday Pestilence that slew

*Court and Fashionable Magazine* for Jan. 1809, pp. 19–20, as White has now ascer-
tained, and which he appended in a note to *Queen Mab* (vii, 67). No use is made of
Schubart's matter in *The Wandering Jew*, which, as Medwin tells us, was 'not found
until some of the cantos had been written' (revised *Life*, p. 12).

[1] Coleridge had taken a rib from him for the Ancient Mariner; see Professor
Livingston Lowes in *The Road to Xanadu*, ch. xiv.

[2] This witch was taken over from *The Nightmare*. The passage relating to her
almost versifies the corresponding text of the romance (revised *Life*, p. 41).

[3] In the manuscript preserved by the Esdaile family living near Taunton.
Shelley's daughter Ianthe married Edward Jeffries Esdaile in 1837. The manuscript contains a number of poems written earlier than *Queen Mab*, and intended
for publication in the same volume with it in the spring of 1813. Here are some
almost verbal echoes of the fragment of Schubart's poem.

The myriad sons of Israel's favoured nation . . .
Or the Angel's two-edged sword of fire, that urged
Our primal parents from their bower of bliss
(Reared by Thine hand) for errors not their own,
By Thine omniscient mind foredoomed, foreknown?

But in the beginning of 1810 this audacious thinking was in front of him, and *The Wandering Jew* hardly or only verges on it. He was still in a leash of religious doctrine that was loosening daily, and the signs point to it that he slipped it suddenly, in the spring or the early summer of that year.

## 4. INTELLECTUAL BEAUTY

In some of his earliest letters to Godwin Shelley related how *Political Justice*, read for the first time, as his words imply, at the close of 1809,[1] wrought a great change in him. It 'opened to my mind fresh and extensive views', and 'materially influenced my character'. 'Till then I had existed in an ideal world; now I found that in this Universe of ours was enough to excite the interest of the heart, enough to employ the discussions of reason. I beheld in short that I had duties to perform. . . . I was at Eton. No sooner had I formed the principles which I profess than I became anxious to disseminate their benefits.'[2] 'To them [Godwin's writings], to you [Godwin] I owe the inestimable boon of granted power, of arising from the state of intellectual sickliness and lethargy into which I was plunged two years ago, and of which *St. Irvyne* and *Zastrozzi* are the distempered, although unoriginal visions.'[3] 'I did not truly *think and feel* until I read *Political Justice*.'[4] And indeed, after *St. Irvyne*, nothing of any bulk or consequence came from his pen of the old 'distempered' kind.[5] Again, there are two short poems in which he writes of vivid moments in his inner life at school, one the *Hymn to Intellectual Beauty* in 1816, and the other the lines *To Mary*, which formed the dedication of *The Revolt of Islam* in 1817.

[1] See footnote p. 25.                    [2] To Godwin, 10 Jan. 1812.
[3] To Godwin, 8 Mar. 1812.              [4] To Godwin, 3 June 1812.
[5] Of the fourteen pieces of *Original Poetry by Victor and Cazire*, dated from Oct. 1809 onwards, three are in the Gothic manner, but none of these indited later than Jan. 1810. The 'Tales translated from the German' which he had in hand when Medwin visited him in the first Oxford term were presumably, and a small Gothic element of the Margaret Nicholson poems, published in the same period (Nov. 1810), was certainly, in the lurid way. These were backslidings.

In the *Hymn* he addresses 'the awful shadow of some unseen Power', which 'visits with inconstant wing' the world of Nature and 'each human heart and countenance', which 'consecrates every thought or form on which it shines', but anon hides itself, and 'leaves this dim vast vale of tears vacant and desolate'. Why is it never in one stay? What is that but to ask why sunlight fades, why 'the daylight of this earth' is clouded by 'fear and dream and death and birth', why hate succeeds to love and despondency to hope?

### III

No voice from some sublimer world hath ever
To sage or poet these responses given—
Therefore, the names of Demon, Ghost or Heaven,
Remain the records of their vain endeavour.
Frail spells—whose uttered charm might not avail to sever,
From all we hear and all we see,
Doubt, chance, and mutability . . .

The only spell to 'give grace and truth to life's unquiet dream' is the light of the 'awful Power'. Man were immortal and omnipotent did it for ever abide. But it comes and goes, and love, hope, and self-esteem vanish with it. Were it to leave us altogether, the grave would be 'like life and fear a dark reality'.

### V

While yet a boy I sought for ghosts, and sped
　Thro' many a listening chamber, cave and ruin,
　And starlight wood, with fearful steps pursuing
Hopes of high talk with the departed dead.
I called on poisonous names with which our youth is fed;
　I was not heard—I saw them not—
　When musing deeply on the lot
Of life, at the sweet time when winds are wooing
　All vital things that wake to bring
　News of birds and blossoming,—
　Sudden, thy shadow fell on me;
I shrieked, and clasped my hands in ecstasy!

### VI

I vowed that I would dedicate my powers
　To thee and thine—have I not kept the vow?
　With beating heart and streaming eyes, even now

I call the phantoms of a thousand hours
Each from his voiceless grave; they have in visioned bowers
    Of studious zeal or love's delight
    Outwatched with me the envious night—
They know that never joy illumed my brow
    Unlinked with hope that thou would'st free
    This world from its dark slavery,
    That thou—O awful LOVELINESS
Would'st give whate'er these words cannot express.

The poem concludes with a prayer that that 'fair Spirit' which
'descended' on the poet's youth 'like the truth of Nature', and
bound him by its spells 'to fear himself and love all human
kind', may supply its calm when life draws on to autumn and
the years 'more solemn and serene'.

The lines *To Mary* recall another occasion—if indeed it was
not the same[1]—'when first the clouds that wrap this world from
youth did pass':

III

I do remember well the hour which burst
    My spirit's sleep; a fresh May dawn it was,
    When I walked forth upon the glittering grass,
And wept, I knew not why; until there rose
    From the near schoolroom voices that, alas!
    Were but one echo from a world of woes—
The harsh and grating strife of tyrants and of foes.

IV

And then I clasped my hands, and looked around,
    But none was near to mock my streaming eyes,
Which poured their warm drops on the sunny ground—
    So, without shame, I spake: 'I will be wise,
    And just, and free, and mild, if in me lies
Such power, for I grow weary to behold
    The selfish and the strong still tyrannise
    Without reproach or check'. I then controlled
My tears, my heart grew calm, and I was meek and bold.

---

[1] Dowden believes this incident recorded in the lines *To Mary* to have befallen
at Sion House, that is before 1804; but does not say on what grounds and appears
to rely only on a statement of Medwin's (revised *Life*, p. 16). Mrs. Shelley, as well
as the *Shelley Memorials* (p. 7), referred it to Eton. I assume with Clutton-Brock
that she is right, for strong probability is in her favour. The words 'when first the
clouds that wrap this world from youth did pass' mean, I suppose, 'when youth was
passing and I becoming wiser'.

V

And from that hour did I with earnest thought
 Heap knowledge from forbidden mines of lore,
Yet nothing that my tyrants knew or taught
 I cared to learn, but from that secret store
 Wrought linked armour for my soul, before
It might walk forth to war among mankind . . .

In April 1810, Shelley and his cousin Harriet Grove were
together, and Shelley, as we know on the authority of Charles
her brother, much in love with her. What the experience of
first love was we may learn from a passage in *The Fragment on
Beauty*:

> 'To feel all that is divine in the green-robed earth and the
> starry sky is a penetrating yet vivid pleasure which, when it is
> over, presses like the memory of misfortune; but if you can express
> those feelings—if, secure of sympathy (for without sympathy it is
> worse than the taste of those apples whose core is as bitter ashes),
> if thus secure you can pour forth into another's most attentive ear
> the feelings by which you are entranced, there is an exultation of
> spirit in the utterance—a glory of happiness which far transcends
> all human transports, and seems to invest the soul as the saints are
> with light, with a halo untainted, holy, and undying.'

Nothing that Shelley says puts a date to the events recorded in
the *Hymn to Intellectual Beauty* and the lines indited to Mary.
They took place in spring or early summer and he may be
writing twice over of the same event: a time of overpowering
beauty, the jar of harsh realities, and a vow to serve the Spirit
of the time in ceaseless war with them. All the probabilities are
that the two entrancements, if two, were in point of time close
together; that they came to pass in his last term at school; and
that the instigation from Godwin's pages half a year earlier and
the light of that first love were gathered into them. True, the
accounts were written six or seven years later on, but it costs us
nothing to assume that the boy was father of the man and felt
and thought on those occasions not much otherwise than his
tale makes out. Here, then, the pattern of his spiritual life took
form. Here emerged the motives that were henceforth, in a
word of his own, 'interfluous' in what he did and what he wrote.
He was sworn to war with the oppressors not from pity but
from fear of himself and love of other men, and from faith in

their immortal destiny. With the hope of immortality stood or fell the strongest sanction of their dignity and their claim to freedom. The pranks in the churchyards came not more of a lust for sensation than of an earnest concern. But 'demon, ghost, and heaven', 'frail spells', 'poisonous names'—the whole tradition, that is to say, of the sinning soul, its judge, its eternal bliss or bail—had no power to defeat for him the plague of his own heart, the wrongs of men upon men, the force of accident, the shadow of death. These requirements only the 'Intellectual Beauty'[1] could answer, and nothing led into touch with it like the experience of the passion in which in those rememberable summer days he rejoiced. He knew now what to live for; he had bound himself in his three-corded girdle: Justice and Faith and Love. And if the vivid moments could not supply him with a new theology there and then, if they fled away, and left him for a while simply mistrustful of the frail spells, that would be an instance of delayed action; his atheism, as he wantonly called it, was already on the border of his mind.

[1] 'Intellectual' in the sense so often carried by the word in the eighteenth century of 'spiritual' or 'behind the senses'.

# IV

# OXFORD

## 1. Hogg[1]

THOMAS JEFFERSON HOGG, who enters at this point into the story, was of an old North Country family on the Tory side. His father, John Hogg, D.L. and barrister-at-law, lived at his hereditary seat of Norton House, near Stockton-on-Tees. Born in May 1792, and intended for his father's profession, Jefferson was sent to the Royal Grammar School at Durham, and thence to University College, Oxford, where he came into residence in February 1810, by two terms earlier than Shelley. He was already a vigorous reader, with a turn for languages which ultimately made him free of all the greater literatures of the Western world, and he read discerningly. And in his Oxford days he had other qualities at use which as time went on were to fall away. He had liberal inclinations, and was not afraid of breaking bounds. The writings which he put before Stockdale dismayed the publisher by their speculative audacity, and so, no doubt, would his *Leonora* have done—his 'piteous story' of one Mary of whose wrongs and sufferings he had learnt at first hand. It was not only in a fine loyalty to his friend, but on absolute grounds, and for the liberty to think, that in the matter of *The Necessity of Atheism* he forfeited his University by hoisting his flag. Yet the Tory in him can never have been less than latent, and in after years was much in evidence. He was at one time numbered with the followers of Bentham and the friends of Stuart Mill, and contributed to *The Westminster Review*; but in 1858 he 'had always been ignorant respecting all the varieties of religious dissent', and 'would not walk across Chancery Lane in the narrowest part to redress all the wrongs of Ireland past, present, and to come'.

Indeed, he had not been made for the soldier of a faith, as even his earliest publication shows. In 1813 appeared his *Memoirs of Prince Alexy Haimatoff*.[2] The hero is a young Russian

---

[1] I have drawn for this section on the Introduction and the contents of *After Shelley : The Letters of Thomas Jefferson Hogg to Jane Williams*, edited by Sylva Norman, Oxford University Press, 1934.

[2] Published by the Hookhams: preface dated 4 Feb.

of exalted rank who passes from one European country to
another on intellectual and amatory adventures, so as sometimes to remind us of Don Juan. Well versed in the humanity
of the ancients, in the science of the moderns, and in all manly
and military accomplishments, handsome in person as he is
rich in mind, he devotes himself now to the cause of liberty and
universal reform, now to love and pleasure, till love changes
him, and he settles down at last as the son-in-law of a Tory
magnate in an English shire. On these crude first-fruits of
a real artistic power Shelley wrote an article in *The Critical
Review* for December 1814, with much praise, both well and ill
bestowed, and with vehement reprehension. He noted in the
character of two or three of the women the delineative subtlety
which was to make a masterpiece of his own portrait, and the
impressive episode of the Sultana, who inveigles the Prince to
her seraglio, and would have murdered him in the manner of
the female spider; but he ran a-tilt at a moral laxity in the hero
set down apparently with cynical tolerance. The philosophical
tutor who travels with the Prince advises him to cultivate his
heart by gallantries among peasant women:[1] and, the advice
being readily taken, 'the effects were by no means very mis-
chievous, at the worst a day of weeping to a few families'. 'A
blind idolatry', writes Shelley, to 'worship the image [of love]
and blaspheme the deity.' The Prince, again, is a novice in a
revolutionary Society, severely tested in principles and virtues.
And yet, to Shelley's detestation, he throws himself in England
into the Tory cause, reprobating it in his heart, that he may
win the favour of Mary's father and, marrying Mary, descends
thereafter from a seeker of perfection to a moderate man.

That Hogg should contemplate so cavalierly all these
lubricities and knaveries was in character. For all the finer
metal in him he had more than a few ounces of what he singles
out as his hero's greater faults, sensuality and pride: a more
than medium sensuality that on one or two occasions carried
him grievously away[2] and came out in his biography of Shelley

---

[1] It has been absurdly and gratuitously supposed that some insinuation was
here intended against Dr. Lind (see R. Garnett, art. Hogg in *D.N.B.*).

[2] In *Harriet and Mary*, 1944, Mr. Walter Sidney Scott denies, what has been
hitherto accepted without question, that Hogg attempted to seduce Harriet
Shelley when her husband, on a visit to Field Place, had left her with him at York
in Oct. 1811. He denies the charge on the evidence of the letters which Shelley

in all that harping on foods and firesides, and the particular memories of teas and dinners fifty years afar. Not the heroic line in morals, and not martyrdom, though he tried it once, but the life of a well-to-do scholar was his natural choice; and pride and a fancy to be cynical fell in well with it. With his keen perception of the ludicrous and the uncouth, he had only to think of the supporters of any creed or cause to take it warily. His comment on men and things often brings to mind the sketch of him in his middle years, sitting at a game of chess,[1] face deeply trenched, nose like a big bent blade, firm-set mouth, and eyes of grim perusal. Yet, if Shelley's first devotion abated somewhat as time went on, there never wanted some incentive to the love and praise that flowed across the distance in the lines to Mrs. Gisborne:

> You will see Hogg—and I cannot express
> His virtues—though I know that they are great,
> Because he locks, then barricades the gate
> Within which they inhabit:—of his wit
> And wisdom you'll cry out when you are bit.
> He is a pearl within an oyster shell
> One of the richest of the deep.[2]

About the year 1855 Sir Percy and Lady Shelley entrusted him with a biography of the poet, and lent him the material, only to recall it when the freedom of the two volumes of 1858

wrote to Hogg from Keswick in the ensuing November and December, and *Harriet and Mary* produces for the first time in their authentic form, and not in the greatly abridged and falsified version in Hogg's biography. Few readers, I imagine, will be persuaded by this defence, or see aught else in the letters but its clear disproof, to say nothing of the evidence in the Hitchener letters, which Mr. Scott arbitrarily minimizes. On 7 Jan. 1815, Mary Shelley—or Mary Godwin, as she still was—in one among several letters produced in *Harriet and Mary* promises Hogg (to take her words in their obvious meaning) that, after the birth of her expected child, he shall be her lover in the full sense of the expression, taking Shelley's acquiescence for granted. Again Mr. Scott will have it that Hogg intended no more than a judicious flirtation. It is at least an open question.

[1] Reproduced in Mrs. Julian Marshall's *Mary Wollstonecraft Shelley* and Mr. Roger Ingpen's editions of Shelley's Letters.

[2] I take it the Julian edition is right in its printing of a passage in Shelley's letter to J. and M. Gisborne, 26 May 1820: 'To know H(ogg), if anyone can know him, is to know something very unlike, and inexpressibly superior, to the great mass of men.' 'Our divine Shelley . . . one who always loved you the best.' (Mary Shelley to T. J. H., 28 Feb. 1823.) In the beginning of a fragment on Friendship, printed by Hogg, Shelley alludes to some estrangement between them and asks to be forgiven for it. I cannot refer this to the estrangement at York in Nov. 1811.

offended them. He was then in his sixties, and twenty years married (or living as married)[1] to Jane, the companion of Edward Williams, and Shelley's 'Miranda'. Some practice as a Counsel on the Northern Circuit, a place on the Board of the Corporations Commissioners in 1833, and a spell of twenty years as revising barrister for the northern boroughs were the rather scant achievements of his professional career. And the laurels that he thought to be his due in the field of letters had been withheld. In '32 and '33 he had indeed made some impression with his papers on Shelley at Oxford in *The New Monthly Magazine*; but there were other articles by which the editors and the public had set little. His *Two Hundred and Nine Days*, an account in two volumes of a tour in Italy in 1827, fulsomely insular and tiresomely funny, deserved no life and had none. Under these and other disappointments he increased, as time went on, in the 'spleen and melancholy' that Peacock noted in singular union with a kind heart; and before the death of Mary Shelley in 1852 he appears in her letters, and in other notices, with a certain malice under his tongue, his temper now depending on little things—the children not noisy or the dinner not amiss[2]—shy of others, as others were of him,[3] and fat and gouty. Before the end he had lost almost all his friendships, including that with Peacock and that with Leigh Hunt, and had wrapped himself in his staid devotion to the mistress of his home. But in the fragmentary book by which the world knows him, as in the papers of '32 and '33, which he absorbed into it, he revived his wonderful days and his saving admiration; and death overtook him in 1862 pursuing the sacred task to the end of a third volume.[4] The book has many faults—inaccuracy,

[1] See *After Shelley*, pp. xiii ff. and *infra*.

[2] Sylva Norman is almost certainly right in supposing that Hogg was meant by Humphry Hippy of Hypicon House, Durham, in *Melincourt* (1817). Hippy is fond of chess and wine, and 'the tinkling of spoons and the divine song of the tea-urn', and prefers these sounds to the music of winds and waters.

[3] 'Shy, reserved, and disappointed', says Thornton Hunt. In 1824 Crabb Robinson objected to including Hogg among the members of a dining club. 'He is a scorner', he writes in his diary, 'and I am uncomfortable in his presence.' (*After Shelley*, xiii.)

[4] Sylva Norman writes on p. xxx of *After Shelley*: 'The date May 29, 1841, which stands at the head of Chapter XXV, suggests that Hogg was actually working on his biography long before the family's invitation'; and on xxxii–xxxiii collects evidence that before his death he had completed a third volume, which his brother John offered to Moxon, having obtained Sir Percy Shelley's consent to its publication. As she also states, there is reason to believe that the manuscript still exists.

disorder, facts distorted or suppressed, letters garbled, conversations of which the words, if not the drift, are unhistorical. But, above the shrewdness and the excellent rendering of incident, the creative power, the power to call back the integral Shelley, is there. If his doings and sayings, as recorded in these pages, be not entirely 'what did happen', they are certainly 'what ought to have happened'; and we have Trelawny's witness to the living identity of this Shelley with the man he knew. Nor, unless Hogg himself had intruded so often into the story, would its abundant comedy have distinguished it even among the famous biographies—the interplay of its two main actors, and its festive appreciation of 'the divine poet' united with the incorrigible child.

## 2. THE UNDERGRADUATE

Shelley went into residence at University College in October 1810, and made acquaintance with Hogg at his first appearance in Hall. The two men, who had not before seen one another, disputed over the merits of the German and Italian literatures, in equal ignorance of either, till the tables were deserted. The talk being then renewed in Hogg's rooms,

'I had leisure,' he writes, 'to examine and, I may add, to admire the appearance of my very extraordinary guest. It was a sum of many contradictions. His figure was slight and fragile, and yet his bones and joints were large and strong. He was tall, yet he stooped so much that he seemed of a low stature.[1] His clothes were expensive, and made according to the most approved mode of the day; but they were tumbled, rumpled, unbrushed. His gestures were abrupt and sometimes violent, occasionally even awkward, yet more frequently gentle and graceful. His complexion was delicate and almost feminine, of the purest red and white; yet he was tanned and freckled by exposure to the sun, having passed the autumn, as he said, in shooting. His features, his whole face, and particularly his head were, in fact, extremely small; yet the last *appeared* of a remarkable bulk, for his hair was long and bushy, and in fits of absence, and in his agonies of anxious thought, he often rubbed it fiercely with his hands, or passed his fingers quickly through his locks unconsciously, so that it was singularly wild and rough. At times when it was the mode to

---

[1] 'Like an elegant and slender flower, whose head drooped from being surcharged with rain', as de Quincey heard him described (*Tait's Magazine*, Jan. 1846).

imitate stage-coachmen as closely as possible in costume, and when the hair was invariably cropped, like that of our soldiers, this eccentricity was very striking. His features were not symmetrical (the mouth, perhaps, excepted), yet was the effect of the whole extremely powerful. They breathed an animation, a fire, an enthusiasm, a vivid and preternatural intelligence that I never met with in any other countenance. Nor was the moral expression less beautiful than the intellectual; for there was a softness, a delicacy, a gentleness, and especially (though this will surprise many) that air of profound religious veneration that characterises the best works, and chiefly the frescoes (and into these they infused their whole souls) of the great masters of Florence and of Rome. I recognised the very peculiar expression in these wonderful productions long afterwards, and with a satisfaction mingled with much sorrow, for it was after the decease of him in whose countenance I had first observed it.'

One other of these contrasts Hogg has omitted to observe; for the voice, which he found so 'intolerably shrill, harsh and discordant, of the most cruel intension', seemed to others—to Peacock, for instance—shrill only under excitement, but ordinarily, and especially in reading, 'soft and low, but clear', and 'good both in tone and tune'.

On the following day Hogg called on Shelley in his rooms.[1]

'I remarked', he writes, 'the same contradiction which I had already observed in his person and dress; the rooms had just been papered and painted; the carpet, curtains and furniture were quite new. . . . The general air of freshness was greatly obscured, however, by the indescribable confusion in which the various objects were mixed; . . . books, boots, papers, shoes, philosophical instruments, clothes, pistols, linen, crockery, ammunition, and phials innumerable, with money, stockings, prints, crucibles, bags and boxes were scattered on the floor and in every place, as if the young chemist, in order to analyse the mystery of creation, had endeavoured first to reconstruct the primeval chaos. The tables, and especially the carpet, were already stained with large spots of various hues, which frequently proclaimed the agency of fire. An electrical machine, an air-pump, the galvanic trough, a solar microscope, and large glass jars and receivers were conspicuous amidst the mass of matter. . . . Two piles of books supported the tongs, and these upheld a small glass retort above an argand lamp. I had not been seated many minutes before the liquor in the

---

[1] On the first floor in the corner of the quadrangle next the Hall.

vessel boiled over, adding fresh stains to the table, and rising in fumes with a most disagreeable odour. Shelley snatched the glass quickly, and dashing it in pieces among the ashes under the grate, proceeded with much eagerness and enthusiasm to show me . . . the electrical apparatus; turning round the handle very rapidly, so that the fierce crackling sparks flew forth; and standing upon the stool with glass feet, he begged me to work the machine, until he was filled with the fluid, so that his long, wild locks bristled and stood on end.'

In this 'magician's den' they usually forgathered. They spent the mornings separately; then, at one o'clock, went out together, usually by the Isis or Shotover way, to strike at some point or other on a bee-line across the fields, till even Shelley knew what tiredness was. There was dinner in Hall at five; then tea in rooms; supper at ten; and bed—for Hogg at any rate—punctually at two. Into this programme we must insert an interval of from two to four hours, after dinner and tea, when Hogg read or wrote, and his companion slept, 'stretched on the rug before a large fire, like a cat, in a sweet and mighty oblivion until ten, when he would suddenly start up, and rubbing ·his eyes with great violence, or passing his fingers swiftly through his long hair, would enter at once into a vehement argument, or begin to recite verses with a rapidity and energy that were often quite painful'. But the day's course was not invariable; for Shelley disliked Hall, and the country ramble might not finish till the night hours. In that case they ate the supper that awaited them, laid before the fire to keep hot—unless Shelley overturned it—and proceeded, with or without the slumberous intermission, to read, singly or together, or talk.

With these manners and pursuits, they were strange apparitions in a College that numbered, if Hogg has reported truly, a bare half-dozen reading men, and could stand for a pattern of drunken youth and dull and formal age. The College was in steep decline after its brilliant epoch of nearly fifty years from about 1745, in which a remarkable number of men eventually eminent in letters or affairs taught or studied within its walls. It had reverted to the common level of the Colleges in the eighteenth century, when Lord Chesterfield would not send his son to Oxford 'because he had been there himself'. The

Master, James Griffith, a shy and solitary man, a dilettante in music and painting, had left the reins of discipline to George Rowley, the unpopular Dean, who did more to exasperate than to put down the prevailing unruliness and viciousness. Nor were the personal relations that sweeten College life cultivated by the Fellows of the society or by the Master, who were all at pains 'to keep the persons of the students at the greatest possible distance'.[1] Even in the undergraduate world the two friends kept much to themselves. A few of their neighbours called in upon them at times, but they were generally left alone and not undeservedly misliked. For, apart from Shelley's 'madness' (which was the general idea of him, as it had been before at school), the two friends, as time went on, were more and more a world to themselves, 'never dined in College, dressed differently from all others, and did everything in their power to show singularity',[2] or so it seemed to those about them. They were ideally, however, in the right place. If the studies officially prescribed for them were a by-work, and the tests for graduation 'hardly worthy of a senior schoolboy',[3] they could approach in their own reading, thinking, writing to the ideal of the scholar's life. In the years when the Honours system had not yet taken root, and when 'Greek learning', in particular, was still 'at the lowest point of degradation', and 'no part of the works of Plato was studied'[4], an undergraduate could only make up for the negligence of his superiors by private enthusiasm; and private enthusiasm in Shelley's case could hardly have run higher. We read of the 'awe', the 'mighty emotion', with which he would 'approach for the first time a volume which he believed to be replete with the recondite and mystic philosophy of antiquity; his cheeks glowed, his eyes became bright, and his whole frame trembled'. He would talk wistfully of the medieval Universities and the seven years' course of study, and lament the long holidays. ' "Then the oak[5] is such a blessing!" he exclaimed

[1] *Memoirs of a Highland Lady, the Autobiography of Elizabeth Grant of Rothiemurchus*, ed. Lady Strachey, p. 125. The authoress was the Master's niece, and was residing with him in Shelley's time.

[2] Report to Hogg's father by a friend, C. R. Clarke.       [3] Hogg, i. 259.

[4] See Thomas Frognall Dibdin, *Reminiscences of a Literary Life*, 1836, i. 92; and Henry Fynes-Clinton, *Literary Remains*, 1854, p. 229; both cited in *Reminiscences of Oxford by Oxford Men 1559–1850*, ed. Lilian M. Quiller-Couch.

[5] The thick oaken outer door of College rooms, latched on the inside, and in that event impassable.

with peculiar fervour, clasping his hands, and repeating often—
"the oak is such a blessing!" slowly and in a solemn tone.' Indeed,
these University days, or at any rate the first of his two terms,
fall with the previous summer into an enchanted episode.
Shelley had 'begun to think and feel', and for a little while—
until the Christmas of 1810—he was at peace, unpersecuted,
unembroiled, a heady but not yet an angry inquirer.

However, he was spoiling for action. In February 1811
he was one of the first three residents in Oxford to join in the
public subscription for the Irish patriot and Castlereagh's sworn
enemy Peter Finnerty.[1] In the following month, when Leigh
Hunt was triumphantly acquitted from a charge of seditious
libel for an article against army flogging in his *Examiner*,
Shelley wrote to him with a plan for a society like that of the
*Illuminati*, a union of liberal-minded men to resist the legal
strangulation of opinion and 'to establish rational liberty on
as firm a basis as that which would have supported the visionary
scheme of a completely equalised community'. As an undergraduate, he told Hunt, he might not then 'avow all that he
thought', but when he came of age, and succeeded to his father's
seat in Parliament, his 'every endeavour should be directed to
the advantage of liberty'. Meanwhile his pen was running, and
in several directions. He had already practised the lyric equiva-
lents of Gothic romance in half a dozen pieces in *St. Irvyne*, and
in the summer holidays, before his arrival in Oxford, had
appeared in a volume of fourteen short pieces, *Original Poetry
by Victor and Cazire*. Cazire was his sister Elizabeth, who, for
one of her two contributions, had imposed upon him by lifting
'The Black Canon of Elmham' from Lewis's *Tales of Terror and
Wonder*; whereupon Stockdale, the publisher, on discovering
the cheat, suppressed the entire edition, saving a few copies

---

[1] Finnerty, when a youth of twenty years of age, was a printer in Dublin and
concerned in a paper called *The Press* when Castlereagh was acting Chief Secretary
to the Viceroy in 1797–8. The fearless indictment in that paper of the cruelties of
the Administration cost him a spell in the pillory and a sentence of two years
imprisonment. After his release he commenced agitator and journalist. Appointed
special correspondent on the Expedition to Walcheren in 1809, he sent home strong
criticisms of the muddles therein perpetrated and was summarily recalled by Lord
Castlereagh. He vented his feelings in a letter to the Secretary for War published
in *The Morning Chronicle* in which the atrocities in Ireland were recalled. For this
he was tried for libel and condemned to a fine of £20 and eighteen months in
Lincoln jail.

previously sent out.[1] The pieces of Shelley's writing, besides three of terror and wonder and two of political insurgency, were poems inspired by the fair or broken weather of his first love, none in the whole volume excelling juvenility. Medwin, on a visit to Oxford in November, found him occupied with 'Tales from the German' (or a French translation from the German); and in the same month the *Posthumous Fragments of Margaret Nicholson edited by John Fitzvictor*, a sumptuous quarto, from the press of John Munday, aroused in academic circles a day's wonder. The reputed author was the mad laundress, at that time living in Bedlam, who attempted the life of the King in 1786, and the reputed editor her pious nephew. Hogg tells us that one day, looking through the proof-sheets of these poems, he demonstrated by a few alterations that what was unpresentable as poetry might be soon remoulded into good burlesque. The poems were altered accordingly, and Peg Nicholson put upon the title-page with the intent 'to ridicule the strange mixture of sentimentality with the murderous fury of revolutionists so prevalent in the compositions of the day'. But fustian prepense and fustian unbidden who shall distinguish? Of the six poems—one gothically weird, three amatory, and two revolutionary—only *An Epithalamion of Francis Ravaillac and Charlotte Corday* is unmistakable parody. It is hard to conceive how Munday so approved of the work that he published at his own risk, or how it sold rapidly, as Shelley declared; much more intelligible that, as others have reported, it 'failed' and was voted 'dull'. Even the colloquy of the two tyrannicides, though peppered with indecency, is dull, and only worth having as a mark of intellectual sobriety in the midst of zeal.[2] So far the main stock in prose or verse had been romance. But before *St. Irvyne* came out in mid-December Stockdale had before him a 'novel to convey metaphysical truth by way of conversation';[3] and troubles at Field Place evoked, before Christmas, 'a satirical

---

[1] The sheets were printed by C. and W. Phillips of Worthing and sent on to Stockdale. One of the distributed copies turned up in 1898, to be reprinted and edited by Richard Garnett.

[2] Slatter in his Notes to the fourth edition of Montgomery's *Oxford*; Shelley to Graham, 30 Nov. 1811; and Hogg.

[3] It was refused by Stockdale, then by Slatter and Munday, as heretical; printed by an Abingdon printer named King, in whose hands it was on the fatal Lady-Day of 1811. The sheets were then sent to Longman, but in vain. Henry Slatter, in Notes to Montgomery's *Oxford*, confuses it with Hogg's *Leonora*.

poem',[1] and, after Christmas, *A Poetical Essay on the Existing State of Things by a Gentleman of the University of Oxford*. In the second week of March 1811, the *Essay* was advertised to be published in London by B. Crosby & Co., and the proceeds assigned to the fund in aid of Peter Finnerty. The book, however, if it appeared, is lost, and the questions concerning it ask themselves in vain.[2]

All this time he read endlessly, and in what he read we can see more clearly than in what he wrote the synthesis of his inspirations coming about, and of what nature the inspirations were. He is occupied with romance, with Godwin, and with metaphysics. Homer and Euripides are much in hand, but more especially *The Curse of Kehama*, and *Gebir*, 'repeatedly perused and recited with tiresome iteration'; and 'narratives of travellers in the East and marvellous tales of Oriental fancy'. It was a remote and fantastic world that took his fancy, peopled with human or divine or monstrous figures, huge cloudy sym-

---

[1] Buxton Forman in *The Shelley Library*, pp. 23 ff., thought he had discovered this poem in a pamphlet entitled *Lines Addressed to His Royal Highness the Prince of Wales on his being appointed Regent by Philopatria Jun.*, dated 1811, and printed by Hamelin and Seyfang, the printers of *Laon and Cythna*, Seyfang being also the printer of *Swellfoot the Tyrant*. It consists of some 250 verses of ironical adulation, much, as Forman considered, in Shelley's style. But, though the King's madness occurred in October, and the matter was before Parliament from 12 Dec. onwards, the Regency Bill did not pass until 5 Feb. 1811. The undated letter from Shelley to Graham, which Forman quotes as evidence, is to ask Graham not to find him a publisher for his satire, but to set to music his translation of a stanza of the Marseillaise.

[2] The title-page, with a quotation of four lines from the sixth part of *The Curse of Kehama* on the ravages of Famine, and the words: 'For assisting to maintain in Prison [Mr. Peter Finnerty] imprisoned for a libel', is given in an advertisement in *The Oxford Herald* for 9 Mar. 1811, as discovered by D. F. MacCarthy (*Shelley's Early Life*, pp. 100 ff.). It was subsequently advertised in *The Courier, The Morning Chronicle, The Times*. MacCarthy also found that *The Dublin Weekly Messenger* of 7 Mar. 1812, in an account of Shelley, stated that he had published a poem on Finnerty's behalf, and the profit paid to Finnerty was £100, which is hardly credible. Shelley sent a copy of this number of the newspaper to Godwin on 8 Mar. Further, in the first volume of Lady Charlotte Bury's anonymous *Diary illustrative of the Times of George the Fourth* is a letter, written by C. Kirkpatrick Sharpe, and dated 15 Mar. 1811, from Christ Church, Oxford, on the new 'literary Sun—a Mr. Shelley of University College, who lives upon arsenic, aqua fortis, [and] half an hour's sleep in the night'. The Margaret Nicholson poems are then mentioned, 'a pamphlet in praise of atheism', *St. Irvyne*, and 'Shelley's last exhibition, a Poem on the State of Public Affairs'. No allusion to the *Essay* can be found in Shelley's letters, unless, as MacCarthy supposes, the 'satirical poem' above mentioned was identical with it, and unless he is speaking of it to Hogg on 11 Jan. 1811, as the poem he has sent (or is sending) to Longman.

bols of a cosmic drama that he has already more or less conceived, and for which Godwin and Condorcet had delivered
the doctrine. Further, all depended on the Intellectual Beauty.
To support the intimations of that Power, he resorts continually
to Plato, proceeds from the *Symposium* to the *Phaedo*, the *Phaedrus*,
the *Republic*. And to uphold its claim against the 'poisonous
names on which his youth was fed', he takes up the philosophers
in whom the deists or the materialists had put their trust, and
especially Locke and Hume, together with the Christian
apologists, Paley before all others, for an idol to shy at. He is
'vehemently excited', says Hogg, by the strange doctrine un-
folded in the *Phaedo*, and especially by the argument that all
our knowledge consists of reminiscences of what we have learnt
in another world. He uses Hume to level the road to Plato. In
'saying yes', as the Germans phrase it, he is bound also to say no,
and in saying no he has started to say yes. Under the stronger
avocation of the theological search science begins to slacken its
hold on him and declines to an appanage of his estate.

Further, he flowed in talk. He would prophesy the coming
age, the indefinite increase of the earth's fertility, a perfect
climate all the world over, the conversion of all manner of
substances to serviceable fuels, and balloons to explore Africa.
'The shadow of the first balloon as it glided silently over that
unhappy country would virtually emancipate every slave and
annihilate slavery for ever.' He would put forward the nega-
tions of Locke or Hume with a dialectical prowess and a logical
severity strangely assorted with the credulous and the fanciful
in other regions of his mind. And in all this Hogg noted a
certain sobriety, a certain conservatism. 'The ideal republic
where his fancy loved to expatiate was adorned with all the
graces which Plato, Xenophon, and Cicero have thrown around
the memory of ancient liberty.' 'He was in theory wholly a
republican, but in practice so far only as it is possible to be one
with due regard to the sacred rights of a scholar and a gentleman.' Likewise in theology, he knew indeed the joy of carrying
all before him, but apart from that, 'his whole frame of mind',
writes Hogg, 'was grave, earnest, and anxious, and his deport-
ment reverential'. 'In politics', wrote Shelley in the summer of
1811, 'I am enthusiastic, I have reasoned and my reason has
brought me to the end of my enquiries. On the other hand, in

theology, enquiries into our intellect, its eternity and perish-
ability, I advance with caution and circumspection.' 'It delights
me to discuss and be sceptical', he once said; 'thus we must
arrive at truth.'

That blend of daring and militant with peaceable and
humble appears in the moral aspect of his character with equal
clearness. The open war on Christianity and the political and
social powers called for the will about which Trelawny once
declared that he never fell in with another so strong. It was
strong in the smallest as in the greatest things. Hogg is always
dancing attendance on a man 'of the whimsical agility of a
kangaroo', dashing after him into shops, alleys, by-paths. Or
on winter days, if it should please the elf to play at ducks and
drakes or sail his boats of paper on roadside ponds, Hogg has
nothing for it but to stand and shiver. Or he must get by
stratagem what he cannot otherwise; must stop the pistol
practice, for instance, by secreting the cartridges. Indeed the
circumventing of Shelley became to so keen a humorist a very
relishable art. When the furious dog had ripped off the coat-
tails of 'the divine poet', all but a shred, and the enraged
victim, having torn them clean loose, would leave them on a
hedge-top to testify to Gods and men, how enjoyable to argue
with him on the nature of anger, and finally, in a calmer
atmosphere, to produce the coat-tails, recovered, and in the
meanwhile hidden from sight, with mobility and with leger-
demain! In the gravest matters it is the same tale. The young
prophet is in the main solitary, his own counsellor indivertible.
And all the while, 'as his port had the meekness of a maiden,
so the heart of the young virgin who has never crossed her
father's threshold to encounter the rude world could not be
more susceptible of all the sweet domestic charities than his'.
'I have had the happiness to associate with some of the best
specimens of gentlemen, but Shelley was almost the only
example I have yet found who was never wanting even in the
most minute particular of the infinite and various observances
of pure, entire, and perfect gentility.' So he comes before us in
Hogg's vivid stories, that, for instance, of the boy beating the
ass and the flaming intervener, or that of the hunger-bitten
child and the 'solemn and earnest' rescuer feeding it with a
spoon. And he has already begun the practice of sharing his

purse or his prospects with needy men of letters. But the Oxford days were not over before his irrepressible mind embroiled him with authority, nowhere as harsh and hasty as in his home, and the unslackening storm broke over him whose effect must needs be to assist his natural frailties, and in the crucial stages of his own and most men's lives

> To cross the curious workmanship of Nature,
> To mingle beauty with infirmities,
> And pure perfection with impure defeature;
> Making it subject to the tyranny
> Of mad mischances and much misery.

### 3. A TROUBLED VACATION

By 15 December he seems to have been once more at Field Place, having called, in the course of his journey, on J. J. Stockdale, and conversed with him all too freely. Stockdale had still to sustain some fifteen years of a rather venturesome business before he came out as a blackmailer, or the accomplice of blackmailers, and fluttered society with the *Memoirs of Harriette Wilson* and with *Stockdale's Budget of 'all that is good, noble and amiable in the country'*, the scandalous *farrago* in which he has set down, amid a 'mass of maculacy', his few transactions with the Shelley family.[1] He was dense, stolid, pompous, wordy, a man of some kindness and a copious religiosity, and a knave who never thought that he was one; one of Browning's men. He had perceived from letters, conversations and orders for books before the December of 1810, that his young client, whom he admired and liked, was theologically in no good way, and now determined to betray the matter to Timothy Shelley, who had apparently no wind of it. Mr. Shelley had once or twice appeared with Bysshe in the office in Pall Mall, and Stockdale had noted that the father was 'not bright', and rasped his son's

---

[1] See the *Dictionary of National Biography*, *sub* Harriette Wilson. Harriette Wilson was the main article of the entertainment. She was a minx with a host of titled lovers, and the *Memoirs* reported the behaviour and the conversation of some of the highest personages in unguarded hours, and went through thirty editions in a year. A swarm of troubles enveloped Stockdale in consequence, and he replied by purveying still more scandal and more matter from Harriette, in the *Budget*, published weekly from 13 Dec. 1826 down to the following June. The Shelley material begins in the first number and ends on 7 Feb. Hogg had never seen, or had forgotten, this piece of Shelley's history, which was recovered by Richard Garnett in an article entitled 'Shelley in Pall Mall' in *MacMillan's Magazine* for June 1860.

temper by superfluous peremptoriness. But the publisher of *St. Irvyne* had a reason for standing well with him; for the author of that work, now on the eve of its appearance, had undertaken the printer's bill, amounting easily to £100, and it would be good business to do some favour to *le banquier*. Whether on this account, or rather out of pure goodwill, he saw Mr. Shelley, and apprised him of the open infidelity of his son. The perturbed father, though he would not pay the bill, was very much obliged,[1] and there was no slight stir at Field Place. No sooner was Bysshe at home than an angry letter came to hand from his father in London, with a threat to withdraw him from college, and throughout the vacation the puzzled and agitated parents molested him with argument and reproach. 'I am reckoned an outcast', he writes. 'My mother imagines me to be in the high road to Pandemonium, she fancies I want to make a deistical coterie of all my little sisters.' 'I attempted to enlighten my father, *mirabile dictu*! He for a time listened to my arguments; he allowed the impossibility (considered abstractedly) of any interference by Providence. He allowed the utter incredibility of witches, ghosts, legendary miracles. But when I came to *apply* the truths on which we had agreed so harmoniously he started at the bare idea of some facts, generally believed, never having existed, and silenced me with these words: "I believe because I do believe." ' The worst of it was that his parents with their very natural displeasure set him upon crooked ways. 'There is now need of all my art; I must resort to deception. . . . Inconveniences would now result from my *owning* the novel which I have in preparation for the press.[2] I give out, therefore, that I will publish no more; everyone here but the secret few [? Elizabeth and Graham] who enter into its [? my] schemes believe my assertion. I will stab the wretch [religious intolerance] in secret.'[3] And the fatal tract on atheism was a fruit of this resolve.

But a sharper adversity supervened. In the previous Easter holidays he had been deep in love with his cousin Harriet Grove. She was a daughter of Thomas Grove, the proprietor of Ferne House, Donhead, Wiltshire, and of the large estate of

---

[1] His letter of thanks from Field Place, dated 23 Dec., is given in the *Budget*.
[2] The novel 'to convey metaphysical and political truth'. See p. 52.
[3] To Hogg, 20 Dec.

Cwm Elan, some five miles from Rhayader; whose wife, Charlotte Pilfold by her maiden name, the sister of Shelley's mother, had borne him a family of five boys and three girls. Harriet, born in 1791, inherited from her mother the type of beauty that marked the Shelley children, and particularly resembled Bysshe.[1] Medwin says she was 'like one of Shakespeare's women or some Madonna of Raphael's'; and events were soon to prove that she carried under a gentle appearance not a little of the firm and shrewd. Bysshe and she had seen each other occasionally since childhood, and during a particularly enjoyable holiday in the spring of 1809.[2] Her journal, which covers the years 1809 and 1810, proves that for most of 1809 they carried on a busy correspondence, and then, from September onwards, all but entirely dropped it, as if the authorities had suddenly ruled it out. But, if so, all was well again in the Easter holidays of 1810, when they were together for a month at Field Place and in London. There was a large party and many amusements, and Bysshe, writes Charles Grove, 'was more attached to my sister than I can express'. When they parted, the correspondence was resumed, and Bysshe rejoiced, if not in a definite engagement, at least in 'successful devotion'. Then, it would seem, she began to beware of him. His letters, as we have reason to guess,[3] discoursed to her not only of divine providence, but also of the golden rule of 'free' love,[4] and her reactions, or those of her environment, may be indicated in two or three of his

---

[1] He perhaps remembered this fact when writing *Fiordispina*, 11–14.

[2] Dowden (i. 48), on the strength of an unpublished poem, dated 28 Feb. 1805, thinks they may have been devoted as early as that. In the last of the Margaret Nicholson poems, published in Nov. 1810, and by all the marks of it addressed to his cousin, Shelley speaks of the past 'two years of speechless bliss'; and Medwin (revised *Life*, pp. 47–9) puts the beginning of the intimacy in the summer before the writing of *Zastrozzi*—the summer of 1808.

[3] We do know definitely, from his letter to Hogg of 4 July 1811, that he wanted a 'free' union with her, and that he raised the issue we may be fairly sure. He canvassed the problem of marriage in *St. Irvyne* (ix, xii). [Since this note was written the true text of the letter to Hogg has been given by Mr. W. S. Scott in *Shelley at Oxford*, p. 45. It shows that not his own free union with Harriet Grove, but Hogg's with Elizabeth, was in the writer's mind.]

[4] In *Original Poetry by Victor and Cazire* the two Songs (xii, xiii) addressed to her, and dated August 1810, are tranquilly affectionate; but *Despair*, dated June, may record an embittered episode. The *Melody to a Scene of Former Times* in the Margaret Nicholson poems, published in Nov., is unquestionably about Harriet. It laments the surcease of the 'speechless bliss' of the two past years. She has so behaved that reason bids him blot her from his memory, but he will not.

poems, dating from the summer and autumn, on 'torn affection's tie' and the loss of a blissful dream. He was still her suitor, however, when, on his return from Oxford to Field Place in December 1810, she sent him word that the tie between them was broken by her own and her father's will on account of his scepticism. But she seems to have acted from another motive. 'Her nature', writes Shelley, 'was in all probability divested of the enthusiasm by which mine is characterised.' 'When in her natural character, her spirits are good, her conversation animated, and she was almost in consequence ignorant of the refinements in love which can only be attained by solitary reflection.' They were, in fact, well rid of one another; and it would be small blame to her if the real reason for breaking with him was a neighbour in Wiltshire, a Mr. Helyar of Coker Court, whom in the subsequent November she married. She effected the dismissal firmly. To Elizabeth, who came to take her brother's part, she said: 'Even supposing I take your representation of your brother's qualities and sentiments, which . . . I may fairly imagine to be exaggerated . . . what right have I, admitting that he is so superior, to enter into an intimacy which must end in delusive disappointment, when he finds how really inferior I am to the being which his heated imagination has pictured.' In a personal interview with him on 30 December[1] she was no less inexorable. By 6 January he had learnt the truth—she was another's, and for a certain time at any rate he had been deceived. It seems that she had no further correspondence with him, and made it a complete and final severance.

Too much, says Peacock, has been made of this affair. Too little has been made of it. Certainly in the dozen letters that he wrote to Hogg before and after the crisis, he strikes an attitude:

'Is she not gone? And yet I breathe, I live! . . . I have wandered in the snow, for I am cold, wet, and mad.'. . . Yet here I swear—

[1] She must have been staying in the neighbourhood—at Horsham with the Medwins, or at Cuckfield with the Pilfolds. On Wednesday, 2 Jan., he writes to Hogg he is 'but just returned to Field Place from an inefficient effort'—i.e. a personal appeal. Hogg's previous letter was 'put into my hands at the moment of my departure on Sunday morning', 30 Dec. It appears by his letter of 3 Jan. that he was back at home on the Monday—'I could not come to London on Monday, my sister would not part with me'. On 6 Jan. he writes: 'I have tried the methods you would have recommended. I followed her. I would have followed her to the end of the earth.' This may mean that Harriet set out for Wiltshire from wherever she was, and that Shelley overtook her and tried the effect of another interview.

and as I break my oaths may Infinity, Eternity blast me—here I swear that never will I forgive intolerance. . . . Oh, how I wish . . . that it were mine to crush the demon; to hurl him to his native hell, never to rise again, and thus to establish for ever perfect and universal toleration. I expect to gratify some of this insatiable feeling in poetry. . . . She is no longer mine! she abhors me as a sceptic, as what she was before. . . . Is suicide wrong? I slept with a loaded pistol and some poison last night, but did not die. . . . But can the dead feel; dawns any day-beam on the night of dissolution? . . . I am very cold this morning, as I have been most of the night pacing a churchyard. . . . She is gone! She is lost to me for ever! She is married;[1] married to a clod of earth; she will become as insensible herself; all those fine capabilities will moulder.'[2]

But it would be ignorance of humanity to suppose therefore that the hurt was inconsiderable. Nor may we so conclude from the fact that Harriet Grove, as he writes of her, is all but a pure transparency, *nominis umbra*. Not a word of her face or form, or of things that in other days she did or said; nor more than a few mere scraps about her character and manner of mind. He writes more of bigotry than of her; it is bigotry he will not forgive. In one letter he has himself noted how impersonal a being he had made of her. 'The question is, what do I love? It is almost unnecessary to answer. Do I love the person, the embodied identity? . . . No! I love what is superior, what is excellent, or what I conceive to be so.' And in another place he defines love as 'that feeling which arises from an admiration of virtue when abstracted from identity'. Are these the words of a real lover? They are words that he might have used at any time in any instance when the passion had hold of him. Not that the woman, corporeal and concrete, was ever superfluous. But she verged upon transparency. She performed the function

---

[1] Peacock thought this should read 'She married!' She did not marry till the following November. But the received text is more in character.

[2] Citations from the letters dated by Hogg 3, 6, and 11 Jan. 1811. The exact text is printed for the first time in *Shelley at Oxford*, ed. Walter Sidney Scott, 1944. This shows that 'never will I forgive intolerance' should be 'never will I forgive Christianity'. The holographs, so printed, throw more light on the tentative approaches made by Hogg to Elizabeth, who refuses to read his first letter to her (pp. 20, 21). And the tirades against Christianity are fiercer than Hogg allowed them to be in his versions. In the letter of 24 Apr. 1811 occurs a paragraph on Christ himself, as 'this horrid Galilean' who shall 'rule the *canaille*'. Hogg has modified this passage with audacious (or pusillanimous) disguises.

of the crystal by means of which the seer sees. Or, to be more exact, and to use a figure of his own, she was the other of the twin flames that, when united, burn into blessedness, and one has nothing in it foreign to the other. The body dislimns to a 'splendour and wonder' of looks and tones; the spirits rise, each to the 'anti-type' of the purest being of the other; until at last the body, nay, the individuality, is in the way:

> We shall become the same, we shall be one
> Spirit within two frames, oh! wherefore two?

And it was Shelley's propensity to hug the summit and wish for the ecstasy all the time; whereof came many troubles. For to desire the trance for ever, to convert the two to one, to supersede the very self on either side,[1] excludes that 'just exchange' that love should be. You must give me what is yours, and I must give you what is mine. And this is why Shelley was an inobservant lover, and why in respect of love as a harmony and not a unison, or in other words as a discipline of humanity, he was neither a master nor a poet. For the same reason he was doomed to misadventure. He was to find too often that he had set his heart on Echo, and she failed him sadly, for a short while mimic, and thereafter mute.

Yet love was for him a great awakening, the lamp of the mind, 'a seeking all sympathies in one', and a want that is fatally put by. How its first coming and departing shone and loomed in his memory we know from *Alastor* and from the still more superb poetry of *Epipsychidion*. And biographically the incident has weight. It is more than a guess that in the autumn and summer of 1810 it fired the train of luminous divinations and high resolves. In that dismal Christmas holiday his sister Elizabeth would not leave him to take his gun afield. Four months later he wrote of himself as 'deprived of all he cared for';[2] and seven months later, brooding on this and other sorrows, loathed his life.[3] And there was fire enough under the smoke to bring on a morbid disquiet that, gathering force from other

---

[1] Hogg discoursed to him of perfectibility through love in this life and in lives to come. 'I am sick to death', he answers, 'at the name of self. Your theory caused me much reflexion. Is it not founded, however, on that *hateful* principle? Is it *Self* which you propose to raise . . .?' (2 Jan.) As if selfhood and selfishness were all one!

[2] To Hogg, 26 Apr. 1811.  [3] *The Retrospect: Cwm Elan.*

quarters in the summer of 1811, goaded him to his marriage.
And, though the wound was not immedicable, the passing of
the years never entirely relieved it of its lingering pain.[1]

There were, however, other things running in his head. He
had already determined that his sister Elizabeth should be
Hogg's wife, not at present requiring her, as a little later he did,
to forgo the rite of marriage. A high-spirited, noisy, good-
natured, sensible girl, not above fibbing, she had played Cazire
to his Victor in the book of poetry under those names, and had
given to his speculations an indulgent ear; till he beheld her a
poetess and a child of light. Hogg was willing, and even ardent;
she was wary, but not adverse. Harriet, Elizabeth, Hogg:
these are the burden of the letters, and with these the nature of
divinity, and the nature of love, and what to live for, and his
and his friend's books, and which publisher for them. He is
living excitedly. Some Christian, enticed to disputation, sends
him a defence of the faith—and he sits up all one night to
answer it. At last and suddenly the wind at Field Place veered
to the south. On some date before the 14th of January, Stockdale once more played the interloper, prompted this time by a
composition touching religion which he had received from
Hogg, and from which he argued worse things of the writer
than he had already hinted. It had been posted from the house
of the Rev. John Dayrell, of Lymington Dayrell in Buckingham-
shire, close to Mrs. Stockdale's home. Mrs. Stockdale remembered that Hogg had sometimes stayed with Mr. Dayrell (who
was in fact his relative) and she made inquiries in the neighbourhood, with a result which convinced her husband that he
must 'instantly rush forward' and save Shelley from his baleful

---

[1] In a Notebook now in the possession of Shelley's great-nephew Sir John
Shelley-Rolls, there are lines of a stanza of the 'Dedication' to the *Revolt of Islam*
roughly corresponding to stanza VI of the poem as printed. Here, after three lines
nearly identical with 51–3 of the received text, there are three running as follows:

> One whom I found was dear but false to me,
> The other's heart was like a heart of stone
> Which crushed and withered mine.

(*Verse and Prose*, ed. Shelley-Rolls and Ingpen, p. 16.)
Harriet Grove is clearly meant in the first of these lines, and as clearly in line 271
of *Epipsychidion*:

> And One was true—oh! why not true to me?

It has often been pointed out that she was in his mind when composing *Fiordispina*
(1820). The lovers are cousins, like each other in face, and the cousinship is a
stricter bond of love, only less strict than that between twins of the same mother.

friend, and from 'the precipice from which he hung by a hair'. He had presently still more reason for alarm. For early in January Shelley, in renewed confidence, sent him 'a metaphysical essay of atheism',[1] which he intended to 'promulgate throughout the University'. 'I represented that his expulsion would be the inevitable result of so flagrant an insult to such a body, and that such a disgrace must probably remain an incubuss [*sic*], and for ever keep down those talents which might otherwise render him an ornament to society. He, however, was unmoved, and I instantly wrote to his father.' And he wrote not only about Shelley but also about Hogg, his impious deliverances and his ill repute. The Squire, however, had perhaps had too much of Stockdale, and left the letter for a fortnight unanswered. In the meanwhile he inquired about Hogg and his family in London, and was immediately a changed man. 'He came from London', writes Shelley, 'full of your praises. Your principles are *now* as divine as before they were diabolical . . . and, to sum up the whole, he has desired me to make his compliments to you, and to invite you to make Field Place your headquarters for the Easter Vacation.' In an interview with Mr. Shelley, and by wrathful letters from the two young men, Stockdale discovered that 'as but too often happens, all concerned became inimical to me'. The amnesty to Hogg was extended to Bysshe also, and in the ensuing term he wrote to his father from Oxford on religion and other things with a fearless candour and in a cordial tone.[2]

### 4. *THE NECESSITY OF ATHEISM*

By the February of 1811 Shelley had taken an onward step in his theology, and wished by means of *The Necessity of Atheism* to try his footing. The propositions of his little pamphlet were bound to follow in his mind on the surmises set down so humbly and anxiously in the vacation letters. Accepting with relish and with entire assent all the conclusions of Hume's essay *Of Miracles*, he had refused to imitate Hume and remain orthodox, whether ironically or otherwise, by faith. In the letters of the

---

[1] Presumably the metaphysical novel and not *The Necessity of Atheism*. Shelley's offence during the vacation was deism. Stockdale was using a violent and inaccurate term.

[2] See his letters of 6 and 17 Feb. in *Shelley in England*, pp. 168, 173.

Christmas vacation he discourses now and then of his theology.
Does not the word 'God', he asks, imply 'the soul of the universe,
the intelligent and *necessarily* beneficent actuating principle?'
'This it is impossible not to believe in. . . . The leaf of a tree, the
meanest insect on which we trample are in themselves arguments that some vast intellect animates infinity. I confess that
I think Pope's

> All are but parts of one stupendous whole

something more than poetry.' But on which attribute of deity
does the future state (of every individual) depend? Not on its
omnipresent being, but on its purposive will. As the future
punishment of the wicked will surely be a chilling imprisonment in a sort of body, so the reward of the good is as surely
the power of love, infinite in extent, eternal in duration, per-
fectible. That reward, however, cannot 'arise spontaneously
as a necessary appendage to our nature', but can only come
from an awarder or governor of the world.[1] And an intelligent
will, a prime mover or first cause is equally necessary to the
physical universe; for if beneficent energies are busy on all
hands in nature, 'there must be something beyond' to direct
them, some will that uses them. Then:

> 'Why is it not at the same time the soul of the Universe; in
> what is it not analogous to the soul of man? If the principle of
> life be *soul*, then gravitation is as much the soul of a clock as
> animation is that of an oyster. I think we may not inaptly define
> *soul* as the most supreme, superior, and distinguished abstract
> appendage to the nature of anything.'[2]

Again, after insisting on the necessity of a first cause:

> 'Was not this first cause a Deity? Now nothing remains but
> to prove that this Deity has a care, or rather that its only employ-
> ment consists in regulating the present and future happiness of
> its creatures. . . . Oh, that this Deity were the soul of the Universe,
> the spirit of universal, imperishable Love!'

And that so it is we have reason to believe, since we must judge
of it by the attributes of our own nature.[3]

For the source of these speculations Shelley might almost
have gone no farther than the book which sets down in exemp-

---

[1] This and the preceding argument occur in the letter to Hogg of 3 Jan. 1811.
[2] 6 Jan.          [3] 12 Jan.

lary clearness and fullness the main theistic argument of the Newtonian era—the *Natural Theology* of William Paley. Newton had declared that 'this most beautiful system of the sun, planets, and comets could only proceed from the counsel and dominion of an intelligent and powerful Being', and that the Being who is the world's first cause 'endures for ever and is everywhere present, and by existing always and everywhere he constitutes duration and space'. Further, the argument of a prime mover, on which Locke and many of his successors in the main relied, was enlarged and supported by the argument from design which Paley elaborated with a hundred instances in animal and vegetable life, in the elements, and in the heavens. And, like Newton, Paley affirmed that the divinity is 'intelligent', that is a person, and omnipresent at the same time:

'Contrivance appears to me to prove everything which we wish to prove. Amongst other things it proves the *personality* of the Deity, as distinguished from what is sometimes called Nature, sometimes called a principle; which terms seem to be intended to admit and express an efficacy, but to exclude and to deny a personal agent. Now that which can contrive, which can design, must be a person. These capacities constitute personality, for they imply consciousness and thought. . . . They require a centre in which perceptions unite, and from which volitions flow, which is mind. . . . We have no authority to limit the properties of mind to any particular circumscription of space. These properties exist in created nature under a great variety of sensible forms. Also, every animated being has its *sensorium*; that is, a certain portion of space within which perception and volition are exerted. This sphere may comprehend the universe; and, being so imagined, may serve to furnish us with as good a notion as we are capable of forming of a Being infinite as well in essence as in power; yet nevertheless a person.'[1]

Again, a little later on:

'In every part and place of the universe with which we are acquainted we perceive the exertion of a power which we believe to proceed, mediately or immediately, from the Deity. . . . In what accessible portion of our globe do we not meet with gravity, magnetism, electricity, together with the properties also and powers of organised substances, of vegetable or of animated nature? Effects are produced by power, not by laws. A law

[1] *Natural Theology*, ch. xxiii.

F

cannot execute itself. . . . An agency so general that we cannot discover its absence may be called universal; and, with not quite the same, but with no inconsiderable propriety, the Person or Being in whom that power resides, or from whom it is derived may be taken to be *omnipresent*.'[1]

Now anyone who knew Shelley well enough might have prophesied at this point that he would soon remove the attributes of personality from his notion of the cosmic soul. For deism involved—or involved for him—so much that he transcended and abjured at the 'visitation' of the Intellectual Beauty, if that experience was really what it seems to have been. If it was a first revolt from the idea of a Master of the World, with his commandments, and his sleepless watch, and his dread account, it might, and it did, die down; but only to come again. The mystic in Shelley would take no interest in a deity who must be argued to exist, and stands in a relation to us, as one being to others, a king to his vassals, or a father to his sons. And the libertarian, or antinomian rather, and the imagination that ever abhorred a limit would dislike the moral governor, with the probation and the reward, as well as the Lord of all things, who made a beginning and set a bound. These suppositions depended in the argument on the certainty of a prime mover or first cause, and Shelley, though he had not yet read, it would seem, Hume's *Dialogues on Natural Religion*, might have been counted on sooner or later to call it in doubt. *The Necessity of Atheism* should have been entitled *The Uncertainty of Deism*.

The little pamphlet with seven pages of text and a short 'Advertisement', printed by E. & W. Phillips of Worthing, the printers of his *Original Poetry*, was intended, as the title-page declares, to be 'sold in London and Oxford'. But he may well have primarily designed it, as Hogg explains to us, for his own convenience. He had learnt from Dr. Lind to challenge authorities, major or minor, on physics or on theology through the post, and was at this time posing clergymen with his heresy; whereby it would save labour to send his argument in a printed form. He received the copies by February 13,[2] and sent a

---

[1] *Natural Theology*, ch. xxiv.
[2] See letter to Graham of that date. The pamphlet had been advertised as 'speedily to be published' in the *Oxford Herald* of 9 Feb. In the letter to Graham of the 13th directions are given to advertise it in 'eight famous papers and in the *Globe*'.

number of them to heads of colleges, professors of the University, and to all the bishops; not only in the hope of vanquishing these dignitaries, should they engage him, but in the spirit of his Advertisement:

> *As a love of truth is the only motive which actuates the Author of this little tract, he earnestly entreats that those of his readers who may discover any deficiency in his reasoning, or may be in possession of proofs which his mind could never obtain, would offer them, together with their objections, to the Public, as briefly, as methodically, as plainly as he has taken the liberty of doing.* Thro' deficiency of proof, AN ATHEIST.

Crude and meagre as the pamphlet was, it put clearly the issue that was dawning on him. In this matter, he pleads, the conclusion will depend in no way on the moral will, nor merit either praise or blame; belief being a clear perception, received passively and involuntarily, of the agreement or otherwise of two ideas.[1] We obtain truth in the first degree of clearness from the senses; in the second by reasoning on that which they supply; in the third from the words or records of other men. By the first means there is no knowing God; by the third no certainty; by the second only a choice between believing that the world is from all eternity or from some almighty hand; and the first alternative is the easier. Finally, it cannot hurt society to know that there is no such proof, for Truth is the benefactor of mankind.

These pellets for the priests were hardly composed before the 12th of January, for they do not consist with the argument in the letter of that date. It is probable that just after his return to Oxford, the untenableness or unlikelihood of a first cause flashed upon him from some book and in his talks with Hogg, and so indeed he confessed to his father when the tragedy came.[2] That the pamphlet was in his hands by 13 February proves how quickly he threw his problem upon paper, and

---

[1] This favourite proposition of his may have come from Rousseau's Savoyard Vicar: 'I believe in God as fully as I believe in any other truth because to believe or not to believe are the things in the world that are least under my control.' At the same time the disbeliever cannot be refuted or blamed. 'It is not reasonable to say to any man, "You ought to believe this because I believe it".' For that matter Shelley's proposition follows inevitably on the thesis that mind is merely a recipient of impressions.

[2] In the letter of 29 Mar. (Ingpen, p. 214): 'You well know that a train of reasoning has induced me to disbelieve the scriptures—this train myself and my friend pursued,' &c.

urged it through the press. It was perhaps in hurry more than
in hesitation that he does not deal explicitly with the argument
from design, of which the January letters had made so much.
It is now ignored; but in taking up the negative import of
the illumination in the summer, he had retained the positive,
nor had Hume or any other weaned him from his intuitions.
A prefatory note to the pamphlet limits the argument 'solely
to a creative Deity', while 'the hypothesis of a pervading spirit
co-eternal with the universe remains unshaken'.

## 5. EXPULSION

After receiving the copies, he sent out a number by the post
to adversaries and friends, and appeared one day with a good
few on the premises of Munday and Slatter, the booksellers.
Here he strewed his tracts in the windows and over the counters,
telling the shopman to sell them off as fast as possible at sixpence each. Twenty minutes later the Rev. John Walker,
Fellow of New College, entered the establishment, looked at
the pamphlet, and sent forthwith for the principals of the firm.
Mr. Slatter and Mr. Munday had before now distressed themselves over Shelley, and set upon him an amateur philosopher,
a Mr. Hobbes, who had argued with him in vain. They came,
and seeing with dismay what ware they had on sale, and what
displeasure it had kindled, carried the copies to the back-
kitchen, and burned them all in Walker's presence. They now
sent a messenger to ask Shelley to their house; where he soon
appeared, and confronted, among other anxious well-wishers,
a 'Counsellor Clifford of O.P. notoriety', who had undertaken
'by entreaties and next by threats to dissuade him from the
error of his ways'.[1] Shelley, however, seemed to them to glory
in his doings; and it is small wonder that after this episode his
reputation as an atheist went abroad. By 15 March Charles
Kirkpatrick Sharpe, of Christ Church, in one of his dandified
letters, mentions the pamphlet as among its author's works;
and the autograph letters that went with it to the bishops and
others, under the name of 'Jeremiah Stukeley', were a clue to
the open secret. And what in the meantime had Mr. Walker
been doing? It is hard to think that he did not ask and learn

---

[1] From the reminiscences of Henry Slatter in the Appendix to Montgomery's
*Oxford.*

who the pamphleteer was, and, knowing that, did not communicate with the Master and Fellows of University College. If he did so, the Master and Fellows held their hand, hoping, perhaps, to evade the trouble.[1] But when Edward Copleston, afterwards Provost of Oriel and Bishop of Llandaff, showed the copy that was sent to him, and presumably the letter, to the authorities of University College, the handwriting would point to the offender[2] and it would be necessary to act.

On the morning of Lady Day Hogg went over early to Shelley's rooms, and found that he was absent. Presently he rushed in, terribly agitated. 'I am expelled,' he said, as soon as he had recovered himself a little. 'I am expelled! I was sent for suddenly a few minutes ago; I went to the Common Room, where I found our Master and two or three of the Fellows. The Master produced a copy of the little syllabus and asked me if I were the author of it. He spoke in a rude, abrupt, and insolent tone. I begged to be informed for what purpose he put the question. No answer was given; but the Master loudly and abruptly repeated, "Are you the author of this book?" "If I can judge from your manner", I said, "you are resolved to punish me, if I should acknowledge that it is my work. If you can prove that it is, produce your evidence; it is neither just nor lawful to interrogate me in such a case and for such a purpose. Such proceedings would become a court of inquisitors, but not free men in a free country." ' The question was again repeated; the answer again declined; upon which the Master exclaimed, 'Then you are expelled, and I desire you will quit the College early to-morrow morning at the latest'; and one of the Fellows handed Shelley a paper with 'a sentence of expulsion drawn up in due form'. 'I have been with him in many trying situations of his after life', Hogg continues, 'but I never saw him so deeply shocked and so cruelly agitated as on this occasion. . . . He sat on the sofa, repeating with convulsive vehemence the words "Expelled, expelled!" his head shaking with emotion, and his whole frame quivering.'[3]

[1] This was recently suggested by Sir Michael Sadler to Mr. Edmund Blunden. See Mr. Blunden's essay, 'Shelley is expelled', in *On Shelley*, Oxford, 1938.

[2] Shelley himself states that Copleston was the informer in his letter to Godwin of 10 Jan. 1812, and he told Southey so when he met him at Keswick. See Southey's letter to G. C. Bedford, 4 Jan. 1812, quoted by Mr. Blunden in *On Shelley*, p. 17.

[3] I can see no ground for distrusting Hogg's narrative, as some writers do. He

Upon this Hogg dispatched a note to the Master and Fellows 'expressing my sorrow at the treatment my friend had experienced, and my hope that they would reconsider their verdict, since by the same course of proceeding myself or any other person might be subjected to the same penalty and to the imputation of equal guilt'. The conclave in the Common Room was still sitting, and summoned him before them. He thought he saw upon them 'the angry and troubled air of men assembled to commit injustice according to established forms'. Their manner to him was overbearing, but, if his account is trustworthy, he had much the better of the encounter. Taking up the pamphlet, the Master asked him, 'Did you write this?' and he answered that the question was unfair, so unfair that no gentleman in the University would comply with it. He was then bidden to retire, and reconsider his reply; but had 'scarcely passed the door' when they called him back, and put their question once again. Once again, in respectful terms, he declined to answer. 'Then you are expelled', said the Master, and a paper containing the sentence, which had lain, apparently, all the time upon the table, was put into his hands. It stated his offence as a contumacious refusal to disavow the pamphlet. He protested that the word 'contumacious' was not justified by his behaviour; but had not finished speaking when the Master broke in: 'Am I to understand, Sir, that you adopt the principles contained in this work?' ' "The last question is still more improper than the former", I replied, "and since by your own act you have renounced all authority over me, our communication is at an end." "I command you to quit my College to-morrow at an early hour." '

During the morning, and before all the formalities were complete, the two culprits 'made themselves conspicuous by great singularity of dress, and by walking down the centre of the quadrangle, as if proud of their anticipated fate'.[1]

is surely the witness most likely to have remembered what took place, though, no doubt, he has not exactly reported what was said.

[1] From an account by C. J. Ridley, then Junior Fellow, produced by Dowden, i. 123–4. Hogg, however, tells us (i. 42) that calling on his Etonian friend Halliday Shelley said: 'Halliday, I am come to say good-bye to you, if you are not afraid to be seen with me.' Shelley told Peacock that 'his expulsion was a matter of great form and solemnity; there was a sort of public assembly before which he pleaded his own cause in a long oration, in the course of which he called on the illustrious spirits who had shed glory on those walls to look down on their degenerate successors'.

Towards afternoon the decree of expulsion, on 'a large paper, bearing the College seal, and signed by the Master and Dean' was affixed to the Hall door, and the doom was in force.

Recently published letters have thrown a light—or a mist— on these unhappy doings. On 17 February Bysshe wrote to his father that, when examined in divinity, he would conceal his heresy, easily as he could prove it.[1] But the itch to publish and declare in some way or other was irresistible. Yet to declare and publish atheism, or even to hold it, in the exact meaning of the word he seems to have regarded as a crime. In the following May, after his visit to Cuckfield, he wrote to someone who had refused to see him after his disgrace—perhaps Miss Hitchener—complaining bitterly of the excessive penalty for what had been written as 'the amusement of a rainy day', and 'carried perhaps a little too far some of the arguments of Locke'. He had been classed with 'wretches, the bane of society' whose openly professed atheism was 'the last effusion of depravity' and a menace to all virtue and happiness.[2] The publicity, it seems, was not the offence, but its aggravation. When he abhorred his grandfather as 'a complete atheist' he meant one who, openly or not, rejected a divine principle of some sort or other. That he should nevertheless have taken the name upon himself in the same way—to quote his words to Trelawny— 'as a knight takes up a gauntlet', and run to strew his pamphlets on the shopman's counter it needs not much psychology to understand. Nor was there any disingenuousness in the alternate attitudes of defiant assertion and humble inquiry.

But about the inwardness of his behaviour the authorities, when they called him before them, had no occasion, and surely no wish to ask. They knew he had written the pamphlet, and it made nought of the profession of orthodoxy that, when matri-

---

And Peacock states that he showed him an Oxford newspaper containing an account of these proceedings and his speech. The newspaper has not been traced. The assembly was beyond doubt a myth, and the speech, as Peacock puts it, 'in the potential mood'. In his letter of 10 Jan. 1812, Shelley told Godwin, 'I was informed that in case I denied the publication no more would be said. I refused, and was expelled.' This, too, is in every probability a construction of his. Neither are the authorities likely to have so informed him, nor Hogg to have forgotten it. Out of a notion that so much was somehow signified he has jumped to a statement that no less was plainly said.

[1] Julian Shelley, xxxvii; viii. 54.
[2] *The Athenians*, ed. Walter Sidney Scott, 1943, p. 11.

culating, he had duly made. Moreover, the Shelley visible to the Master and Fellows differed greatly from Hogg's description of the scholar and the saint. They had heard, no doubt, what a character he bore at Eton; and themselves had constantly found him 'very insubordinate' and apparently contumacious.[1] In respect of the prescribed studies he had given them no reason to think well of him, and on the social account 'no one regretted his departure'.[2] Nay, in point even of the moral rudiments his name was unsavoury; for they believed him a loose liver who, by indulging his passions, had undermined his health.[3] Hogg foolishly supposes that the Master and Fellows were revenging on a Whig family the election of Lord Grenville to the Chancellorship, and the defeat of Lord Eldon, their collegian, in 1809, and were demonstrating their Toryism and their orthodoxy to the dispensers of preferment. There is no reason for doubting that they rose from their conclave convinced that they had done their duty on impiety and effrontery and undesirability.

Yet there were not wanting Fellows of Colleges, even at that period, who, had they been congregated in one society, might have retained Shelley to the end of his course to his immense advantage. One such, who may have been a Fellow of Wadham, once saw him from his windows standing in the rain, called him in, and on that and other occasions fell to arguing freely

[1] *Memoirs of a Highland Lady*, by Elizabeth Grant (the Master's niece), ed. Lady Strachey, 1898, p. 129. 'He was a ringleader of every kind of mischief', she says, no doubt exaggerating. '. . . He was slovenly in his dress, and, when spoken to about these and other irregularities, was in the habit of making such extraordinary gestures, expressive of his humility under reproof, as to overset first the gravity, and then the temper of the lecturing tutor. . . . These scenes reached unpleasant lengths.' Miss Grant's reminiscences are erroneous in detail, but she, no doubt, conveys what Shelley was in the eyes of his superiors.

[2] Ridley again.

[3] *Memoirs of a Highland Lady*, p. 129; where, in rather cryptic words, which Professor Peck has made clear, the charge is given as having been insinuated in a conversation by Rowley, Fellow and Dean of the College. It is supported by Thornton Hunt in a paper entitled 'Shelley as I knew him' in *The Atlantic Monthly* for Feb. 1863: 'Again, accident has made me aware of facts which give me to understand that, in passing through the usual curriculum of a college life in all its paths, Shelley did not go scatheless—but that, in tampering with venal pleasures, his health was seriously, and not transiently injured.' A reaction followed, says Hunt, 'marked by horror'. Professor Peck (*Life*, ii. 191) would, with some hesitation, connect this evidence with the lines on 'One whose voice was venomed melody' in *Epipsychidion* (256–66). But these are slender foundations. 'The purity and sanctity of his life', says Hogg, 'were most conspicuous.' See Dowden, i. 76.

and candidly with him. Tutors of that sort would have soon discovered what manner of man he was, and might have made clear to him how much he had to learn; and how well it would be for a year or two longer to keep the peace. It happened, however, that he came to the University at almost the lowest ebb of her usefulness and her repute, and in the centre of a time when, according to John Stuart Mill, orthodoxy was more powerful and more vindictive all England over than in the times before and since.[1] Nowhere was this temper as much pronounced as in the Common Rooms of Oxford, in the little circles of well-provided clerics, many of whom were as sluggish in their duties as they were narrow in their minds.[2] The Oriel 'Noetics', headed by Copleston himself a few years later, might dare to ask and speculate, to the perturbation of those around them; but to Shelley in his standing, and in his time and place, there was hardly a way open but martyrdom—perhaps improved in manner—soon or late. That the governing body of his College should be exceptionally good was not to be asked of them, but of the world they were at home in their young impossible outcast is now and for ever an historic victim and an indelible reproach.

[1] 'It would have been no small thing had he (James Mill) done no more than to support himself and his family during so many years by writing; holding, as he did, opinions, both in politics and in religion, which were more odious to all persons of influence and to the common run of prosperous Englishmen in that generation than either before or since.'—*Autobiography*. James Mill lived from 1773 to 1836.

[2] See the description of Common Room society in the early thirties in Mark Pattison's *Memoirs*, pp. 74 ff. Schopenhauer says somewhere in *Die Welt als Wille und Vorstellung* (1818), of the difference in the spiritual status set by theologians between Christian and heathen, that no philosopher would recognize it, and, if any man would, 'er kann nach England gehen und sich in Oxford niederlassen'.

# THE FIRST MARRIAGE

## 1. THE PLOT IS LAID

ON the morning of 26 March the two friends left Oxford by the London coach, and late in the day presented themselves before Shelley's cousins, John and Charles Grove—John a medical practitioner, Charles a medical student—at their dwelling in Lincoln's Inn Fields. 'Here', says Hogg, 'we passed a very silent evening', though Bysshe 'attempted to talk'. In the night, at a coffee-house in the neighbourhood of Piccadilly, Bysshe was sleepless. 'I remember', writes Medwin, 'as if it occurred yesterday, his knocking at my door in Garden Court in the Temple at four o'clock in the morning the second day after his expulsion. I think I hear his cracked voice, with his well-known pipe, "Medwin, let me in, I am expelled"; here followed a loud half-hysteric laugh.' The 27th was spent in looking for lodgings, which they eventually found at 15 Poland Street, and here day by day they continued, as before, to read and write and walk and talk together.

Timothy Shelley had been informed of the expulsion by the College. For some days he made no sign, except by a brief and stately letter to Hogg, written on the 27th, to withdraw the invitation to Field Place. On the 29th Shelley broke the ice with as tactful a letter as he was able to write. He enclosed a copy of *The Necessity of Atheism*, and drew attention to the Advertisement with its humble petition for more light, 'which surely deserved an *answer*, not expulsion', and protested his sorrow at inflicting so much pain on others with an evident sincerity. But on the main point—the tenor of *The Necessity*—he was impenitent. Whereupon, alarmed by the contents of the pamphlet, and afraid even of a legal prosecution for atheism, Mr. Shelley repaired to London, and started at once to mismanage him. For about a fortnight what may be called exchanges went on, on the one side from Poland Street, and on the other from Miller's Hotel by Westminster Bridge. The Squire began, it may be assumed, with a demand—that Bysshe should retract the pamphlet and sue for pardon to the College.

He should furthermore renounce all intercourse, personally or by letter, with Hogg. It may have been at this point that there was some talk of his travelling to the Isles of Greece; it would, his father expected, call off his thoughts from 'objects tending to produce Temporary Insanity', and chasten him with the taste of danger. These demands having been rejected (as we may suppose) at an interview on the 31st of March, were repeated in part and supplemented in a formal letter on the 5th of April. Bysshe was 'to go immediately to Field Place, and to abstain from all communication with Mr. Hogg for a considerable time'; he was to place himself under an appointed tutor, and 'attend to his instructions', to the end that he might 'abandon his errors'. The terms of peace were necessary, declared Timothy, to his own character, to the welfare of his other children, and 'above all to his feelings as a Christian'; and, should they be rejected, 'I am resolved to withdraw myself from you, and leave you to the punishment and misery that belongs to the wicked pursuit of an opinion so diabolical and wicked'. Shelley answered with a curt and firm refusal, once for all, either to separate from his friend or to take his opinions from another. Perhaps the acidity of the refusal was due to what had been reported to him of his father's talk. The poor flustered man was blabbing at large. It may have been at this time that he blurted something of sending Bysshe to foreign service in the army, and something of John inheriting the estate if Bysshe were outlawed; and on these sayings someone put the worst complexion and passed them on.[1] He had at any rate talked of Hogg as his son's 'original corrupter', and in the letter from Shelley to the elder Hogg,[2] to deny that charge, the formal style of writing breaks down in indignation.

The Squire was of a variable temper, however; on Sunday the 7th he had his son and his son's evil genius to dinner; and some of Hogg's liveliest pages tell the story. If the host's inconsequent chatter, his scattered intelligence, his laughing, swearing, weeping—but not his mellowing mood—are in this picture overdrawn, they were enough to account for the misery in which Shelley endured the evening. 'What do you think of my father?' he whispered after a while. 'Oh, it is not your father', returned Hogg, 'it is the God of the Jews—the Jehovah you have been

[1] Shelley's letter to Godwin of 10 Jan. 1812.  [2] 5 Apr. 1811.

reading about.' And seething impatience and sore distress took relief in Shelley in a wild fit of laughing. When after the dinner he had gone out on an errand for his father, the Squire turned to Hogg as to a man 'very different from what I had expected to find', and begged for his counsel. 'Tell me what I am to do with my poor boy.' The boy was wild, was he not? Yes, Hogg answered, he was a little wild, and the remedy would be marriage. But he must be enticed, not commanded; introduced by a seeming chance to the right person, 'and if he did not like her, you could try another'. The Squire's agent, Mr. Graham, was present, and was engaged with his master in an earnest deliberation over a list of young women, when Bysshe came in again. By this time the president of the feast was 'jolly', proposed a bottle of a still choicer port, drank tea, and launched into a long rigmarole of his popularity in the House of Commons and the County of Sussex, his excellence as a magistrate, and an unintelligible tale of his sending two poachers to prison, 'and one of them came and thanked me'.

    ' "There is certainly a God", he then said. "There can be no doubt of the existence of a Deity; none whatever."

    'Nobody present expressed any doubt.

    ' "You have no doubt on the subject, sir, have you?" he enquired, addressing himself particularly to me. . . .

    ' "If you have, I can prove it to you in a moment."

    ' "I have no doubt." '

But he would not be baulked of his argument, and after fumbling in his pockets, drew out a paper, and began to read. Bysshe leaned forward intently, and presently said: 'I have heard these arguments before.'

    ' "They are Paley's arguments", I said.

    ' "Yes", the reader observed, "you are right, sir, they are Palley's arguments; I copied them out of Palley's book this morning; but Palley had them originally from me."

    'When we parted, Mr. Shelley shook hands with me in a very friendly manner. "I am very sorry you would not have any more wine. . . . Tell me the truth, I am not such a bad fellow after all, am I?"

    ' "By no means."

    ' "Well, when you come to see me at Field Place, you will find that I am not." '

'Oh, how I wish that you would come to Field Place', said Shelley, as the two guests went bedwards. 'You would set us all to rights.'

More and more bewildered, Timothy Shelley changed about from hour to hour. The very day before the dinner he had written to Hogg's father to ask his help in separating the two friends. The very day after he took the disastrous step of bringing in his starched and stiff-lipped lawyer, William Whitton. Reminded, as it would seem, by Whitton[1] of what had frightened him at the beginning of the trouble, that Christianity was 'a part of the law itself'[2] and to strike at it an indictable crime, so that if the law were put in motion, his own good name would suffer, he now acted as in a panic. He promised to be guided only by the lawyer's advice, to send on to him all letters concerning the affair, and to communicate with his son through him only. But he did not keep his word. In the days following the convivial Sunday one person after another appeared at Shelley's door as his father's emissary and advocate: a Mr. Hurst from Horsham; John Grove; a Mr. Clarke, a friend of the elder Hogg's; and Shelley's uncle, Robert Parker. They found him eager to go home, full of affection to his mother and his sisters—'never to me', commented poor Timothy—and grieved for their sakes, and though determined to relinquish his heresies only upon conviction, 'very willing to be put right'.[3] But an agreement became yet more remote when on the 11th Mr. Shelley went home, leaving the solicitor to act for him.

The strife now went forward on the previous questions, and on another which had supervened. Bysshe, it seemed clear, must take up some profession. The family had intended that on coming of age he should accept his father's seat in Parliament, and the Duke of Norfolk had a lively interest in him. At several times during this spring he went to see the House of Commons and its unlovely members, 'and my father so polite to them', and once at least dined at the Duke's table, who told him that

[1] See Timothy's postscript to John Grove's letter of 11 Apr., forwarded to Whitton (Ingpen, p. 231): 'my answer was that I had plac'd the business in your hands, to guard my honour and character against Prosecutions in the Courts.' On 14 Apr. he gave the same reason for his conduct in a letter to R. Clarke (ibid., p. 238). That some rumour of a prosecution had gone about appears from a sentence in Shelley's letter to Hogg of 15 May: 'All danger about prosecution is over; it was *never* more than a hum.'

[2] See *Encyclopaedia Britannica*, *sub* 'Blasphemy'.

[3] Letters to T. S. from John Grove, 11 Apr., and R. Parker, 12 Apr.

Parliament, with the mediocrities in it, was the shortest road
to consequence for a man of parts. But he had soon angrily
rejected the role of the Duke's henchman in an assembly of
which he could not bear the sight, and wavered in his mind
between following John Grove in his career of surgeon, or following Hogg as a probationer in the law. For a while he joined
Charles Grove at the lectures on anatomy at St. Bartholomew's.
But he could not choose a profession against his father's will and
became impatient. On 14 April Timothy Shelley at Field Place
was astounded by a letter from Poland Street, 'as from one
belligerent to another'. It contained counter-proposals, drawn
up by the two young men, with the approbation of the elder
Hogg, but apart from a tone not over-modest, it asked for
nothing that a wise man would not have given. The writers
undertook to return to their homes, and neither to obtrude on
anyone nor to publish atheistical opinions, or even speculations.
They asked, however, that they should be free in future to
correspond with each other, and Bysshe should be free to choose
his own profession, when Hogg had entered at the Inns of
Court, or had taken up some other line. Angry as the Squire
was, Whitton evidently feared his giving way. He lectured
him on paternal indulgence; he made the most of a son presenting his father with demands; he obtained a letter from old
Sir Bysshe against relenting. Moreover, as if to strengthen
Timothy's hands, on 16 April Hogg left Poland Street for a
short stay at Ellesmere, and afterwards for a conveyancer's
chambers at York, leaving Bysshe, as Bysshe's father trusted,
to his better judgement. But the trust was soon shattered. On
the 22nd, or a day or two before, Mr. Shelley had news from
the lawyer that shocked him 'infinitely more than when I heard
of his expulsion'. Bysshe had wearied of his dependence, and
made, as it were, a dash for complete freedom. On the 17th he
had written to the solicitor proposing to resign the entail of
certain estates in Sussex, if his father would promise to divide
the property between his mother and sisters, and pay him forthwith an annuity of £200 or £100, of the exact amount he was
quite careless. The effect of this suggestion was powerful. It
brought a rebuke from Whitton, and there was indeed some
sting in the reminder that, as an infant, 'you have not the
value of 6*d.* to relinquish', and in the question who had made

him guardian of his mother and sisters. So hot was the temper on either side that nothing could now be done by the way of personal intercourse, which Whitton had intended trying, and all negotiation was in suspense. Timothy Shelley was deeply enraged, not only by the attitude in Bysshe's letter towards himself. To a man so stuffed with feudal pride this proposal of his son's to escape from his family and his heritage to irresponsibility and a pittance was a mystery of evil. 'To cast off all thoughts of his Maker, to abandon his Parents, to wish to relinquish his Fortune, and to court Prosecution, all seems to arise from the same source [the "diabolical publications that have fallen in his way"]. . . . He wishes to become what he would term a martyr to his sentiments—nor do I believe he would feel the Horrors of being drawn upon a Hurdle, or the shame of being whirl'd in the Pillory.' He now decided that Bysshe was not to be received—or at any rate not to stay—at Field Place. 'If I please', writes Bysshe, 'I *will*.' 'This resolution of mine was hinted to him. "Oh! then I shall take his sister [Elizabeth] away before he comes." But I shall follow her, as her retirement cannot be a secret.'[1] On 24 April, meeting his father in a passage in the Groves' London house, 'I politely enquired after his health. He looked as black as a thunder-cloud, and said, "Your most humble servant!" I made him a low bow, and wishing him a very good morning—passed on.'

Bysshe was by now miserable. At first, while Hogg was with him, he had thought of dwelling 'for ever' in the pleasant room in Poland Street, with its wall-paper pattern of vines and grapes, and the charm of the Oxford days might seem to be replaced by the studious mornings and the long walks in the afternoons. For more company there were Tom Medwin in the Temple, and John and Charles Grove; and there was the Reading Room of the Museum and the idyllic corners of Kensington Gardens. We do not hear of him poring on the life of the great City, as Wordsworth had done when he first stayed in it, and mused 'most feelingly' before the quick dance

> Of colours, lights, and forms; the deafening din;
> The comers and the goers, face to face,
> Face after face.

We hear of Shelley gliding through the dense crowds, intent

[1] 24 Apr.

upon some book. 'Sometimes a vulgar fellow would attempt to insult or annoy the eccentric student in passing. Shelley always avoided the malignant interruption by stepping aside with his vast and quiet agility.' Or, he is either the child at his paper boats on the Serpentine, or the enthusiast who harangues a dinner party on the superiority of the female sex, or electrifies with his eloquence the British Forum ('a spouting club, in which Gale Jones and other Radicals abused all governments'), or writes to ask Rowland Hill for a turn in his pulpit in the Surrey Chapel. When on 16 April he was left alone, the dangers of this inward-looking and withdrawing nature began to assail it. Left to himself he took to heart the unreason and the overbearing with which he had struggled for freedom and for self-respect, and committed himself even further to that estrangement from the majority of men, and their loyalties and ideas, which went back to his boyhood, and had taken a new form and impulse with the failure of his first love. The hate that, as Aristotle tells us, is deeper than anger, that goes out, not to individuals, but to classes of men, we can see in his now frequent letters fast ripening. That Christianity is a system of punishments and rewards, that it is comprehended in its abuses, that the crimes men have done in its name have flowed out of it, that reason abhors it—all this cake of rash conclusions was setting firm. Hogg writes to him that Christians may be amiable, that popular religions must be superstitious, and that the few should leave the many, not in anger, to themselves. Shelley replies that he will indeed keep himself apart, but with a hope that all men shall be one day perfect; and how can they be amiable who regard free thinking as a state of sin, and say with Bishop Warburton that, unless he cultivates faith, a man has lost one-third of the moral virtues? But there was another and a deeper disquiet. In this loneliness and adversity the 'social flame' craved for an answer. He still suffered from the loss of his cousin's love. 'Solitude is most horrible', he writes, 'I cannot endure the horror, the evil which comes to *self* in solitude.' 'What a strange being I am, in spite of my boasted hatred of self; this moment thinking I could so far overcome Nature's law as to exist in complete seclusion, the next starting from a moment of solitude—starting from my own company, as if it were that of a fiend—seeking anything rather than a continued communion with self.'

Three weeks of this existence resulted, fortunately, in nothing worse for a while than a rather deep flirtation. On the north side of Clapham Common was Mrs. Fenning's—afterwards Mrs. Hawkes's—school for young ladies, where Mary and Hellen Shelley were pupils, and Bysshe would at times appear to see his sisters, and on occasion to intervene vehemently against the punishments that he found in use—black badges at the throat and iron collars around the neck. Mary and Hellen had a special friend among their school-fellows, by name Harriet Westbrook, who on the 1st of August in this year 1811 would arrive at the age of sixteen. She was the younger of the two daughters of John Westbrook, 23 Chapel Street, Grosvenor Square, who had retired on comfortable means from the tenure of the Mount Coffee House in that neighbourhood. His wife played only a minor part in her own family, and in this drama none at all; but the elder daughter, Eliza, was a woman who would have her way, and ruled Harriet, her junior by thirteen years,[1] like a child. Eliza Westbrook left on Shelley's life so deep a mark that it is well to envisage her with the appropriate mitigation as Hogg saw her:

'She looked much older than she was. The lovely face [as Harriet thought it] was seamed with smallpox and of a dead white; as white, indeed, as a mass of boiled rice, but of a dingy hue, like rice boiled in dirty water. The eyes were dark, but dull and without meaning; the hair was black and glossy, but coarse; and there was the admired crop—a long crop, much like the tail of a horse. The "fine figure" was meagre, prim, and constrained. . . . Her father was familiarly called "Jew Westbrook", and Eliza greatly resembled one of the dark-eyed daughters of Judah.'

Harriet, on the other hand, was the beauty of the school and, when she went abroad, the mark of all eyes; 'with hair', as Hellen remembered, 'quite like a poet's dream, and Bysshe's peculiar admiration'. 'She had a good figure', writes Peacock, who knew her later on,

'light, active, and graceful. Her features were regular and well-proportioned. Her hair was light brown, and dressed with taste and simplicity. In her dress she was truly *simplex munditiis*. Her complexion was beautifully transparent; the tint of the blush rose shining through the lily. The tone of her voice was pleasant; her

---

[1] She was born on 4 June 1782; Harriet on 1 Aug. 1795.

speech the essence of frankness and cordiality; her spirits always cheerful; her laugh spontaneous, hearty and joyous. 'She was well educated. She read agreeably and intelligently. She wrote only letters, but she wrote them well. Her manners were good; and her whole aspect and demeanour such manifest emanations of pure and truthful nature that to be once in her company was to know her thoroughly.'

Shelley had made her acquaintance in his Oxford days in the previous January, when, accompanied by Charles Grove, he called in Chapel Street with an introduction and a gift from Mary; and thereupon sent her a copy of *St. Irvyne*, and began to correspond with her. For Harriet he had about him a pleasing awfulness. Since her childhood she had 'thought the military the best as well as the most fascinating men in the world', though she would vow never to marry one, 'not so much on account of their vices as from the idea of their being killed'. If she married anyone, it should be a clergyman. When, then, it was given out at Clapham that Shelley was an atheist, she was 'petrified', 'wondered how he could live a moment, professing such principles', and in writing to him 'tried to shake them'. The fear of even 'listening to his arguments' disturbed her dreams with apparitions of the Devil—'the effect of a bad education and living with Methodists'.[1] When, however, the culprit came to London in disgrace, there were good reasons for seeing him. From time to time she was employed by Hellen and Mary to bring him their pocket money when she paid a visit home. On this account, if on no other, he would call occasionally at her father's house, and his letters to Hogg, after Hogg had left him, betray the plot that Eliza was now weaving, and John Westbrook at any rate not preventing. On 18 April, in the school holidays, 'Miss Westbrook has just called on me with her sister. It certainly was very kind.' On the 23rd Harriet has seen the last of her freedom and returns to School, 'her prison-house', looking unwell. Shelley accompanies her and her sister to Clapham Common, and walks with them there for two hours. 'The youngest is a most amiable girl; the eldest is really conceited, but very condescending. I took the sacrament with her [Harriet, apparently] on Sunday. You say I talk philosophically of her kindness in calling on me. She is very

[1] From her letter to Elizabeth Hitchener, 14 Mar. 1812.

charitable and good. I shall always think of it with gratitude, because she exposed herself to much possible odium.' Ought he to point out to her the road to perfection—the road, that is, of 'atheism'—to make her perhaps unhappy in this life, but perhaps happier in the life to come? He is not sure. On the 24th he dines with Eliza in her father's absence. A day or two later Harriet is again at home, and ill, and her (Harriet's) sister sends for him. 'I found her on a couch pale; her father is civil to me, very strangely; and the sister is too civil by half. She began talking of *l'Amour*. I philosophized, and the youngest said she had such a headache that she could not bear conversation. Her sister then went away, and I stayed till half past twelve.' He has now resolved to indoctrinate her with Godwinism, and Eliza also, for, 'with some taming, she will do'. On the 28th Harriet, at her father's order, returns to school, Shelley accompanying her; and for days afterwards he 'spends most of his time' with Eliza, who is studying Voltaire's *Dictionnaire philosophique*. He has criticized Eliza too hastily. 'I really now consider her as amiable, not perhaps in a high degree, but perhaps she is'; 'very clever', he presently adds, 'though rather affected'. On 1 May, or soon before, he saw Harriet under a halo. Visiting the school again, he learnt that, evidently for some opinion the echo of his own, she was 'in Coventry', and counted 'an abandoned wretch', only Hellen daring to converse with her. 'There are some hopes of this dear little girl; she would be a divine little scion of infidelity, if I could get hold of her.'

But before Eliza's web had quite enclosed him, it was torn. In the middle of April Mrs. Shelley had braved the consequences of urging him to come home and sending him money. That he might do nothing that smacked of surrender, he had refused to come, and sent the money back; but as time wore on the longing to see his mother and sisters grew upon him. And now, half-way through May, a strong and saving hand came to help him. Whitton's design to starve him out of his principles was too tyrannical and too dangerous not to provoke at last one or two of the onlookers. John Grove, though Bysshe had thought him rather neutral, was moved to interfere, and by the end of April had persuaded Mr. Shelley to reverse his policy and allow his son unconditionally £200 a year. And when, on

Whitton's advice no doubt, the promise had been retracted almost as soon as made, Shelley's favourite Uncle Pilfold effectually stepped in[1]—Captain John Pilfold of the Royal Navy, who, after serving in the Battle of the Nile and commanding a frigate at Trafalgar, had settled with wife and children at Cuckfield, some ten miles distant from Field Place. He was of an open and generous nature, and had a cordial and, as it proved, a constant liking for the severely bullied boy. He knew the fine mettle that was in him, and, with his own breezy unstableness in theology, could not comprehend what enormity he had done. On his counsel and insistence Bysshe went down to Cuckfield, probably on 12 May; and two or three days later his father waived his terms and scruples, and agreed a second time to pay him £200 a year, and leave to him the choice of his abode. Nothing was said of his future career, and the question whether he might meet his friend in person was left unsettled. Even the promise not to publish or to propagate 'atheism', which Shelley had previously offered as a means to peace, was not apparently asked for in explicit form. Yet Timothy's surrender was in one particular not without hesitation, and for a good reason, as events were soon to show. The last concession was that Bysshe might come home and associate with his eldest sister; and that was only granted in the certainty that he would otherwise invade the house. There was indeed some reason to fear for Elizabeth if precept and warning had not by now secured her against 'free notions'; and she was to be kept away, as far as might be, from the source of mischief. But Bysshe had won his battle, and on 15 May was at Field Place once more. That a truce had been made, and not a peace, however, was evident in the attitude on each side. 'He looks rather blue to-day', he writes, 'but the Captain keeps him in tolerable order.'

## 2. SUSPENSE

### (a) *In Sussex again*

He remained at home, but for brief visits to Cuckfield, during two months, with nothing to do but kill time. He was still

---

[1] He had been moving on his nephew's behalf before 18 Apr., when Shelley reports 'a very civil letter' from him. On the 24th he writes: 'I wait for Mr. Pilford's arrival with whom I shall depart [for Sussex].'

hoping to enter the medical profession;[1] but the profession should be secondary to his main purpose of waging war on 'faith and custom' by any means within his power, and chiefly by the pen. For the present no opportunity called him, and his purposes hanging thus in stays, and no real comrade at his side, he fretted at his dull days and his disingenuous companions, for so they seemed. 'I am a perfect hermit', he writes; 'not a being to speak with! I sometimes exchange a word with my mother on the subject of the weather, on which she is irresistably eloquent. Otherwise all is deep silence.' And all the time, no doubt, he had to endure the plain man's distrust of him, implicit or avowed. But that which before all else amazed and repelled was a fact which now impressed him for the first time. These dogmas that had set up all the trouble—not a soul of his acquaintance believed them entirely, or even, as it seemed, at all. 'It is most true', he writes, 'that the mass of mankind are Christians only in name; their religion has no reality. . . . Certain members of my family are no more Christians than Epicurus himself was.' There was Uncle Pilfold in a conversation chivying an irate antagonist with *The Necessity of Atheism.* There was his mother, who had once told him that 'prayer is of no use', and that, pagan or Christian, a man fares equally well or ill. Yet more astonishing there was a conversation between his father and his uncle of which he had heard at first hand. 'Says this Wiseacre: "To tell you the truth, *I* am a sceptic." "Ah! eh!" thought the Captain, "old birds are not to be caught with chaff." "Are you indeed?" was the cold reply, and no more was got out of him.'

In the lack of other conversation he wrote many letters. The Rev. George Stanley Faber, at this time Vicar of Stockton-on-Tees, a Bampton Lecturer, and in later years a prominent controversialist, had intervened in the Oxford trouble in a letter to his friend, the elder Hogg, and proceeded to a long epistolary debate with the two apostates. Shelley had not yet done with him, and continued to return his fire. But the joy of battles like these left unquieted the ache of loneliness, the want of the deep communion with a 'not impossible She' who should blend in herself mind and beauty, love its own law, and reason its own light. She would burn with a hate like his for the

[1] To Elizabeth Hitchener, 8 Oct.

Christian superstition and the system that had come of it. And could she lack the flower and sign of the freedom-loving nature —the intuitions of a poet, or even the art itself? To be joined in free love to a poetess would be all that he could ask. As early as his schooldays, he had 'persecuted' Felicia Browne, afterwards Felicia Hemans, 'with extraordinary letters',[1] till her mother took alarm; and in the same mood perhaps on 16 May he wrote from Field Place to Miss Janetta Philipps, repeating an offer he had made at Oxford to print her poems at his own expense. But the poetess resolved to owe no favour to an infidel.[2]

## (b) Elizabeth Hitchener

For these repulses, however, he was presently comforted; for a month later, if not an Aspasia, certainly an Egeria might seem to have come his way. This was Elizabeth Hitchener,[3] who kept a school at Hurstpierpoint, and had among her pupils a child of Captain Pilfold's. She had now, in her twenty-ninth year, made good her ascent from the family of a publican and smuggler, and fearlessly aggrieved her neighbours by her outspoken liberalism and her zeal for the Rights of Women.[4] Prim and formal to strangers, she was lively with her friends, and wrote and spoke on the things she had at heart with fluency and fire, with a high pitch of sentiment, and, as Shelley at one time considered, 'a penetrating mind'. Her volume of poetry,

[1] Her own expression, in a letter quoted by Mr. Ingpen, *Shelley in England*, p. 80. Medwin (revised), p. 58, says that this happened in 1808, on his introducing Shelley to her poems, published in that year.

[2] *Poems*, by Janetta Philipps, appeared, however, later in the year, printed by Collingwood & Co., Oxford, with a long list of subscribers, including Shelley, his sisters Elizabeth and Hellen, Mr. Grove, Miss H. Westbrook, and Thomas Medwin.

[3] On leaving this country for Austria, later in her life, Miss Hitchener left Shelley's forty-six letters to her in the hands of a solicitor, Henry J. Slack, whose widow bequeathed them in 1907 to her nephew, the Rev. Charles Hargrove, with instructions that they should go ultimately to the British Museum. He, however, gave them to the Museum straight away where they now form Add. MS. 37496. They were privately printed by T. J. Wise in two volumes in 1886–90 and published in one volume in 1908 by Bertram Dobell. This text was collated with the autographs by Ingpen, who in many places completed or improved it. (From *A Bibliography of Shelley's Letters*, by Seymour de Ricci, 1927, pp. 105, 106.)

[4] Shelley told Godwin on 5 July 1812, that 'by the patronage of a lady whose liberality of mind is singular, this woman [E. H.] at the age of twenty was enabled to commence the conduct of a school. She concealed not the uncommon modes of thinking which she had adopted, and publicly instructed youth as a Deist and a Republican.' But all this is improbable, and she was evidently a Christian when she encountered Shelley.

*The Weald of Sussex*, issued in 1822, with learned notes, was thought by Buxton Forman 'respectable' as versified topography, though it has lines, like that in her ode on Women's Rights, which her poet friend, when he thought of her profanely, would quote with tears of laughter:

All, all are men—women and all.

Some clue to his early captivation by her is afforded by the scraps of her spinsterly letters that have come into print. 'The wickedness of the world', she writes to him, 'has too often frozen my heart's blood, and more than any other cause acted upon my feelings to accept a religion which promised a purer nature. . . . Oh! the ecstatic idea of the society of "just men made perfect" and a being more holy than the human mind can conceive affords the heart such real bliss that my feeling knows not how to forego what my reason is not ready to accept.' Although loath to keep step with him either in religion or in politics, she would always listen with understanding and with unction, as to one who 'rose above human nature'. 'Oh, lovely sympathy! I owe thee much, and the few months I have drunk of the reanimating cup atone for the blank of years I had endured.' If he had not, as she once wrote, 'waked the slumbering lyre' of her heart, she would hardly have been human. But probably not one ray of love-liking ever sped from him to her. One witness speaks of her 'fine dark eyes' and 'well-formed Roman countenance, full of animation'; the others report her as tall, 'very dark, with a quantity of black hair', and otherwise signally unattractive—bony and masculine. But beauty was a capital requirement with Shelley for the role of Cythna; and indeed, by all the signs of it, the worship that he paid her, before her unlovely faults peeped through the nimbus, was conjured. Again and again he protests to her that the 'love' between them is 'friendship, which has as much to do with the senses as with yonder mountains'; and that these sexless passions are the higher kind; and the letters that poured her out his mind— from 6 June 1811 till 18 July of the year following—abound in rhapsody and in pose.

But of his schemes and speculations they are precious documents. In June 1811 the Prince Regent feasting his Bourbon guests in the great conservatory of Carlton House; the throne of gold and crimson; the high table two hundred feet in length; the channel in the midst of it, where water from a silver fountain flowed by mossy banks, and gudgeon and goldfish sported in the stream—all this 'ludicrous magnificence' puts him on his version of the *Marseillaise*,[1] and reminds him of 'the natural death of great commercial Empires' in dire catastrophes. And, apart from such high folly, the daily facts of wealth and poverty and leisure and toil carry into his heart the hope of equality, intended by nature, and prescribed by justice as at the least our aim and rule. But it is of religion, the root of evil, he has most to say, and at no other time of his life did he write of his divinity, if it now deserved that name, in terms so cold and costive: 'the stony power to stones, . . . the existing power of existence'. He feels the cold. 'I recommend reason. Why? Is it because, since I have devoted myself unreservedly to its influencing, I have never felt *happiness*? I have rejected all fancy, all imagination.'

## (*c*) *Impregnations*

### (i) '*Thalaba*' *and* '*The Curse of Kehama*'

That he had 'rejected all imagination' was not true, however. It pushed up, like buried seed; not in his own words and visions, but in the romance and the sentiment of two or three favourite books devoutly appropriated. There was much in Shelley's genius that found its element in *Thalaba the Destroyer* and *The Curse of Kehama*. For his insatiable fancy here was a magazine: gods or heavenly creatures speeding on resplendent wings, or tabernacled in mist and fire on the face of waters;[2] sea nymphs in pinnaces of shell;[3] ships or boats self-wafted through air or flood;[4] chariots on any element with yoke of dragon or empyreal steeds;[5] horses, or birds, or meteors even, that in the hour of need present themselves, as with a human consciousness, to save

---

[1] He sends this version to Graham, and asks him to set it to music in an undated letter after the banquet.

[2] *Kehama*, vii. 10; *Witch of Atlas*, liii. He assuredly remembered Ereenya's wings when he made those of his Hermaphrodite.

[3] *Kehama*, vii. 2; *Prometheus Unbound*, II. v. 20 ff.

[4] *Thalaba*, xi. 31 ff.; *Kehama*, vii; *Witch of Atlas*, xxxvii ff.; *Prometheus Unbound*, II. v. 72 ff.

[5] The instances are too many to quote; Shelley's chariots are easily swifter and fierier.

or guide;[1] and the like.[2] And not less than to such bright and
dream-like things he would thrill to the exotic beauty or weird-
ness or terror of Southey's scenes—the heights and spaces, the
paradises and wastes, the flora and fauna of Eastern lands;
mighty waters, interminable caves, lakes of fire, and ruined
cities, real or fabulous, in oceans or in desert sands. It was
from these two poems, perhaps more than other sources, that he
learned to send the persons in his poetry on lonely voyages
through similar scenes.[3] But what Southey did for him in the
first place was to set out in form and beauty, and so strengthen
and settle, a certain conception of the world of men that had
been long harbouring in his mind. In the summer of 1811 he
called *Kehama* his 'favourite poem'.[4] Kehama is the almighty
Rajah, the man-fiend, ruler in the Earth and prince of evil
spirits, and the world sickens under his sway. The God of the
elements and his attendant deities flee from their mountain
paradise and from their sphere, and the souls of dead worthies
from their resting-place, while down in Hell the giants and
demons expect the invader and deliverer. On Earth the dreadful sorceress, whose tread is plague and famine, and all her
crew of devils, thrive and triumph. But to this unholy dominion

---

[1] *Thalaba*, vi. 3 ff., vi. 8 ff., xi. 4 ff.; *Revolt of Islam*, VI. xx ff., xliii; VII, xiv ff.;
*Unfinished Drama*, 125 ff.

[2] It would be easy to add to these parallels. Some are very likely accidental; but
not, perhaps, those between *Thalaba*, x, and *The Witch of Atlas*—the Witch, to
cheer her solitude, makes the Hermaphrodite, an animated image, partly of snow;
Laila's father, for the same purpose, places round her figures of men and women,
made of snow, and 'breathes into them motion and life and sense'. The Witch is
amused by the fire in her cavern, and Laila by the fire-fountain in her garden.
In at least three places in Shelley (*Revolt of Islam*, x. xxxvi; *Prometheus Unbound*, II.
iii. 95–7, and IV. 565–7) a 'doom', bad or good, is said to lie coiled like a snake
under God's throne, and God may loose it, either against men or for their benefit,
or perforce against himself. This seems to be explained by *Kehama*, xxiii. 5. 88:
> And that the seven-headed snake, whereon
> The strong Preserver sets his conquering feet,
> Will rise and shake him headlong from his throne.

[3] The similarities between Southey's and Shelley's landscapes, in respect of the
material features—but not the expression—are many, but naturally general and
inexact. A good few have been noted in *Alastor* only by Professor Harold Leroy
Hoffman in *An Odyssey of the Soul*. But, as the author shows, some can be as well or
better matched in other books in prose or verse. The subject was to some extent
investigated by R. Ackermann in *Quellen, Vorbilder, Stoffe zu Shelley's poetischen
Werken*, Erlangen and Leipzig, 1890.

[4] See letters to Miss Hitchener, 6 and 11 June 1811. He had been devoted to
*Thalaba* at school (p. 23), and it was one of the poems chosen for the evening
readings to his family and friends at the end of 1814 (Dowden, i. 472).

a term is appointed; Seeva, the supreme and the omnipotent, watches it in anger; and at the fated hour, when Kehama descends into the womb of the Earth, to dethrone Yamen, the judge of souls and King of Hades, a beam from Seeva's eye, striking the insolent one, claps him into torment, and the world is saved. In the centre of the story moves Kailyal, the gentle maiden, whom Kehama cannot terrify or seduce, and whom her heavenly lover Ereenia, one of the Glendoveer or most beautiful of the Good Spirits, receives at last into love and bliss for ever. Much the same thing happens in *Thalaba*: the destroyer and deliverer quells in the depth of the Earth the sorcerers and powers of evil; and over Thalaba also the banner is love. A twilight of man and nature; a mass-enslavement, with the multitude prostrate or self-immolated in the cities and the temples as the tyrant or the idol goes by; and love in God, and love and faith in man and woman preparing the end of it all: to that design the drama of the world about him was more and more conforming in Shelley's eyes, and Southey's chief personages invaded his day-dreams, as they did afterwards his dramas and tales. He thought he knew what Kehama stood for, and who might be one of the deliverers, if the woman, the long-expected, the genius of the adventure, would only come. There was some deficiency and some flatness in Southey's harp, but also certain strings that gave out the spirit of his theme;—'piety', as Carlyle defines them, 'gentle deep affection . . . soft pity . . . and chivalrous valour finely audible too'.[1]

## (ii) '*The Missionary*'

If we suppose that he sought in books the expression of his deeper mind and mood, and found it where he was best pleased, we must have regard to another romance that in this same summer had laid a charm upon him—*The Missionary: an Indian*

---

[1] Carlyle's *Reminiscences*, 1881, ii. 311, quoted by Maurice H. Fitzgerald in the Preface to his Oxford *Southey*, 1909. Of the appeal of these tenderer notes to Shelley we have a sign perhaps in the description of the love-lorn Arab maiden in *Alastor* (ll. 129–39), which falls in, roughly but evidently, with the story of Oneiza, when Thalaba goes from her and her father in the desert (iii. 14 f., and especially 24). Another favourite passage was that of 'Kailyal despising the leprosy' in *Kehama* xix (to Elizabeth Hitchener, 25 July 1811); and he 'contemplated with republican feelings' the statues of Avarice, Conquest, and Priestcraft under the throne of Yamen in the last canto (26 Dec.).

*Tale*, by Sydney Owenson, afterwards Lady Morgan.[1] The author of *The Missionary* had much in common with Rosa Matilda, as well in the rhetoric of her book as on the emotional and the moral sides; but she was a better artist who vigorously daubed her Indian background, and raised the phantom of a charming character in a situation worthy of a finer hand. Hilarion, the Franciscan monk, a kinsman of the kings of Portugal, has a face and a presence answerable to his royal blood and the saintliness of his life. He goes to convert India to the Catholic faith with the rank of Papal Nuncio, and as a solitary dweller in the Vale of Cashmire falls in with Luxima, the Brahminical high-priestess, renowned far and wide for her beauty, her piety, and her prophetic powers. They live near each other, he in a cave under a mountain, she in a forest-girt pagoda, and accidents and inward promptings draw them close, until all his heart is set upon converting her, and all hers on pleasing and obeying him. The conversion having come to pass, she is solemnly cast out of the Brahminical communion, and fares with her spiritual father to Goa, to be immured in a nunnery. In Goa Hilarion's enviers and enemies, Dominicans and Jesuits, accuse him to the Inquisition of being an apostate and the seducer of his disciple, and he is sentenced to be burnt alive. But as the fire is lighted in the place of execution, Luxima, escaped from the nunnery, breaks through the crowd and throws herself into his arms, with a prayer to Brahma to receive and unite their souls. She is scorched by the flames and stabbed on the breast; but at her cry of 'Brahma!' the native Goans rise against the Inquisitors and the other Europeans. In a sea cave, to which they have stolen away, Luxima dies in Hilarion's arms, confessing the faith of Brahma, and Hilarion thereupon repairs to the beloved mountain grotto in Cashmire, and, in obedience to her last commands, becomes the apostle of reconciling love between caste and caste and between Christian and Hindu. Within this outline the main part of the story is a protracted war between passions. The priest is often nearly the lover, to his grievous shame; and in the priestess it is love that works the conversion and silences—but not constantly—her old allegiance, and the memory of her lost renown. Shelley

[1] 'Since I have read this book, I have read no other. But I have thought strangely' (to Hogg, June 1811).

remembered this book when he wrote of Cythna bursting through the soldiers and priests to die with Laon at the stake, of Asia waiting in the paradise of the 'Indian Caucasus', the mountain girdle of Cashmire, and in *Epipsychidion* of the pleasure-house in the deep woodland. Luxima, with all her tenderness, her delicate speech, her long dusk hair and 'dove-like eyes', her 'bright and ethereal form', is a frequent type in Shelley's verse from *Alastor* onwards. And here he might refresh or enlarge ideas that were now or later sovereign with him, 'warm and vivifying' ideas, as Hogg puts it: of the divinity radiant in every soul and sunbeam, or of love 'purified by an intelligence that seemed to belong to mind alone', and making always for oneness between creed and creed, or soul and soul, or thought and sense.

## (d) Elizabeth Shelley

Four years afterwards he described in *Alastor* how love first befell him in his solitary youth, how it went from him like a dream, and how he pursued its phantom under the mastery of desire. In the spring and summer of 1811 he was deep in that predicament. His cousin's unkindness was a memory still unsalved, though losing poignancy; and the other Harriet no more as yet than fancy's toy. Meanwhile, in the interval between their reigns, fifteen weeks or more before and after returning home, he plagued himself with his sister Elizabeth in a condition of mind so far approaching the courtship of a lover, so memorable, that in time to come the relation of Laon and Cythna, in the original version of the poem, represented to him, as a poet, an ideal bond. He once told Hogg that the intimacy that love is or should be is perfect only between sister and sister; but feminine as in so high a degree he was, he could easily imagine himself or a double of himself on one side of the alliance and indulge the thought of it as the holiest of all espousals. 'Sister' was his dearest word, and consciously and unconsciously he often used it for the heart's desire. He used it of Harriet Grove and was pleased and surprised to be told by Hogg that he did so; and after his friends in despite of him had cleared his *Laon and Cythna* of its dangerous element, could not, in his subsequent poetry, abstain from it. The tragic incest of a youth and a maiden is one of the motives to the pity and sorrow of *Rosalind and Helen*; and in the heart of the Aegean paradise of *Epipsychi-dion* lies the pleasure-dome of the 'tender-hearted Ocean King',

> Made sacred to his sister and his spouse.

Once more, 'identity', in his own expression, was for Shelley the roof and crown of love; a merging as of two flames born of one substance and nursed by the same food. It was the fierce demand of a solitary; and if we add that for him, in his prevailing mood, the physical union in love was the type and seal of the mystery, and further bear in mind his heedless logic and the haste of his desires, that incestuous strain of his will be seen as naturally appertaining to the pattern of his mind. But there is more to say before the passion towards his sister—his own word for it—will have been defined. It did not vanquish his moral sense. Feverish as it was, it consisted in sympathy, and not in the appetence of flesh and blood. He would join her to his friend, his second self, in the free alliance in which love would be love indeed, and their joy would echo in his, and brother and sister mystically unite. Had Shelley's mother been less uncongenial to him, she in all probability would have been the paragon and the magnet, as so often happens with natures moulded like his, and there would then have been no conjoint lover, no vicarious unrest, and no running to be relieved of it into the greatest error of his life.[1]

In the Christmas holidays Elizabeth had listened to the letters and other effusions of the prince of men, and allowed her verses to be sent to him. She had been 'enthusiastically alive to the wildest schemes, despising the world'. But her brother's disgrace had changed her. There had been 'machinations'; she had gone over to religion and the enemy. Having told him as much after the Oxford tragedy, and reported her father's order not to write to him, she was taken with a fever, and for some three weeks the post to London brought nothing from her. Not knowing the cause of her silence, he gave her up for 'lost';

[1] *The Quarterly* for Apr. 1887 charges Shelley with an incestuous design upon his sister, basing the accusation on the letter to Hogg of 4 July 1811. Dowden wrote of this letter in *The Athenaeum* for 14 May 1887, offering a different interpretation and vouching for the veracity of the version given by Hogg. As now appears from the reprint of the holograph in Mr. W. S. Scott's *Shelley at Oxford*, p. 45, the version is highly mendacious, and Shelley's meaning plain: 'I desired, eagerly desired to see you and sister irrecoverably united where you have no priest but love.'

and the letters to Hogg from Poland Street waver between a fear that she never was or will be lovable or illuminable, and a resolution to try instantly some 'experiment' to recover her. Then Hogg begins to falter, and writes that practical consequences, especially to the woman, forbid the venture of free love, and is vehemently answered.[1] Is not the hate of matrimony quite instinctive in those who adore virtue, is expediency worth one thought? At first, after his return home, his hope is rekindled that 'things shall be as I order them', but in less than a week drooped once more. She is 'apathetic to all things except trivial amusements' and despicable conversation. She to whom on the ground of her sentiment and her poetry he once ascribed 'all the properties which the wildest devotee ascribes to the Deity' is now 'not worthy of us'; but, if she is dead, are there not hopes of a 'resuscitation'? Yes, or he would not 'tear his heart'—but no, he 'will think no more of her, she has murdered thought'—but yes, he *will* think, and 'ardently devote himself'. But a few days later she is again the body of a departed soul, 'carried to the dung-heap as a mass of putrefaction'.

Hogg, meanwhile, the appointed lover of a lady he had never seen, was eager to pursue the enterprise, but in hope and patience, and towards matrimony, and occasionally gave counsel or made demur on the handling of his cause. On 25 May he sends Shelley a letter for her asking why she forbids a correspondence. If she would favour him with an answer, how soundly he would sleep in his grave, were his troubles to end there. Could it stand in his epitaph that she had smiled upon him, how would time and the weeds spare the inscription, and the moon shine upon it as the Howlet flitted by.[2] But by the middle of June Elizabeth was out of hand, and Bysshe wincing under 'scorn the most virulent, and neglect and gaiety equally contumelious';

'Would it not be a general good to all human beings that I should make haste away? . . . Where is she whom I adored?

[1] Mr. Ingpen is manifestly right in ascribing to 13 May, or thereabouts, the letter from Shelley that Hogg has dated 9 Aug. It was written, as the contents make clear, on the day before he at last went home. It contemplates, therefore, the free union, not of Harriet Westbrook and himself, but of his sister and his friend.

[2] 25 May. *The Athenians*, p. 16.

Alas! where is virtue? Where is perfection? Where I cannot reach. Is there another existence? Yes! Then I shall live there rendering and rendered happy. . . . Why do I write madly? Why has sleep forsaken me? Why are you and my sister for ever present to my mind?'

And he could neither spare her his screeds on free love, nor support the answering scorn.

On 23 June he fairly lost his wits. His mother pressed him at table into taking wine; he 'began to rave'; and she gave him a sedative in the form of pen, ink, and paper. He thereupon wrote to Hogg, entreating that, 'to soothe me and restore my peace', he would at once set out for Horsham and come, under cover of midnight, to Field Place.

'There are two rooms in this house which I have taken exclusively to myself. . . . These you shall inhabit with me. You must content yourself to sleep upon a mattress; and you will be like a State prisoner. You must only walk with me at midnight for fear of discovery. My window commands a view of the lawn, where you will frequently see an object that will amply repay your journey—the object of my fond affections. Time and opportunity must effect that in my favour with [her] which entreaties cannot. . . . I almost *insist on your coming*.'

He did not come, and Bysshe presently confessed he had been 'mad'; he was in a state of mind that only his friend's company would remedy. 'I have been thinking of Death and Heaven for four days. . . . Is there a future life? Whom shall we injure by departing? But I do not talk thus, or even think thus, when we are together.'

### 3. Solution

### (a) *In London: July 1811*

Bysshe was now resolved to visit him. By the middle of June he had one invitation from John Westbrook to join the family in Chapel Street, and accompany them to a house of theirs in Aberystwyth; and another to Cwm Elan, the estate near Rhayader, where his married cousin, Thomas Grove, was master; but, whether or no he accepted either, he would go to York. On 21 June he purposes to fall in with the wishes of the Westbrooks, and, after a week in Aberystwyth, join his friend. On the 25th, he thinks of going to London and thence to Wales, travelling on foot that he may 'better remark the manners and dispositions of the peasantry', to spend the summer, first 'a week or two' with the Groves, and then with the Westbrooks.[1] On the 27th, he tells Hogg he will come at once to York—'on my way to Wales, where possibly I shall not go'[2]—and with that destination, after a last appeal to Elizabeth, he left home for London on some day later than 4 July. But he did not escape trouble; for in London 'days of urgent business that would neither admit of delay or rest' and several sleepless nights exhausted him, and resulted, after his arrival at Cwm Elan, in 'a short but violent nervous illness'.[3] Hogg, having waited for his coming for some days in vain, received an undated letter to say he was at Cwm Elan; and soon afterwards another to explain his movements. In London angry letters had come from his father; the invitation to Hogg to invade Field Place in secret had been discovered; and if Bysshe were to visit his friend, he should have no money. But 'the old buck' should be thwarted; 'Mr. Peyton' would do for a *nom de guerre* and Mr. Peyton would swallow Mr. Shelley and some fine day happily arrive at York. At length, whatever the reason was, he disappointed the Westbrooks and betook himself to his cousins.

Why could he find no time for writing to Hogg from London, no time for seeing Miss Hitchener, who was then in town, as he had promised? What had been the pressing occupation and the worry? In all probability the trouble arose in Chapel Street, where the Westbrooks were still at home.[4] In the two months past they had not let go of him. They had plied him with letters, and he had written as regularly, under injunction from Eliza that 'you will take no notice to any of your family of your intimacy with us'. In this correspondence the elder sister so won upon him that he at times wondered which of them he liked the better. But the younger was after all 'the larger diamond', albeit less polished, and her contempt of surrounding prejudice 'fine'. On Harriet and surrounding prejudice much of the correspondence must have turned, for, as the fond

---

[1] To Elizabeth Hitchener, 25 June; to Hogg, 25 ? July.

[2] He speaks (25 ? July) of having intended to 'accompany Hogg to York' presumably, if Hogg should have come, in the mad way, to Field Place.

[3] To Elizabeth Hitchener, postmark 15 July.

[4] He did not, apparently, lodge with them in London, but at John Grove's.

disciple of an atheist, she was in such trouble at Clapham School
that her father at one time thought of withdrawing her. But
he had not yet resolved to do so, and when Shelley came to
Chapel Street in those early July days, he no doubt championed
his martyr and responded once more, and more impressionably,
to her charm. It would be strange if, a month afterwards,
Harriet Westbrook should have prevailed upon him, as she did,
had there been no occasion for renewing her influence, except
by letters, since the early part of May. Nor can we wonder
that all the coil and the worry should have made him ill.

## (b) Cwm Elan: ? 15 July–? 5 August

Cwm Elan is a mountain glen, deep and narrow all the way,
and especially at the point where the Groves lived, some five
miles to the south-west of Rhayader. The Elan swirled and
tumbled on its rocky path to meet the Wye, through densely
timbered hills or barren and precipitous walls; but where the
gardens of the manorial house extended along its banks, 'the
special charm of the landscape lay in its union of wild loveliness
with the grace and ornament of human culture . . . meadow
and lawn, corn-field and clover-field, clear pathways and the
abode of man'.[1] Here was Nature as Shelley instinctively loved
her best, and now beheld her for the first time, but he was in
no receptive mood. The lines entitled *The Retrospect*, which he
wrote while living for a time close to the same spot in the following summer, describe how, when he first came to it, he would
hide from the daylight in the deep woods, and

> Would close mine eyes, and dream I were
> On some remote and friendless plain,
> And long to leave existence there,
> If with it I might leave the pain
> That with a finger cold and lean
> Wrote madness on my withering mien.

But at fall of day or under the moon or in the noon of night he
would wander far, and lose the 'sense of overwhelming woe'
before the coming on of the dark or in the sound of the waters
or the mountain wind. And the cause of his sorrow was 'the
soul's solitude', the heart unanswered, and the want of kindred
minds superior to custom and the world's pleasure and pride.

[1] Dowden, i. 162.

This torment near to madness is not betrayed in the letters written at Cwm Elan, where he arrived probably on 15 July, but he has much to say about monotony. It is not entirely unrelieved, however. As at all times since boyhood, his pen is active: at a novel in epistolary form to be composed by turns with Hogg; at 'essays, moral and metaphysical',[1] that Stockdale, with his unpaid reckoning for *St. Irvyne*, may have for nothing, if he will. And, as at all times, he is 'the friend of the unfriended poor'; walks with an old beggar man, asking a thousand questions, and receiving at last one memorable answer: 'I see by your dress that you are a rich man. They have injured me and mine a million times—you appear to be well intentioned, but I have no security of it, while you live in such a house as that, or wear such clothes as those. It would be a charity to quit me.' Did the words remind Shelley of a little pinnace on the Elan with a bank note for a sail? He rides to Rhayader with Mrs. Grove, 'a very nice woman'. But, 'I am all solitude', he writes, 'as I cannot call the society here an alternative of it.' 'I am what the sailors call banyaning. I do not see a soul.' The post on three days in the week, neither regular nor safe, reminds him of Tantalus and the waves in hell, and his heart is on the road to York.

But on the causes of the unrest the letters throw a light, and the main cause is, as before, the loss to him of his sister's grace. Had he been suing for her hand, and hurt by her disdain, he could hardly have written in other terms. But although desirous that another man's affection should carry on and crown, as it were, his own, he stood to suffer all the shock of love rejected for the second time, unless his sister should at length relent. And the letters to his friend, when they touch upon the matter, persist in the curious interchange of 'you' and 'me':

'Now, there is Miss F. D. Browne[2] . . . that lovely extract of her poems certainly surpasses any of Elizabeth's, and it was Elizabeth's poetry that charmed, and, as you were pleased to say, bewitched me. . . . For the rest, it is *now* far from being *my* wish that you should think more of the past. I foresee that all regrets cherished on that head will end in aggravating disappointment;

---

[1] Presumably the essays mentioned in the letter to Miss Hitchener of 26 Dec. and 2 Jan., to be published, he hopes, in the summer.
[2] Afterwards Mrs. Hemans.

I do not say despair, for I have too good an opinion of my firmness to suppose that I would yield to *despair*. Besides, *wherefore* should I love her? A disinterested apprehension of what is in itself excellent; this is good if it is so—but what I felt was a *passion*. . . . Is it not[1] then the *business* of reason to conquer passion, particularly when I received *all* the evidences of her loveliness from the latter. . . . Let me *hope* that I shall be dispassionate; I did *execrate* my existence once, when I first discovered that there was no chance of our being united.'[2]

It is a strange confusion. 'Should I despair?', or 'Should you despair?' it is one. And the great end is 'our being united', they with each other, and therefore he with her. Later, when in London, early in August, he hears that John Grove is Elizabeth's suitor, and in all the tumult of deciding to abscond with Harriet Westbrook, dashes into Sussex for a word with her. He is reassured: Hogg need not tremble; she has no fondness for her cousin John. Yet neither has she any for her other wooers (for some there are), or for Hogg himself. 'I must still think', he adds, 'how unfortunate it is you ever mentioned her very name, still must I long for the time when you will forget her, but which now you say can never come.'[3]

So then he had loved and lost, if that be a way to love, the second time, and his tribulation had now thrown him into a mood for folly. So teased and desolated, he was bound to think more and more of the kinder maiden who heard him gladly, and for his and his gospel's sake had estranged the whole world. He knew that she must be, for the present at any rate, a poor companion in the paths of thought; but there was always in one mode of his loving a strain of guarding and fostering. And were he still to teach, and she to listen, what might she not become? Was she not already his martyr, lonely, almost desperate, as her letters ever and again declared? And there were other appeals, renewed at every meeting with her: a face 'fresh as the morning, all light and sweetness', as even an enemy wrote of it.[4] Suddenly, in this sea of temptation, he was hit between wind and water. In his own story of the event, given to Miss Hitchener on 26 October following, he began with the letters for some time exchanged

[1] The text is: 'It is not then'; which was evidently wrong.
[2] To Hogg, n.d., ? 28 July.
[3] 15 Aug., text garbled by Hogg, and first corrected in Koszul: *La Jeunesse*.
[4] Mary Shelley in *Lodore*.

with Harriet in his endeavour to win her over to 'the good, the disinterested, and the free.' 'The frequency of her letters became greater', he continues, 'during my stay in Wales. . . . They contained complaints of the irrational conduct of her relations, and the misery of living where she could *love* no one. Suicide was with her a favourite theme; her total uselessness was urged in its defence. . . . At length one letter assumed a tone of such despair as induced me to quit Wales precipitately.'

### (c) *In London again: ? 6 August–? 25 August*

Until the last week in July he had meant to join the Westbrooks in Aberystwyth; but they had left that place for home earlier, perhaps, than had been at first intended. It was for London, therefore, that he left Cwm Elan, most probably on Monday, the 5th of August, with money lent by Hogg. In an undated letter of one of the last days of July he had replied to his friend's jesting about Harriet that 'if I know anything about love, I am *not* in love'. Now, writing probably on 3 August, after the summons and on the brink of the journey, he has chosen his course. Harriet, he informs Hogg, had been ordered by her father to go back to school, where her life was unendurable. Asked for his advice, he had advised her to resist, while pleading with her father at the same time. 'She wrote to say that resistance was useless', he continues, 'but that she would fly with me, and threw herself upon my protection. We shall have £200 a year; when we find it run short, we must live, I suppose, upon love! Gratitude and admiration all demand that I should love her *for ever*.' That he, of all men, should be 'a protector', was a 'flattering distinction', he says, but 'quite ludicrous'. However, the die was cast and Hogg might expect Harriet and himself at York immediately or in three weeks' time, as Harriet might decide. And he has almost resolved to commit matrimony, his friend's argument for that institution having suddenly put on weight. 'Hear it not, Percy,' he quoted to Charles Grove, after telling him of her appealing letter, 'for it is a knell that summons thee to heaven or to hell.'

'I arrived in London', he continues to Miss Hitchener. 'I was shocked at observing the alteration of her looks. Little did I divine the cause; she had become violently attached to *me*, and feared that I should not return her attachment. Prejudice made the confession painful. It was impossible to avoid being much affected. I promised to unite my fate with hers. I stayed in London several days, during which she recovered her spirits.' Hogg meanwhile, alarmed at the imminent catastrophe, tried the one shift that might avail. He would seem to have reckoned that Harriet or her conspiring family might be countered only were Shelley to insist on the sacred duty of free love; and wrote in all haste to plead for it. No, Shelley answered: Hogg's own repeated argument—that free love would not do, as asking of the woman by far the heavier sacrifice—stood for him firm, however pure and free the principle in itself. He could now stifle the 'ineffable digust' which the idea of matrimony had but a few weeks before excited in him. It was in these days that he heard from Charles Grove that his brother John intended to marry Elizabeth. On the 10th of August, under promise to Harriet of returning whenever she might call him, he departed for Field Place. He was in Sussex for five days;[1] saw Elizabeth and talked to his comfort with her; saw Miss Hitchener; and called at Horsham on the elder Medwin, who lent him money. On the 15th he was again in London on Harriet's summons. She had written that her family were once more urging her to return to school. And now, having already promised 'to unite his fate with hers', he 'proposed marriage', and she, after some demur as to the immediacy of the venture, consented. For nine days after his return from Sussex he remained at the Groves' house in Lincoln's Inn Fields, 'embarrassed and melancholy', as Charles Grove relates, as if engaged 'in exerted action rather than inspired passion'; until Harriet's indecision was overcome and a plan devised for flight.

On the evening of Saturday, 24 August,[2] accompanied by Charles Grove, he removed from Lincoln's Inn Fields to a coffee-house in Mount Street, close to Harriet's home, where the cousins spent the night. Early next morning they awaited Harriet's coming, with a coach in readiness before the inn, and

---

[1] He writes from London to Elizabeth Hitchener on Saturday, 10th: 'I shall be at Field Place tomorrow.' On the 15th, he writes to Hogg: 'I left London yesterday, though now returned.' Here the date of his leaving must be wrong. Dobell thought that the letter to Miss Hitchener, evidently of the 19th of August, discussing the propriety of his dining with her in her home, was written in Sussex, i.e. from Field Place or Cuckfield. But it is not necessary to suppose so.

[2] See Dowden's note on the date of the elopement, i. 176.

breakfasted. Still she did not come, and the hero of the adventure amused himself by flinging oyster-shells across the street. 'Grove', he exclaimed, 'this is a *Shelley* business!'[1] When at last she joined them, the three together drove to the inn in Gracechurch Street, or thereabouts, whence the coach for Edinburgh started in the evening.

### (d) Marriage in Edinburgh: 29 August

The two fugitives made the journey without a break, Shelley dispatching a hasty note to Hogg, as they passed through York, with an appeal for money; and another to his father to ask for his clothes to be forwarded, and to admonish him that 'it is little worth the while of its inhabitants to be affected by the occurrences of this world'.[2] A Scottish advocate in the coach told them how to be married in Scotland, and, arriving in Edinburgh not sooner than the evening of the 27th, they lost no time in forging the necessary certificate of the due period of residence and the proclamation of banns. Then, on 29 August, they presented themselves before the Rev. Joseph Robertson, Minister of the Church of Scotland, who in due form made them man and wife.

What had been his real or main inducement? Her charm and beauty? Or her woes and troubles, as he afterwards made out? Surely neither. Her manner and person had a certain candle-power, enough to attract him, but not enough to burn his wings, and much misgiving disheartened his knight-errantry. Yet an overmastering force had hold of him, knowing in his heart that he did not love her, and now and then dimly suspicious of his being entrapped. Had he respected her in the due degree of love, the 'ineffable disgust' that the idea of marriage had excited but a week or two before would not have been so easily put by. And he may have told himself at times, what in the bitter sequel he confessed, that against her also his rashness was a sin. The blinding compulsion is not far to seek. It was the effect induced by the loss of his cousin's love, exasperated by the futile passion in the summer months at Field Place, a passion no less fervid for having been deflected and side-tracked by a saving slant. It was the twice whetted hunger of one in whom love, or the illusion of love was indispensable to every exultation, and not 'a thing apart', but his 'whole existence'.

---

[1] A business with no core or substance in it.        [2] *Shelley in England*, p. 306.

# VI

## DISTRESSES AND RESOLVES

### 1. HARRIET SHELLEY

SHELLEY's first marriage, from the wedding day to the act by which he definitely abjured it, lasted for three years all but a month. For nineteen months or more it was happy; and then a turn to unhappiness can be seen clearly after the April of 1813, when for many weeks he lived in or about London, and in the society of accomplished friends discovered his privations. For a long while at first there was an immense relief from vain longing, and the Godwinian and the philanthropist came out in free and fervent play. To reason his desires and hopes, to demonstrate 'atheism' and rights and wrongs, was at this period of his life a rage upon him. In all the excitement of August 1811 he could go aside and write letters on wealth and wickedness, and on aristocracy and equality. And behind this opinionated assurance was the pure love of man, the young and knightly passion to help and save; so that he burned not to think only, but to 'mix with action'. Within the happier nineteen months he had set forth his creed in the poem and the notes of *Queen Mab*, and had brought away a sore sense of the difficulty of doing good from his plunges into Irish politics and into the endeavour to mend the embankment at Tremadoc. These blended energies of mind and will were an overmastering current that received and dispersed within it the cares and joys of his married life. The marriage was one among other pieces of his missionary labour, with a special blessing on it and the promise of a rich reward. 'Blame me if thou wilt, dearest friend,' he writes to Miss Hitchener, 'for *still* thou are dearest to me: yet pity even this error [of the marriage], if thou blamest me. If Harriet be not, at sixteen, all that you are at a more advanced age, assist me to mould a really noble soul into all that can make its nobleness useful and lovely. Lovely it is now, or I am the weakest slave of error.' Once his demand for freedom and a small competence had been again conceded, to evangelize society, and Harriet by the way, seemed not to be overmuch.

All was glad, confident morning, the feverish night gone by, sure ground, and nothing impossible. There were sore disappointments, but he went on indivertibly in his high purposes. There are many aspects of Shelley; and one reminds us of the most effectual angel who brought swift aid to Virgil and Dante in the nether world, 'waving the gross air from his countenance', and 'seemed as one whom other care urges and incites than that of those who stand before him'.

Yet only fondness kept it from him that he had built his house on sand. For he had fallen away from his high idea of love. He wanted, as he once put it, 'an all-sufficing passion', and descended to a pupil and mistress. He had taken her for what she might become, with a bond of marriage to assist her weakness and the minority of her soul; and until that future should have shaped itself he must wait and want. At first, however, she gained upon him. She was glad and eager that he should 'superintend the progress of her mind', and help her to 'an elevated philosophy'.[1] She took over with no stint of fervency his opinions and his hopes and, with some profane amusement, made herself a party to his sublime futilities. As Hogg and Peacock both testify, she was 'well educated', read assiduously French authors as well as English, and preferred not 'light productions' but 'morality—Telemachus and Belisarius, and other compositions of the same leaven'. Indeed, she would read the morality hour after hour to weary ears, and discourse unconscionably on dreadful temptations and on her special theme of suicide. Yet melancholy was not her shade, and for any such tiresomeness there were all the amends in the character given by Peacock, as already quoted.[2] And Hogg entirely bears him out. Always bright and pretty, as he tells us, well and plainly dressed, and so preened that, whenever you saw her, 'she might have stepped that moment from a glass case', she diffused about her cheerfulness and calmness, and was withal sincere, natural, warm-hearted. In her love for him, declared Shelley, there is not only a shield from the world's scorn, but medicines for the spirit—passion linked with virtue, peace, and truth, 'pure thoughts forcing the quick and warm return', mild eyes that pierced and cleansed the heart; nay,

[1] Letter F, in *Shelley's Lost Letters to Harriet*, ed. Leslie Hotson, p. 41.
[2] See p. 81.

heaven on earth, the consecration of his enterprises, the inspiration of his song.[1]

Yet ingenuousness and kindness were not enough. These graces were indeed in Shelley's eyes the ground of all heart's-ease, and if Harriet had maintained the supply, she would probably not have lost him. But he would have wanted more and more wistfully the other half of the longed-for sufficiency, the communion of aspiring minds, and repaired for it, as from the very first he did, to another woman. For his correspondence with Miss Hitchener was broken for only seven weeks, and he resumed it on a much more eager note.

'My dearest friend, you, who understand my motives to action which, I flatter myself, unisonise with your own, I will dare to say I *love*: nor do I risk the supposition that the lump of organised matter which enshrines thy soul excites the love which that soul alone dare claim. Henceforth will I be yours. . . . Not a thought shall arise which shall not seek its responsion in your bosom; not a motive of action shall be unenwafted by your cooler reason.'[2]

In the second of his letters after his marriage he proposed to share his income with her when he had come of age; by the end of January she was to leave her school at Hurstpierpoint immediately, and reside in his home. Would it not be a reasonable compact between him and the sister of his soul, whom he had loved, for sure, in a former life, and would for ever love, 'intellectually and celestially'? Was it not due to the world at large that her 'great mind' should indite not grammar-books, but books to reform a nation and save it from its imminent ruin? 'I am incapable of writing, compared to what I shall be when I am enlightened with the emanations of your genius. Let us mingle our identities, and burst upon tyrants with the accumulated impetuosity of our requirements and resolutions.'

But the marriage was unfortunate not on the intellectual side only. Harriet's charms and graces easily hid from sight the deficiencies that she had never the opportunity to make good. For example: in all this Hitchener affair she seems at first sight admirable, welcoming under her roof the woman who was to take on the better half of her vocation, and to help in moulding her, if it were possible, to what she ought to be. But in that

[1] *The Retrospect*; *To Harriet*; fragment of Sonnet, 1 Aug. 1812; dedication of *Queen Mab*.	[2] 16 Oct.

behaviour there is all the while and nevertheless an aspect of 'poor little Harriet', as Hogg sometimes calls her. 'What shall I say to bring you to us?'—so she wrote to the luminary, who for some time and for good reasons hesitated to arrive. 'Should we not be more useful all together? You would by your arguments countenance ours; as you are older than I am, therefore people would not think what I say so foolish.' Is it wonderful that, when snares were laid for her honour by her husband's dearest friend, it should have seemed to Eliza Westbrook that the young thing would need to be mothered, as heretofore? So in the middle of October, not two months after the wedding, appeared the duenna, to go with her wards from that time everywhere, to keep their money 'in a hole or corner of her dress', and to coddle Harriet's nerves. Hogg is as lively as ever about this assiduous government, with its instant reprehensions, and 'What would Miss Warne say?'—whoever Miss Warne was; and the superior languors of the person, and how Shelley wilted in her presence. What Shelley's friend sometimes fancied he could do with pleasure, under these circumstances, we may gather from the conversation by the swollen Ouse, one day when the young people were by themselves, and Harriet could receive the blasphemy laughing: 'Dearest Harriet, how nicely that dear Eliza would spin down the river! How sweetly she would turn round and round, like that log of wood! And, gracious heaven, what would Miss Warne say?' And he has no doubt, nor have his readers any, that the only wise course for the chief victim was to forbid the overshadowing and dismiss the intruder. Harriet did very well for a time with her token payments, until, thanks to the vulgar influence of the woman always at her side, she scanted or omitted the comfort that it was in her power to give even when she wearied of things abstruse. But Shelley had no inkling of all that was to come, and the calamity slept in its causes.

## 2. THE EMBROILMENT WITH FIELD PLACE; FROM THE END OF AUGUST TO THE END OF OCTOBER 1811

Shelley had bitterly incensed his parents by marrying the taverner's daughter and by his way of marrying. Without a word to either of them, and by what they could regard only as an act of dissoluteness, the heir of the house, who was to consummate the long labour of building it up, and present an appropriate figure to the world, had bound himself to 'a young female'. They themselves had been treated as in this connexion of no account, and only entitled to pay the bill, and so in his letters after the marriage he virtually told them. And now his father came in and began operating, with wrong to answer wrong.

Mr. Shelley had visited London in the middle of August, perhaps to inquire what game his son was playing; but, if that were his purpose, he discovered nothing of an anxious nature. By the 25th, the day of the lovers' flight, he learnt that Bysshe was dangerously captivated and by whom, and requested Whitton to intervene. But the lawyer demurred: he feared that John Westbrook had either laid the toils, or looked on while others laid them, and that Bysshe himself was 'governed only by his passions'. 'I shall not like to meddle with such a chicken, for he is very confident.' By the 27th news of the elopement came to Field Place by Bysshe's letter from the coach, and probably from John Grove; and the excited father set out for London breathing disinheritance. He at once caused Whitton to examine the settlements of the estates, only to learn that Bysshe 'was tenant in tail in remainder, and there was not any power of revocation and new appointment'. On the same day, and on the 28th, there were conferences in Chapel Street between the lawyer and his client and John and Eliza Westbrook, John Westbrook on his part also in high displeasure. The conversations touched no doubt upon finance, and who should maintain the runaways; with the result that each of the fathers resolved to leave them unsupplied. So Timothy Shelley ordered his attorney to withhold the allowance of £200 a year granted to Bysshe in the previous May, a quarter of which would in four weeks' time fall due; and with that decree and with blabbing and fuming to the inquisitive world, only fomented his own anger. On 16 September Whitton was moved to entreat him to write and talk no more on the irremediable.

At Edinburgh, meanwhile, the Shelleys were well lodged in George Street, where in the first week of September they were joined by Hogg upon a holiday. Harriet, 'radiant with youth, health, and beauty', seconded her husband's 'rapturous' welcome, and for a whole happy month the three of them were together. The wit and gourmand was all the gayer for his excellent food, and very facetious over the Scots. They had books from a public library, and read many, chiefly French. Shelley translated as for publication a treatise of Buffon's, and Harriet the two volumes of Marie Collin's moral and affecting tale of *Claire d'Albe*, writing out her version 'without blot or blemish in a small neat flowing hand'. And she read her 'grave and excellent books' aloud 'very well, very correctly, with a clear agreeable voice', while Hogg was pleased to listen, but Bysshe, to her keen annoyance, sometimes fell asleep. But the place and the tone of the place, the commercial spirit, and the gloom of the Lord's Day were not to their fancy. They were told to take their exercise on a Sunday unintentionally, and Shelley, at his single church-going, 'sat through the psalmody and sermon in deep dejection and with piteous sighs'.

But by the first week of October the policy to reduce him by starvation to a satisfactory abasement was wearing down his patience. He was at his wits' end for money and deep in debt. Since the decision to leave Cwm Elan he had borrowed from Hogg, from a certain Mr. Dunn, from the elder Medwin, and from the landlord of his inn on the eve of the wedding. On 30 August he applied to his father for an immediate advance of £50, with not a word of his marriage, but a few on the desertedness of the Scottish capital and on the rain. With no answer to this appeal, and John Westbrook equally unforthcoming, it was lucky that Captain Pilfold took the view that 'to be confoundedly angry is all very well, but to stop the supplies is a great deal too bad', and sent his nephew 'cheerful, hearty letters' with money. But the relief was transient, and Shelley on the 15th of September knocked for the second time in what was meant for a soothing manner at the bolted door. He could not think for a moment, he told his father, he had displeased him by his 'late proceedings', though he might have acted 'with impoliteness'; but if anger had been kindled, he 'might succeed in pointing out' how unfortunate it was in a mind 'which the duties of legislation demand to be unruffled', and how 'inconsistent with the Christian forbearance with which you are so eminently adorned'. What more conformable to the world's opinion than that two persons mutually attracted should live together by law? What would the world think of a father who on that account should punish a son? And how hard for his mother and sisters to lose his society, if the vanity might be pardoned, knowing that the only cause was matrimony, that 'venerable institution'! Again no answer; and again, on the 27th, he tried the door. Had he not complied with law and with religion? He had not indeed consulted his father when he chose a wife; but a choice like that depended on general tastes, and his father's were the opposite of his own. Even granting that he had really offended: there was still Christianity and the duty to forgive. 'Father, are you a Christian?' Nothing was more common than elopements of young people, and implacable parents were 'now banished to antiquated farces and silly novels'. Finally, having thrown in, as it were, the terrors of the Last Day, since 'it is perhaps too late to appeal to your love for me', he called upon the sinner to 'bring forth fruits meet for repentance', and send him immediately a remittance of £50.

This third appeal was as futile as the others; but in the first few days of October he was able through the Captain's bounty to discharge his local debts, and, Hogg's vacation having now ended, the three companions left Edinburgh for York. Here they took some dingy lodgings from two spinsters, mantua-makers, at 20 Coney Street, the Shelleys intending to reside in the city until Hogg, in the course of his legal education, should move to London, and when that time came to move with him. It was essential, however, that Bysshe should see his father, and bring him, if he could, to terms. From York he addressed him two more remonstrances,[1] in the preceptorial tone, and tried to enforce them by an appeal to old Sir Bysshe.[2] But his long detained and sorely needed wardrobe was consigned to him by his mother without a word, and he learned that command had been given at Field Place that on those premises his and his wife's names were never to be spoken. It was high time to appear in person and 'try the force of truth' on his 'thoughtless' parent. On Wednesday the 15th, therefore, leaving Harriet in his friend's care, he departed for the South, and on Saturday morning arrived in Cuckfield at his uncle's house.

But news that came to hand before his departure from York put him in a rage. Timothy Shelley, it is to be remembered, knew nothing of the marriage until he read the letter from Edinburgh of 15 September. It was therefore in perfect honesty,

[1] 5 and 12 Oct.  [2] 13 Oct.

but in a nasty humour that on 8 September he insinuated in a letter to the elder Hogg that Bysshe had run away with Harriet as his mistress; that his friend had joined him with the intent to share her favours; and that it would be not surprising if the young woman were to be left on the friend's hands. Bysshe, hearing in York of these imputations, immediately dispatched a few lines to speed before him to Field Place. He taxed his father with using calumny as 'a cowardly expedient of persecution', with desiring more than his disgrace, with having once wanted to send him to be killed in Spain. But he was 'not an insect whom injuries destroy'. If his father would not hear his name willingly, he would follow him to London, and hollow in his ear 'Bysshe, Bysshe, Bysshe', till he were deaf. One point at least in the letter made an impression—he protested that the allowance had been granted to him unconditionally, to live upon at his own discretion, and faith had been broken with him.

There had been another and fiercer incentive to the southward journey. Once more Elizabeth Shelley is in the picture. He had heard at York, presumably from Captain Pilfold, that his mother had been at work to marry her to Edward Graham, the Agent's son; that she had acted without her husband knowing it, and had behaved to her daughter 'violently' and 'persecutingly'; and the matter was unsavoury and a public scandal. In fact it was an old scandal swollen. Some six months previously, Bysshe being then at home, an anonymous letter to Timothy Shelley accused the mistress of Field Place of an illicit intimacy with the young musician.[1] Field Place had been much amused, and Shelley in a waggish letter in verse admonished Graham of the peril of 'cornuting old Killjoy'.[2] The scandal, like a rolling snowball, now had it that the guilty lady had been trying to pay off the lover with the daughter's hand, and Shelley, on unknown grounds, if any, was at once persuaded. In a letter to his mother, intercepted and undelivered, he tasked her with what he called to others her depravity,[3] and with urging the match to save her own good name; and in another to Elizabeth, likewise withheld, charged her to 'speak truth', if her father

---

[1] Shelley's undated letter to Graham, certainly written in May 1811; Julian Shelley, x. 416.

[2] Julian Shelley, iii. 92.

[3] To Elizabeth Hitchener, 26 Oct.; to Charles Grove, 29 Oct.

should ask her questions.[1] 'Too ridiculous for a thought' was Timothy's comment when the matter was laid before him; but in an interview, or separate interviews, with his parents on Sunday, 20 October, the devoted brother poured out his mind on this and on his other sores in bitter language and affrighting passion. The altercation was audible, it seems, from beyond the room, for the tattlers of Horsham were soon agog with it.[2] But all the fury profited nothing. The plot for Graham's benefit, if it existed, was left to its barren self, and Shelley's persuasion of his mother's 'baseness' seems presently to have died away. And for the rest, his father not only demanded once more that he should abjure his atheism in a public manner and a contrite tone, but went farther: he would not talk of the allowance, except through Whitton, and in future would not receive his son's letters until Whitton had opened and pronounced them tolerable. After a fruitless interview with Sir Bysshe the invader knew that he had shot his bolt, and there was nothing for it but to see the lawyer, and left Cuckfield for London on the 24th, to his parents' immense relief. Indeed, he had come upon them like an evening dragon: the Master of Field Place was near sending for a guard of constables, and 'the ladies ran upstairs at the barking of a dog'. In London Whitton refused to meet him, and after another blast to his father he departed on the 25th for York. It was well that he did not receive until the 26th the note in which the lawyer assumed the censorship of all his letters to Field Place. He returned it to its sender with the intimation, written on the cover, that in case of any such censoring 'impudence would draw down chastisement on contemptibility'; and received a lecture in reply on his 'boyish warmth' and 'flippancy', wherewith the hostilities ceased. 'I wish he may continue 100 miles off', wrote his father. 'We are all well, but often in sad frights with the ladies' fancies.'[3]

### 3. The Estrangement from Hogg

As if the frustration of his journey were not enough, Shelley returned to the North to encounter a sorrow as disheartening for a while as any that ever befell him. That he had acted

---

[1] Written at Cuckfield on Tuesday, 22 Oct. Both the undelivered letters are printed in *Shelley in England*, pp. 348, 349.
[2] To T. C. Medwin, 26 Nov.          [3] Ingpen, p. 349. Kegan Paul.

improperly and foolishly in leaving his wife to the sole care and company of his friend was immediately apprehended by Hogg's parents, and Mrs. Hogg, on some day before the 21st, sent a letter to Harriet to urge her 'by no means to continue with him', and 'pitying her situation, offered to write to her friends'; to which Harriet sent back 'a very civil answer much in the style of a gentlewoman, thanking Mrs. H. but declining her service for the present'. The apprehensions were too well grounded. Shelley, who was to have come back in the company of Eliza Westbrook, must have heard in London that she had preceded him to York. He found her at her sister's side, not with Hogg in the lodgings in Coney Street, but without him in some rooms in Blake Street.¹ And Harriet's bearing to his friend had changed and become inimical. In a day or two he had found out the reason. Hogg, he learned, had been enamoured with her in Edinburgh, and avowed his passion when they came to York. She had repelled him and, hoping that the matter would be thereby ended, kept it secret. But in Shelley's absence in the South the advances had been renewed with pertinacity and with sophistical argument, until her firmness and her reproaches had shamed the tempter, and he was eager to write to Shelley and beg forgiveness. This, however, she would not allow, fearing that the letter would distress her husband overmuch and spoil his journey. She even trusted after his return to spare him the perturbing truth and, as is most likely, summoned her sister to come at once and stand by her in the meanwhile. Having heard of these things,

> 'I sought him', writes Shelley,² 'and we walked to the fields beyond York. I desired to know fully the account of this affair. I heard it *from him*, and I believe he was sincere. All I can recollect of that terrible day was that I pardoned him—freely, fully pardoned him; that I would still be a friend to him, and hoped to convince him how lovely virtue was; that his crime, not himself, was the object of my detestation; that I value a human being not for what it has been, but for what it is; that I hoped the time would come when he would regard this horrible error with as much disgust as I did. He said little: he was pale, terror-struck, remorseful.'

¹ He knew of the change of rooms when he was in London, for he gave the new address, to which letters were to be forwarded, at the Turk's Head Coffee House.
² To Elizabeth Hitchener, 14 Nov.

At the same time Shelley declared that for the present there could be no maintaining the old intercourse, and that he and Harriet would leave the city, but did not tell him whither and when. But on those terms he would have the friendship to continue, and urged upon Hogg, and Hogg consented, that they must write to one another in the time in which they should live apart.

Accordingly, on 1 November or thereabout, the Shelleys, with Eliza Westbrook, departed, as they left word, for Richmond, without warning him. They rested at Richmond for a day or two, then went on, and arrived by the 8th of November at Keswick. They had made for Keswick because Harriet and Eliza knew and liked that country, while Shelley was at the time 'indifferent to all places'. But he soon agreed to stay there, and on or before the 12th left his first lodging at Townhead for a furnished house, small, one-storied, on the south-western slope of Chestnut Hill, looking down on the land between Derwentwater and Bassenthwaite. 'Our window', he tells Miss Hitchener, 'commands a view of the two lakes and the giant mountains which confine them; but the object most interesting to my feelings is Southey's habitation.' 'The scenery is awfully grand; it even affects me in such a time as this.'

'I stand alone', he writes to Hogg, 'I feel that I am nothing: a speck in an universe! . . . Oh, how I have loved you! I was even ashamed to tell you how! And now to leave you for a long time! No: not for a *long* time! Night comes: Death comes. Cold, calm Death. Almost I would it were tomorrow. There is another life— are you not to be the first there? Assuredly, dearest, dearest friend. Reason with me still: I am like a child in weakness.'[1]

For seven or eight weeks Hogg poured through the post, upon him or upon Harriet, his remorse and his hurt pride. On the day of the secret flight after discovering that the Shelleys were gone, he had pursued them with 'several letters' and a threat, if Harriet would not forgive him, to 'blow his brains out at her feet'. They must return to York and admit him to the old intimacy. Was a 'mistake' to be scored against him as a crime? Was chastity a virtue to be asked of any man: of any man whose

---

[1] Cited in Hogg's version in the *Life*, and substantially faithful to Shelley's letter as given by Mr. Scott. In the other letters much of the text is carefully falsified.

blood ran warm like his, not cold like Shelley's? Were not Harriet's beauty, and her other graces an excuse for him, and he no 'smooth-tongued traitor', but a victim to irresistible attractions—to his love of excellence—to his own virtue? And if they stayed away, mistrusting his repentance, he would do that which should overwhelm them, but then too late.

To all of which Shelley answers firmly, wisely, more than generously, and in his own pure-hearted vein. At times he wonders if Hogg is not profoundly cunning, or decides that he 'does not love him now'; but that is momentary. Now and then it comes upon him that his reprobation is unworthy an illuminated mind, and that he should be, and in a strange degree in fact is free from jealousy. He attaches 'little value to the monopoly of cohabitation', and for friendship's sake 'would not refuse what he might share', nor 'much care utterly to resign'. But Hogg has basely forgotten the main thing: Harriet's happiness is at stake, and she is deeply 'prejudiced'; he 'hopes she will not always be so'.[1] And yet in himself, he confesses, the 'prejudice' has not been killed, and the letters are more than touched with it:

'Think not', he writes, 'that I am otherwise than your friend: a friend to you now more fervent, more devoted than ever, for misery endears to us those whom we love. . . . Still let us continue what we have ever been. . . . Let us forget this affair: . . . You will say perhaps that it is well for *me* to reason; I am cold, phlegmatic, unfeeling, that I compromise for those sins which I love by railing against those which are matters of indifference. In the first part of this charge there may be some truth, I have more than once felt the force of this. Is constitutional temperament the criterion of morality? . . . Prove to me satisfactorily that virtue exists not, that it is a fabric as baseless as a schoolboy's vision— then take life, I will no more with it. . . . Harriet will write to you tomorrow. May I require that, as one proof of self-conquest, you will throw the letter into the fire, suppressing all thoughts of *adoration*. . . . But the letter will arrive first; it will be pressed to the lips, folded to the heart, imagination will dwell upon the hand that wrote it; how easy the transition to the wildest reveries of ungratified desire! Oh how the sophistry of the passions has changed you! . . . Assert yourself, be what you were.'[2]

[1] Letters II and V of the series given from the manuscripts by Mr. Walter Sidney Scott in *Harriet and Mary*, 1944, pp. 15, 21.
[2] From the 'fragment of a novel in imitation of *The Sorrows of Werther*', which

The drama presently culminated. By 15 December Hogg had challenged him to a duel.

'I have answered his letter', writes Shelley, 'in which I have said that I shall not fight a duel with him, whatever he may say or do; that I have no right either to expose my own life or take his—in addition to the wish which I have on various motives to prolong my existence. Nor do I think that his life is a fair exchange for mine, since I have acted up to my principles, and he has denied his. . . . That if he would show me how I had wronged him, I would repair it to the uttermost mite, but I would not fight a duel.'

On the 26th he writes again:

'Since I have answered Hogg's letter, I have received another. Its strain is humble and compliant; he talks of his quick passions, his high sense of honour. I have not answered it, nor shall I. I leave him to his fate.'

## 4. AT KESWICK, NOVEMBER 1811–FEBRUARY 1812

All this while Shelley had been suffering acutely from his lean purse. After his father had persisted in refusing assistance towards the end of October, his only good hope was in the Duke of Norfolk, who had endeavoured to meet him in London in the last week of October with a view to some mediatory action. Accordingly on his arrival at Keswick he wrote to the Duke; who answered that he 'would be glad to interfere', but had no great hope of prospering, since Mr. Shelley, 'and not he alone', saw the late events otherwise than Mr. Shelley's son. On 23 November, after exchanging letters with Field Place, he invited Bysshe and Harriet with Miss Westbrook to visit him at Greystoke, where he entertained them from the 1st of December to the 8th or 9th. Bysshe found that he 'would be very well as a man' if he were not a Duke, and listened to his good advice. Indeed, it behoved him to listen, for he was on the verge of destitution, and had travelled to Greystoke with his last guinea. A small sum of money had come from John Westbrook, with an intimation that no more would follow, but it would only release him from a few incumbent debts, and enable him to incur a few others. On 13 December, then, he wrote to his father to beg

Hogg printed in his *Life*, and which, he says, Shelley had given him to read and he neglected to return. Instead of 'Harriet' he prints 'Charlotte'. The text as given above is almost faithful to the original reproduced in *Harriet and Mary*.

him to relent, while a letter of the Duke's on his behalf to the same address preceded his by one day's post. Bysshe protested that, though the Duke had prompted him to write, his sentiments were none the less genuine, 'for when convinced of my error no one is more ready to own that conviction than myself'. He recalled the promise that he should enjoy 'the completest free agency', when his allowance had been granted in the previous summer. On the strength of that promise he had married 'a lady of unimpeachable character', and if he had dissimulated in doing so, that had been 'required by the very nature of the action', and had been regretted. If his letters from Edinburgh had given offence, let it be remembered how he was left destitute in that distant city, and how naturally he had felt aggrieved. And now he sincerely entreated to be forgiven. On one point, however, he could retract nothing:

> 'I hope you will not consider what I am going to say an insulting want of respect or contempt, but I think it my duty to say that, however great advantages might result from such concessions, I can make no promise of concealing my opinions in political or religious matters—I should consider myself culpable to excite any expectation in your mind which I should be unable to fulfil. What I have said is actuated by the sincerest wish of being again upon those terms with you which existed some time since. . . . I have not employed meanness to concede what I consider it my duty to withhold. Such methods as these would be unworthy of us both.'

But Shelley had no prudence. On 16 December he wrote to his grandfather's huntsman, Allen Etheridge, enclosing a letter to sister Hellen, whose independent mind had commended her to his hopes, instead of Elizabeth. Allen, who took the letter to his master or to Timothy Shelley, was to hide it in the Summer House at Field Place, and send word to Hellen where to find it. Everyone near her, it ran, believed her brother to be wicked and loveless; but that was false; she need not hate him because all others did. Where she was, she must submit to those who would not let her freely walk abroad and read and think; but if she were with him she might 'run and skip, read, write, think just as she liked'. She could, however, even now write to him, keeping this act a secret, and placing the letter in the Summer House, whence he would obtain it, for 'I watch over you, though you do not think that I am near'. He longed to hear what books she read and above all what she *thought*, for thinking and trusting only to reason was the great thing. They would *tell* her it would be wrong to write to him; but how did she know it was? they could not tell her *why*. And he ended with renewed injunctions to be secret, unless she deemed that Mary, though not so 'firm and determined' as herself, might be taken into confidence, and induced to write as well.[1] This letter his father may have had before him, when on the 19th he replied curtly to his *eirenicon*. He rejoiced, he wrote, that the society of the Duke of Norfolk had wrought a change of heart, and Bysshe could now perceive how wrongly he had used his parents. As to the allowance, it had been granted on condition that he should study for some career, and that he had never done. Still: 'I hope and trust', continued the writer, 'that everything will in due time and with proper Probation be brought to an excellent work.' But the letter concluded in a way which, though Shelley answered it in grateful tones,[2] must have seemed likely to perpetuate the 'probation': 'I never can admit within my Family of the Principles that caus'd your expulsion from Oxford.' So the war was to go on, and Shelley resolved to wage it faithfully. About the middle of December he heard from the Pilfolds that his father and grandfather were concerned—as well they might be—for the family estate when it should fall in due time into his hands, for the entail terminated in his person; and that, while ready to starve him that he might not 'send forth his monstrous opinions', they were equally willing to pay him straightway a lordly income—£2,000 a year—if he would entail the property on his eldest son, or in default of issue on his brother.[3]

'Silly dotards', he writes, 'do they think I can be thus bribed and ground into an act of such contemptible injustice and inutility? . . . Dare one of them propose such a condition to my face—to the face of any virtuous man—and not sink into nothing at his disdain? That I should entail £120,000 of command over labour, of power to remit this, to employ it for beneficent purposes, to one whom I know not—who might, instead of being the benefactor of mankind, be its bane! . . . My indignant contempt has rendered my writing rather illegible.'[4]

---

[1] *Shelley in England*, pp. 369–71.
[2] 23 Dec.
[3] Mr. Ingpen has found no confirmation of this report in the Whitton papers.
[4] To Elizabeth Hitchener, 15 Dec.

But this spirit was not to be tried to the uttermost. Before 23 December John Westbrook had undertaken to pay Harriet a yearly income of £200, and at some date before 20 January Shelley hit by chance on an effective solution of his father's obstinacy—he asked for a loan of £100 from the Duke of Norfolk. It is more than likely that the Duke reported this petition to Field Place and that Timothy Shelley at once perceived that he must provide his son at least with bare necessities. By 26 January Bysshe was expecting £100 from Whitton, the arrears of the old allowance, which was now to be restored, in order, as his father told him, that 'he might not cheat strangers'. And with that arrangement, he entered on his independent life. Whatever conditions tacitly attached to the allowance as originally made, there were none now. The grant was now conceded simply that he might go his ways and let his father be rid of him, and whatever he should do or write, revocation was hardly to be feared. The world was all before him.

He had already purposed what he would do first with his freedom. Keswick was no abiding-place; he had not taken to its people, nor they to him. To some eyes Chestnut Cottage had become the nursery of two wedded children. 'The garden is not ours', said Harriet to one of the Southeys, 'but then, you know, the people let us run about in it.' To others the wild-looking youth was at least uncanny, his hydrogen fireworks on one dark night almost resulting in his summary ejection. His idea of the place was yet more unpleasantly tinged by the assault made upon him, on the evening of Sunday, 19 January, probably by some strolling ruffian, who felled and stunned him at the cottage door, but made off before proceeding to robbery when a neighbour came in sight. The factory system and its attendant evils were installed in the valley, and Keswick, full of the debauched servants of the rich, was 'more like a London suburb than a mountain village'. Shelley's mind was at this time full of his friend's treachery, and the power of evil, and therewithal of the social plagues, and adverted sensitively to such of their results as the many natural children thrown by poor women into the rivers and lakes. The thought of these things troubled him in his walks and usurped on the beauty of the scenes. Among the lakes and hills he must needs muse upon a time 'when this retirement of peace and mountain simplicity was the pandemonium of druidical imposture', or an imaginary time when a 'vast and licentious city' stood in the midst of it. 'These mountains', he writes to Miss Hitchener,

'are now capped with snow, the lake, as I see it hence, is glassy and calm. Snow-vapours, tinted by the loveliest colours of refraction, pass far below the summits of these giant rocks. The scene, even in a winter sunset, is inexpressibly lovely. The clouds assume shapes which seem peculiar to these regions. What will it be in summer? What when *you* are here? Oh, give me a little cottage in *that* scene. Let all live in peaceful little houses—let temples and palaces rot with their perishing masters! Be society civilised, be you with us, grant eternal life to all—and I will ask not the paradise of religionists!'

But out of this dejection came a great resolve. Close by, the fight for Irish freedom 'constituted a part of a great crisis in opinions'. Ireland had been among the subjects of his earliest verse,[1] and in the prevailing spirit of her people seemed to him 'the widest and fairest theatre for the operations of the determined friend of liberty'. By 7 January he had resolved to embark on the adventure straight away.

Another reason for leaving Keswick unregretfully was that he had failed to meet Wordsworth and Coleridge who were absent from the district. For compensation he came upon congenial spirits, greatly attracted by him, in the persons of William Calvert and his wife, of Greta Bank. William was a brother of Wordsworth's benefactor, Raisley Calvert, and himself a friend of the poet's, with whom he lived in the summer of 1793 in the Isle of Wight, and in the spring of the year following at the farmhouse of Windy Brow under Skiddaw, Dorothy Wordsworth and Raisley being one of the party.[2] He was equally intimate with Coleridge, and shared with him a lively interest in electricity and in chemistry. Dowden has plausibly conjectured[3] that he figures in the stanzas based on *The Castle of Indolence* as the second idler, the 'noticeable man with large gray eyes', with pale musing face and forehead 'profound, though not severe', who would entice the 'weary wight' with his 'rare inventions'

---

[1] *The Irishman's Song* in *Original Poetry by Victor and Cazire* is dated Oct. 1809, and sings of the dead patriots and their cry for vengeance.

[2] See Professor Ernest de Selincourt's *Dorothy Wordsworth*, pp. 50–4.

[3] *Life of Shelley*, i. 209, 210; where a full account is given of William Calvert.

and his microscope, and amuse him with his boyish games. With these tastes, and with his liberalism and his zeal for progress, he was the very man for the new-comer on Chestnut Hill, and they were often in company. At Christmastide the Calverts introduced their new-made friend to Southey. A month before Shelley would have run forward to this acquaintance like a thirsty man to the wells, but by what he had heard meanwhile as to the one-time poet of Joan of Arc his expectations had fallen, and the water, when he came to drink it, was brackish.

Southey was at this time thirty-seven years old, and lived at Greta Hall the life of the good man and 'the entire man of letters'. In the many-chambered house the wives and children of three families—Lovell's and Coleridge's and his own—subsisted partly or entirely by his incessant pen. Poems, biographies, histories, essays flowed from it, and the work was done with a devotion and a discipline creditable alike to the human body and the human will, and too much, ultimately, for both. Detractors then and since have put down his cheerful path-keeping, his laboriousness, his Toryism as similar marks of an unadventurous soul, and the Robert Southey who once, as *he* put it, 'believed in the persuadability of man and had the mania of man-mending' as a soul betrayed and lost. There had been a real change. Yet none of the Lake Poets gave up the hope of liberty as for ever, or abated his political solicitude, or his religious freedom. It is true, the memory of things done in France inspired them with fears now seen to be groundless. In 1812 Southey thought of the reform of Parliament as 'the shortest road to anarchy', and of any concessions to the Catholics as fraught with the overthrow of the Church establishment and incurable evils therewithal; and this although he was 'no High Church bigot' and on 'the mysterious parts' of the Articles preferred, not indeed to 'refuse belief', but to 'withhold it'. On the other hand, he had taken the social misery to his heart and the temper that had run in his youth to the heroical enterprise of 'pantisocracy' came out in his age in an impatient looking backward, eye to eye with William Cobbett, to the England of the Tudor times. 'If [in Tudor times] one class were treated in some respects as cattle, they were at least taken care of; they were trained, fed, sheltered, protected, and there was an eye upon them when they strayed. But how large a part of your population are like the dogs of Constantinople, unowned, living by chance, subsisting in filth, mischief, and wretchedness!'[1] And in irresponsible hours he was capable of flings that might well discover to a democrat the remains of grace. Every schoolboy knows how Wordsworth and he, in de Quincey's amazed hearing, concluded that 'no good could be hoped for until the royal family was expatriated', and Southey in extemporal verses entreated 'old George' to remove his sovereignty to 'the great Botanic Bay'.[2] Some of his sayings agreeably surprised Shelley in their earlier interviews. 'He is an advocate of liberty and equality. He looks forward to a state when all shall be perfected, and matter become subjected to the omnipotence of mind.' And then (though upon this point the confession is evidently overstated): 'He thinks that Jesus Christ stood precisely in the same relation to God as himself.' 'He says I ought not to call myself an atheist, since I believe the Universe is God', and 'agrees in my idea of Deity—the mass of infinite intelligence'. He is 'no believer in original sin', but in sin made by institutions. And yet—all was false and hollow: he wanted equality, 'but not in this age', and he was not a real Christian, but took the name. Nor was he at all a philosopher or reasoner. 'Southey says Expediency ought to be made the ground of politics, but not of morals. I urged that the most fatal error that ever happened in the world was the separation of political and ethical science. . . .' But 'he has a knack, when truth goes against him, of saying: "Oh, when you are as old as I am, you will think with me." ' Inevitably, after the earlier encounters they could go no farther with each other. The first impression on Shelley's mind of a man with 'all that characterises a poet', a 'great man' and an amiable, though weak in logic, soon changed to that of one of whom 'it rends my heart to think what he might have been'. One of Southey's least honourable magazine articles about the 'contemptible Burdettites' and 'the best monarch that ever adorned a throne' was read by the young republican, who 'could hardly contain himself', and on leaving Keswick passed by Greta Hall, 'without one sting'.

'Here', writes Southey,

'is a man who acts upon me as my own ghost would do. He is

[1] From *Colloquies on the Progress and Prospects of Society* (1829).
[2] *Reminiscences of the English Lake Poets*: 'Wordsworth and Southey'.

just what I was in 1794. At present he has got to the Pantheistic stage of philosophy, and in the course of a week I expect he will be a Berkeleyan, for I have put him upon a course of Berkeley. . . . I daresay it will not be very long before I shall succeed in convincing him that he may be a true philosopher, and do a great deal of good with £6,000 a year; the thought of which troubles him a great deal more at present than ever the want of sixpence (for I have known such a want) did me.'

But in a few words to Miss Hitchener, Shelley has given his answer, or the answer in his heart:

'Southey thinks that a revolution is *inevitable*: this is one of his reasons for supporting things as they are. But let us not belie our principles. They may feed and may riot and may sin to the last moment. The groans of the wretched may pass unheeded, till the latest moment of this infamous revelry,—till the storm bursts upon them and the oppressed take ruinous vengeance on the oppressors.'

### 5. WILLIAM GODWIN

For this disappointment, however, he could abundantly console himself with the news that William Godwin was still alive. Godwin, now at the age of fifty-six, was already, as Hazlitt has expressed it, in the calm enjoyment of his posthumous reputation. Time had been when half the world looked upon him as a public danger, and the other half as the liberator of mankind; but it had appeared that he was after all no cloud-compeller. And now, as Hazlitt wrote in 1820, and might have written in 1812, 'his person is not known, his opinions are not asked, no one thinks it worth his while even to traduce and vilify him, he is to all intents and purposes dead and buried. He knows this, and smiles in silent mockery of himself, reposing on the monument of his fame.'[1] Since his honourable share in the defence of Horne Tooke and Thelwall in 1794, he had taken no part in political activity, and his best in literature had been done in the seventeen-nineties—*Political Justice* in '93, *Caleb Williams* in the year following, *The Enquirer* in '97, *St. Leon* in '99. Personally also and morally, he had in a measure ceased from living. In his better days the tranquil audacity of his explorations into politics and morals was reflected in his life,

---

[1] *The Spirit of the Age.*

for he lived austerely and dangerously in that high service. It was not for nothing that he had been a Dissenter, a Minister's son, and himself a Minister; for he had not only the logic of the Calvinist, but the missionary zeal. Moreover, the few months of his connexion with Mary Wollstonecraft until her death in August 1797 acquainted him for once and once only with love and anguish, and humanized him, while it lasted. She called him, as she lay dying, the best and kindest of men, and he truly foreboded, after her death, that happiness would never revisit him. And in fact the calamity not only widowed him in spirit, but left him with a practical task that brought enslavement. For the sake of her two children—Fanny, her daughter by Gilbert Imlay, and the Mary of this history, after bearing whom she had died—he married again in 1801; but the woman whom he chose, the cantankerous Mrs. Clairmont, with two children by a former husband in her train, was particularly ill suited to the end he had in view. Poverty ensued; and in 1805 his managing wife launched him into the publishing business known eventually as 'M. J. Godwin & Co.', or as 'The Juvenile Library', with a shop and dwelling-house, after the spring of 1807, in Skinner Street, Holborn. Given better management, he might have done well with his books, with hands like Hazlitt's or Charles and Mary Lamb's to write them and his own strange sympathy with the young flowing into excellent tales and fables. But the enterprise, for the twenty years for which it lasted, was one chain of shifts and failures, and the philosopher soon began to flag wearily and to borrow and beg money in shabby ways. It would be untrue to say that his milder politics after 1793 were induced in him by the wish to improve his market. The amended views amounted indeed, as de Quincey has said, 'almost to a palinode'. In the second edition of *Political Justice* in 1796, and the third in 1798, and in certain unpublished notes of 1798 on the design of a book to be entitled *First Principles of Morals*,[1] he not only spoilt his original trenchancy with circumspection, but, by conceding, among other points, the natural inequality of men and 'the empire of feeling' in the lives of men,

---

[1] See the Introduction to the first edition of *Political Justice*, edited and abridged by Raymond A. Preston, in two volumes, New York, 1926; *The Life of William Godwin*, by Ford K. Brown, 1926, ch. xiii, pp. 135 ff., and de Quincey's Essay on Godwin, *Works* (ed. Masson), xi. 328.

gave away the hope of a swift and absolute redemption of all things by reason. In 1820 he wrote to one of his younger friends that 'the Whigs constituted the party to which a liberal-minded and enlightened man would adhere'. These changes had set in long before his grievous poverty, and were genuine afterthoughts. All the same, the spirit of subscription to the things that are succeeded to the earlier spirit. If he judged himself aright in his observations on his own character, timidity or diffidence was the root of all his faults. And that would lead straight on to what Charles Lamb has called his 'violent and Satanic pride'. His second wife began her courtship by calling to him from a window: 'Is it possible that I see before me the immortal Godwin?' Vanity made him touchy and resentful, formal and preceptorial, and convinced him that in return for his writings other men were bound in duty to supply his wants. Yet he still excelled as a confessor or a guide of young men and women, and would lavish on those who came to him his sagacity and his funds of knowledge. He was now to take in hand a neophyte than whom none could be more ardent, but rather to temper his zeal and to apprise him of wants and weaknesses that no other friend or monitor discerned more clearly; and much of Shelley's intellectual, and much more of his personal history begins on the day when these two were first in contact.

On 3 January 1812 Shelley introduced himself in a letter written in high excitement. He had hitherto enrolled the author of *Political Justice* in the list of the honourable dead; but had now heard that that dazzling luminary had not yet passed from the earth, and 'William Godwin was still planning the happiness of mankind'. One who, though still young, had suffered many things by reason of his ardent philanthropy entreated the friendship of a veteran in similar afflictions, and, failing an answer, would one day seek him out in London to represent himself as not unworthy of the boon. To this letter Godwin answered that it had told him too little of its writer; and Shelley on 10 January sent him a brief account of his career, his reading and his writing, the dayspring from *Political Justice*, and the embitterment at home. The reply was gracious. After a few grave words on the subject of filial duty, and a shrewd warning that 'being yet a scholar, he ought to have no intolerable itch to become a teacher', Godwin tendered his friendship as to a disciple gifted evidently with 'extraordinary powers', and the inheritor of a fortune who might become, if well advised, 'extremely useful to his species'. The disciple was overjoyed; he had taken the hand of one in whom still burned 'the unmoderated enthusiasm of humanity', in whom 'the age of the body had not induced the age of the soul'. On the 16th he wrote again. He pleaded not guilty towards his father: 'I have always been desirous of a reconciliation with him, but the price which he demands for it is a renunciation of my opinions.' He protested that he put his convictions forward in company or in print 'in order that, if they were erroneous, unforeseen elucidations might rectify them', and that he hoped 'in the course of our communication to acquire that sobriety of spirit which is the characteristic of true heroism'. 'I am not ignorant that vanity and folly delight in forwardness and assumption. But I think there is a line to be drawn between affectation of unpossessed talents and the deceit of self-distrust, by which much power has been lost to the world. . . . I will not again crudely obtrude the question of atheism upon the world. But might I not at the same time improve my own powers and diffuse true and virtuous principles?'

'I know not how to describe the pleasure which your last letter has given me; that William Godwin should have "a deep and earnest interest" in *my* welfare cannot but produce the most intoxicating sensations. . . . I am much deceived in myself if love and respect for the great and worthy form not a very considerable part of my feelings. . . . With what delight, what cheerfulness, what good will may it be conceived that I constitute myself the pupil of him under whose actual guidance my very thoughts have hitherto been arranged.'

## 6. LITERARY ENTERPRISES

And now his pen was once more active. On 11 December he writes to Miss Hitchener of the first idea, as we may suppose it, of what he was presently to achieve in *Queen Mab*—'a Poem to be a picture of the manners, simplicity and delights of a perfect state of society, tho' still earthly. . . . I only thought of it last night. . . . After I shall draw a picture of Heaven.' 'I think', he adds, in the same letter, 'I shall also make a selection of my younger poems for publication.' On 26 December: 'I do not proceed with my poem; the subject is not *now* to my mind'; but 'I am composing some essays which I design to publish in the summer';[1] while 'the minor Poems [which we may suppose to be a portion of the so-called Esdaile Manuscript] are to be sent to the Printers'.[2] On 2 January he speaks of the lost romance of *Hubert Cauvin*, a tale 'to exhibit the cause of the failure of the French Revolution and the state of morals and opinions in France during the latter years of its monarchy. . . . Some of the leading passions of the human mind will have a place in its fabric. . . . I design to exclude the sexual passion, and think the keenest satire on its intemperance will be complete silence on the subject. . . . I have already done about 200 pages of this work,[3] and about 150 of the essays.' On 20 January he is writing his *Address to the Irish People*, 'secretly intended, as a preliminary to other pamphlets, to shake Catholicism on its basis, and to induce Quakerish and Socinian principles of politics'. His enthusiasm touched his companions, and he was pleased with them; pleased with Harriet, and persuaded that Eliza herself was 'very amiable' and 'her opinions gradually rectifying'. And like the heroes of his poetry on their lofty missions he longed the more for that second self that should be, as he put it, 'the stronger shadow of that soul'—the divinity within him—'whose dictates I am accustomed to obey'.[4] His distress over the sad event at York drew closer the tie with Elizabeth Hitchener, and made some parts of his letters to her a kind of chrysalis of the *Epipsychidion*, save that they are tinged with a certain fear of the sexual property! 'How much worthier of a rational being

---

[1] These were doubtless the 'series of moral and metaphysical essays' which he was 'engaged in completing' in the summer of 1811 and had offered to Joseph Stockdale in his letter of 1 Aug. They are alluded to in subsequent correspondence under the alternative designations of 'moral and religious essays', or 'my metaphysics'. See *infra*, p. 144. It is likely they were used up, partly at any rate, in the Notes to *Queen Mab*.

[2] On the contents of the manuscript now in possession of the Esdaile family in Somerset, Shelley's descendants through his and Harriet's daughter Ianthe, see pp. 183–4. These 'minor poems', finished at Keswick, were put into the hands of R. & J. Stockdale, printers, of 62 Abbey Street, Dublin, on whose proceedings with them see *infra*, p. 144.

[3] On 7 Jan. he tells Miss Hitchener that he expects to conclude the novel within that month. He based the failure in France, as he states in the *Address to the Irish People* and the *Proposals for an Association*, on the fact that 'violence was employed', and that 'the doctrines of philanthropy and freedom were but shallowly understood'.

[4] To Elizabeth Hitchener, 23 Nov.

is friendship', he writes, 'whose sensibility is celestial and intellectual.'[1] It was in this January that he conceived the unhappy purpose of inducing her to share his home. If that were for the present impossible, could she not come with him to Ireland to move mountains?[2] 'You have said you are not handsome, but though the sleekness of your skin, the symmetry of your form might not attract the courtiers of Dublin Castle, yet that tongue of energy and that eye of fire would awe them into native insignificance.' His intention was now definite: it was to found an association of wise and good men to further both the immediate needs of Ireland and the ends of man's life in that and in every country. 'I, even I, weak, young, poor as I am, will attempt to organise them [sic], the society of peace and love.' In the summer, having carried out his purpose, he would live in North Wales, in 'some antique feudal castle whose mouldering turrets would be fit emblems of decaying inequality and oppression', and entertain the Godwins and their family, and Uncle and Aunt Pilfold and their children, and Miss Hitchener and Mrs. Adams, her aged friend, and children from her school. His friends were not pleased with the venture. Southey and Calvert wished he would not go; his uncle, and even Godwin wrote in some alarm; and there were tremors in his own heart. But, no! they would not assassinate, they would not imprison him; they dare not; what he should have in mind and what he should put in print being so peaceable. By the 29th he had received from Whitton his half-year's allowance of £100, and on 3 February the party of three sailed from Whitehaven, 'in enthusiastic anticipation'. 'I am Irish', writes Harriet, 'I have done with the English.' They had a distressful passage; for the ship, after being detained in the Isle of Man, was driven wide by a storm, so that they landed in the North, and not until the 12th of February arrived in Dublin.

[1] See especially the letters of 23 Nov. and 15 Dec.
[2] Letters of 2, 20, 29 Jan. and 3 Feb.

# VII

# IRELAND

## 1. THE SITUATION

GRATTAN, in one of his impassioned speeches on the enact-
ment of the Union, compared his country with the dead-
seeming Juliet:

> Thou art not conquered; beauty's ensign yet
> Is crimson in thy lips and in thy cheeks,
> And death's pale flag is not advanced there.

By 1812 she was astir, and girding herself for a new phase of
her warfare. The common people of the land were about to
rally at the call of a great leader of men, and, organized under
the Catholic priesthood, to throw into the conflict the blended
motives of Irish nationalism, religious, political, and agrarian.
The Union had been carried by chicane against the wishes of
most Irishmen. It left the Catholics as before with the electoral
vote but with no right to sit in Parliament or hold office under
the Crown. And the hierarchy and the main body of the
Catholic gentry were induced to tolerate it by the promises of
English politicians and because they reckoned that the worst
of their grievances would by that means be remedied and by
no other. They were bitterly disappointed, for Pitt's concilia-
tory intentions were baffled and shelved, and Fox died in 1806.
The Catholics soon apprehended that the Irish Parliament,
Protestant though it was, was more likely to do them right,
could it be restored, for had it not presented them with the
franchise of 1793? It was at this juncture, in 1807 and after,
that Daniel O'Connell came to the fore, being at that time in
his thirties, and the most brilliant of the junior members of the
Bar. By 1810 he was the strong man of the Catholic Committee,
and pressing upon it as much of his forward policy as he had then
conceived: the incessant petitioning of the House of Commons
for emancipation, the recruiting and organizing of the Catholic
endeavour throughout the country, and especially the rallying
of the whole of Ireland to demand repeal. Yet independence,
in the sense of the cutting of every tie with the British Crown
and Parliament, was never his aim. The last flicker of the spirit

of 1798 had been easily douted in the insurrection under Robert Emmet in 1803. Only a remnant of 'the United Irishmen' nursed in dispersion their bitter memories and their republican dreams.

Shelley had come on the morrow of a crisis. The Catholics had been challenging the power of the Government to hamper agitation. It would have greatly helped the agitators if they had had the legal right to assemble in Dublin conventions of Catholic delegates from the whole country. From this to a delegation from all creeds and classes to demand emancipation, or at any rate repeal, might be only a short road. One thing was in the way: in 1793 the Government had directed against the United Irishmen a Convention Act, which prohibited all committees or assemblies of a representative or delegate character that should purpose, 'under pretence of petitioning', to change the constitution in Church or State. The Act had been long unused, and in 1810 the Catholic leaders boldly disregarded it. O'Connell established local boards of managers throughout the country, to act in union with a General Committee, and a General Committee was elected of thirty-six delegates from the parishes of Dublin and ten from each county. But on the 12th of February 1811 Wellesley Pole, the Irish Secretary, issued a letter to sheriffs and magistrates, requiring them to arrest all persons implicated in the election. The committee was dissolved; but in an aggregate meeting of Catholics in Dublin on 9 July it was determined to appoint another by the same illegal method. In the teeth of a proclamation by the Lord Lieutenant reaffirming the law and the orders of the Secretary, and amid widespread enthusiasm, the election was held; on 19 October the new Committee met; the usual petition was drafted and approved; and the magistrates, appearing tardily on the scene, were informed that they had come too late. In November the Government prosecuted Dr. Sheridan, one of the members, in the Court of King's Bench, but, notwithstanding the conclusive charge of the Chief Justice, failed, amid intense excitement, to obtain a verdict. But a few days before Shelley's arrival another offender was prosecuted, pronounced guilty, and nominally fined. The agitators had nothing for it but to fall back on aggregate meetings.

In the Spring of 1812, then, Dublin was a Cave of Aeolus

with its pent-up winds. But it was not a throng of such patriots as Shelley was looking for. The Irish patriots of that era, excepting the like of Wolfe Tone, were bound to appear in his simple apprehension men of impure motive, stained with religious passion, or with economic prudence, or some other unworthiness. And the man whom he especially wished to meet and whose speeches he had read with admiration proved upon acquaintance to be 'not the choicest soul'. This was John Philpott Curran, the glory of the Irish Bar, the defender of Wolfe Tone and Napper Tandy. Within the lines of Grattan's policy he had fought against the Union with might and main; and when the Act was passed, and there was nothing for it in his own words but that 'Ireland, like a bastinadoed elephant, must kneel to receive its rider', the heart had gone out of him. Then in July 1803 the public troubles broke into his home. His youngest daughter, Sarah, had, without his cognizance, accepted as her lover the earliest of the heroes in Shelley's verse, Robert Emmet; and when his insurrection failed, the romantic youth had lingered too long in the neighbourhood of the Currans' house in the hope of a word with her, and so fallen into the hands of his enemies. The unhappy girl, whose correspondence with him was now discovered, quitted the country, and died in Italy of a broken heart, leaving to Tom Moore the inspiration of one of his best-remembered poems:

She is far from the land where her young lover sleeps.

In 1806 the Whigs appointed Curran to be Master of the Rolls, but the office neither pleased nor suited him, and the connivance with the alien domination tarnished his repute. His melancholy increased, and as a means against it he let himself go at a too convivial board in talk and jest. Shelley eagerly availed himself of an introduction from Godwin, and twice sadly dined with him. Of the Irish leaders he seems to have been in personal intercourse with only this one, and he never spoke with O'Connell, though they were once in the same room. As for the parties, he soon turned cold to the Whigs and the Catholic aristocracy. But, 'the remnant of United Irishmen', he writes, 'whose wrongs make them hate England, I have more hopes of'.

## 2. THE IRISH WRITINGS

In the course of his stay in Dublin he published two pamphlets under his own name, and printed, without issuing them, two anonymous broadsides. An *Address to the Irish People*, already written at Keswick, came from the press on 24 February; intended at first to appear on broadsheets, like the early writings of Tom Paine, and to be posted about the city, it now came out as a tract octavo of twenty-two pages of text in small print and on bad paper. This tract he intended at first 'to distribute throughout Ireland either personally or by means of booksellers'. It was a message to the common people in language which the author designed, but the reader will hardly perceive, to be 'adapted to the lowest comprehension'; whereas the second and somewhat smaller pamphlet, *Proposals for an Association*, delivered by the printer on 2 March, the same in shape as its predecessor and in type and paper even worse, was directed to the more intelligent in an authentic style. The full title was a large one: *Proposals for an Association of those Philanthropists, who, convinced of the inadequacy of the moral and political state of Ireland to produce benefits which are nevertheless attainable, are willing to unite to accomplish its regeneration.* It is evident from the *Proposals* that Shelley's thoughts, as he wrote, were less on the Irish question than on the 'Rights of Man'; and it was in continuance of his argument, therefore, that he threw into thirty-one short clauses the substance of his thinking on that subject and others, and had his axioms printed on a single leaf on some date before the 17th of March as a *Declaration of Rights*. Few, if any, copies of this document were circulated in Dublin, but the attempt to disseminate it at a later time and in another field were to bring its author into personal hazard. Finally, he had printed, but then kept to himself the feeble poem, written in England,[1] under the title of *The Devil's Walk*, and modelled evidently on one a little better and a great deal better known from the conjoined pens of Coleridge and Southey.

Repetitious, badly arranged, with some fustian in places, the Irish writings have also the limpidity and onflow of Shelley's style and a high-mindedness not without charm. But they are the work of one ignorant of the situation. The *Address* especially

---

[1] He had sent it to Miss Hitchener on 20 Jan.

is behind the times or wide of them altogether, and Grattan might have perceived in it an excessive edition of his lost hopes. It recognized indeed the wisdom of what many of the Catholic leaders were now saying—that the first necessity was not Emancipation but the Repeal of the Union, and that between Protestant and Catholic in Ireland there was a compulsive bond not only of a common home, but of the same needs and sufferings. A common front in all Ireland to restore the Irish Parliament and liberate the Catholics thereby and thereafter—that formula will cover equally Shelley's argument and O'Connell's aims. But Shelley writes as if Ireland were still governed by the critical and tolerant humour of the eighteenth century and not once more by the passions of the seventeenth; as if North and South were not embroiled; and as if the English supremacy were to be disposed of by reasoning. Forget—nay, you have forgotten—your religious feud, he tells them, unite, have faith in the principle of liberty, think it out, preach it, argue it with your enemies, and truth, with no pressure but its own, will carry the day. Emancipation is good; Repeal is better; and both are assured to you by the march of Mind. O'Connell could have told him that it was a far cry to the abeyance of the feud and that justice must be wrung from England not by truth but by fear. The two communions were exhorted to forget their discreditable past and admonished that any religion or none is 'good if it makes men good', and that many a rascal goes regularly to Mass and many a good man never at all. With these challenging declarations he threw in a good deal more from the school of the Revolution on the freedom of assembly and the freedom of the press, governments and wars, poverty and crime, not without a sprinkling of loftier and severer precept. Liberty dwells with self-control, and the Irish will only have it if they think more and drink less. 'Husband your time, that you may do to yourselves and others the most real good. . . . Conversation and reading . . . will contribute, so far as lies in your individual power, to that great reform which will be perfect and finished the moment everyone is virtuous and wise.'

The second pamphlet starts by arguing that only a league of philanthropists in continual discussion can keep up the public spirit now burning in Ireland and lead the nation into the peaceable and only wise method of accomplishing its will. It should be an Association of men such as were the salt of the revolution in France, acting openly in the light of day, one which even the bishops, could they 'reassume the dignity of man', would be glad to join, and for which the aristocracy no longer carried the brains. It should be the forerunner of others like it in the sister island. It should purpose to 'examine all projects of reform and forward them if approved'. There would certainly be danger in the enterprise, if that were anything to a good man, for Government, which permits the priest to frighten the dying cottager with Hell-fire, abhors inquiry into the principles on which itself rests. It would be said that the aim was to violate the Constitution; that man is incorrigible; that we must take warning from the Revolution in France; that if the poor do well, they will overstock the earth and starve. But these arguments could not stand against reason, and if the enemy used violence, he would spoil his cause. The Revolution had failed in France because the long-enslaved people could not rise to it. And Malthus had discovered no law to perpetuate vice and misery. Shall we delay to do good for fear of the remote consequences of our beneficence?

The thirty-one numbered clauses of his *Declaration of Rights* put forward the premisses of his policy. It has been thought[1] that he had in mind the declaration moved by Lafayette in the French Assembly in August 1789 and the similar manifesto moved by Robespierre in April 1793. Certainly he had the first of these decrees before him, for it is quoted textually and entirely in the book which lay at the back of his thinking, as well in the pamphlets as in the broadside—*The Rights of Man*. It was in these days at Dublin that he induced Eliza Westbrook to prepare for publication an anthology of the 'useful passages' in Paine, and he frequently echoes him, besides expressly acknowledging his authority.[2] Not that *The Rights of Man* had anything new to teach him or carried his entire assent, or gave

---

[1] W. M. Rossetti in *The Fortnightly Review* for Jan. 1871, 'Shelley in 1812–13'.

[2] Here are some of the slighter echoes: Shelley quotes in the *Address* the words of Lafayette, 'for a nation to be free it is sufficient that she wills it', quoted in *The Rights of Man*; and Paine's own words that 'a religion is good if it makes men good'; and he repeats Paine on Britain 'having no Constitution', and on the false mystery of the State, and on a State religion telling the Almighty how to use His grace. His admiration of Paine was an enduring one: 'that great and good man', as he calls him in 1819 (Letter to Leigh Hunt, 3 Nov.).

him all that he delivered in the tracts. Some of their propositions are distinctly Godwinian: 'Man has no right to kill
his brother. It is no excuse that he does so in uniform: he only
adds the infamy of servitude to the crime of murder.' Or again:
'The rights of man are liberty and an equal participation in
the commonage of Nature.' And since 1791 many hopes of the
Revolution had failed. Paine had then expected that the
United States would presently league with France and Britain
to emancipate the European peoples. Shelley in 1812 has no
such hopes of public action, but sadly confesses that liberty waits,
and may long wait for the self-schooling of the individual. Nor
could he rely, like the doughty man of 'common sense', on
swift and total methods within the State, but commends the
British Constitution for its gradual progression. And yet the
dipping into Paine's mind in these Dublin days refreshed him.
*The Rights of Man* lays down, and Shelley after it, the revolutionary fundamentals: that government acts as a delegate from
the people individually; that it is a necessary evil; that it has
no right against the liberty of conscience and speech and the
primal equality of each and all. Paine grafted these convictions
on a burning sense of the contrast of Europe and America and
on a passionate certainty that man, if he wills it, is straightway
free, and his day even now at hand. And the author of the Irish
tracts, albeit with a chastened expectancy, thought 'every hour'
on the same 'lofty destination' and on the coming day.

### 3. IN DUBLIN: 12 FEBRUARY–4 APRIL 1812

The Crusaders took lodgings in the house of a Mr. Dunn,
woollen draper, 7 Lower Sackville Street, whence they moved
on or before 10 March to a jeweller's premises at 17 Grafton
Street. They spent a few days quietly, while Shelley wrote his
*Address*. When the pamphlets arrived from the printer on 24
February, one Daniel Healey (or Hill) was engaged to sell or
give away copies, and Shelley either dispensed them in the
street, or threw them to passers-by from his window, or dropped
a copy from his balcony 'when he saw a man who looked likely'.
'For myself,' writes Harriet, 'I am ready to die of laughter and
Percy looks so grave. Yesterday he put one into a woman's
hood of a cloak—she knew nothing of it, and we passed her.
I could hardly get on, my muscles were so irritated.' Copies

were sent to discourage custom at sixty public houses; notable persons received them by the post. Of the fifteen hundred copies four hundred were distributed in three days and nearly all in three weeks. The *Proposals*, issued on 2 March, were distributed, it is to be supposed, by the same means, but not so rapidly or numerously.

'Everything proceeds well', wrote Shelley on 27 February; 'my little pamphlets have excited a sensation of wonder'. He would enlarge his operations by 'proselytising the young men of Dublin College', or those of them not entirely dissipated, and by strengthening his tracts with a 'selection of the moral sayings of Jesus Christ'.[1] On the following day, 28 February, he attended and harangued a great gathering of Catholics in the historic Theatre in Fishamble Street, the Earl of Fingal presiding, O'Connell in the list of speakers, and the house crowded with the Catholic *élite*, men and women. The business was to affirm over again the claims to Emancipation and to Repeal and to send a petition in that sense to the Prince Regent. After a speech by O'Connell and several resolutions, the motion to address the Prince was moved and seconded, and to this proposal Shelley spoke for more than an hour. He gave his audience the substance of the *Address*. He spoke, it appears, at first with some diffidence, and then fluently; for one auditor has described his utterance as 'cold and precise', and another as 'rant'.[2] The audience at some of his sentiments as to religion gave him a hiss, but received him on the whole 'with great kindness';[3] and when he declared that as an Englishman he would blush for England's crimes, 'did he not know that arbitrary power never fails to corrupt the heart of man', there was 'loud applause for some minutes'. On the next day he figured in the Dublin newspapers and on Saturday, 7 March,

---

[1] Alluded to, presumably, as 'biblical extracts' in the undated letter to T. Hookham (Julian edition, No. cciv), supposedly 17 Dec. 1812, and in the letter to the same correspondent of the following 2 Jan., when he asks that they shall be sent to the press; the impression to be of 250 copies which might serve for 'small Christmas or Easter offerings'.

[2] See MacCarthy on the proceedings in the Theatre, and the allusions to Shelley in the press.

[3] *The Freeman's Journal*, 29 Feb. Lady Shelley, in *Shelley Memorials*, p. 27, says he was 'interrupted with savage yells', threatened with violence, and advised by the police to quit the country; which, like other statements, speaks little for the accuracy of that book.

*The Dublin Journal* presented a letter from one of his hearers on 'the disgusting harangue of a stripling', a renegade who even at the generous time of life had abjured his own country. On the same day *The Weekly Messenger* gave an account of him and a long extract from the *Proposals*: the heir to one of the richest fortunes in England, says the account, this young man had devoted himself to 'the propagation of those divine and Christian feelings which purify the heart of man', with a 'peculiar fascination' in recommending them; intrepid in affirmation and in rebuke, charitable, rational, a peace-maker between religions and a withstander of tyrants; not, as some thought him, a dreamer, but a real friend to Ireland. Finally the writer mentioned what he had learnt 'upon *undoubted* authority', that 'a very beautiful poem' of Shelley's had been written for the benefit of the imprisoned patriot Finnerty, and brought in nearly £100.[1] Shelley was not above vanity; he sent a copy of this article to Godwin, and two to Miss Hitchener, begging her to get it inserted in the Sussex newspapers,[2] to prepare the county for an evangelical invasion. On the top of these encouragements came news early in March that set him writing verses[3]—of a liberal revolution in Mexico, and the prospect of a speedy end to the Spanish domination across the seas.

The confidence was soon dashed. The enterprise in Dublin ended in a swift collapse. It collapsed in perplexity and despondency not ten days after the laudation in *The Weekly Messenger*. On 10 March he wrote to Miss Hitchener that the Association 'proceeds slowly and I fear will not be established'; 'I am sick of this city', he adds, 'and long to be with you and peace'. On the 18th Harriet writes to her that 'all hope of an Association is now given up'. After loitering over a fortnight more in the city, he left it on 4 April, sooner by nearly a month than he had at first intended.[4] He had been disappointed in the first place by

[1] See p. 53.

[2] A short reference to the *Address* appeared in a Lewes newspaper for 1 June 1812, and apparently Shelley's doings in Dublin were reported by the same journal in an earlier issue (*Shelley in England*, p. 383).

[3] The poem in the Esdaile MS. entitled *To the Republicans of North America*, dated 1812, must be correctly renamed by Rossetti *The Mexican Revolution*. Shelley evidently supposed that Cotopaxi is in Mexico.

[4] To Elizabeth Hitchener, 27 Feb.: 'We shall leave this place at the end of April.' That he left on 4 Apr. appears from Harriet's letter to Catherine Nugent on 16 Apr.

the many persons who, after his speech at the great Meeting, sought him in his lodgings. Two of them indeed made some mark in his esteem. Catherine Nugent, a furrier's assistant, a little, cordial, vivacious woman, who in '98 had visited the captives in the prisons, and, descending into middle age, looked on Ireland as 'her only love', called frequently and stayed long, whether to 'sit and talk with Percy on virtue', or to pass the time with Harriet, which she would seem to have preferred. A more engaging visitor, for Shelley at least, was the enthusiastic John Lawless, 'Honest Jack', as he was popularly known, at this time in his fortieth year, who having been disqualified for the Bar on account of his intimacy with United Irishmen, divided his life between business in a brewery, the conduct of newspapers and magazines, and a strenuous share in the Catholic agitation. At this particular time he had literary projects in hand in which Shelley and his money might be of use to him. The panegyric in *The Weekly Messenger* was probably of his writing. On 14 March Shelley tells Miss Hitchener that he will 'soon have command of a newspaper with Mr. Lawless', and a week later writes to T. C. Medwin that he is 'engaged with a literary friend in the publication of a voluminous History of Ireland . . . for the completion of which I wish to raise £250 . . . the work will produce great profits'. It would appear that he did receive some money from Medwin, and passed it on to Lawless,[1] and, after abandoning his mission and preparing to leave the city on or before the 18th, was arrested for a while by these literary prospects, fortunately unpursued.

But the Dubliners in general would not do. They were tied, almost all of them, in religion to mere faith, in politics to expediency. They 'hated' their well-wisher as a sceptic, and slighted him as a youth, whom his servant had given out to be fifteen years of age, and the leaders ignored his presence and even his letters. Nor were his callers alone or chiefly disheartening. The Irish experience was poignant and perplexing; it discovered the world about him in dreadful novelty; it blew cold on his assumptions and laid his indecisions bare. He had forgotten what was said in *Political Justice* about Associations,

---

[1] As the sequel will show, Shelley occasionally made drafts of money on Lawless. At least one of these was unhonoured and he considered Lawless to have acted dishonestly to him in some way or other.

and the wise who are fit for them and the vulgar who are not;[1] and had written as if the crowd also might study the laws of society in clubs and circles, and advance themselves *pari passu* in self-enlightenment and self-control. These hopes were rudely shaken by the spectacle of a state of things which, says Shelley, 'might excite impatience in a cooler temperament than mine'. The *Address*, he writes, 'was principally designed to operate on the Irish *mob*. Can they be in a worse state than at present? Intemperance and hard labour have reduced them to machines. The oyster that is washed and driven at the mercy of the tides appears to me an animal of almost equal elevation. . . . I had no idea of the depth of human misery until now . . . in their narrow streets thousands seem huddled together—one mass of animated filth.' 'It is indescribably painful to contemplate beings capable of soaring to the heights of science with Newton and Locke, without attempting to awaken them from a state of lethargy so opposite.' The law was cruel to these outcasts. Shelley found 'a poor boy and his mother' in some noisome den and 'rescued them'; but the boy whom he intended teaching to read, was 'snatched to a magistrate of Hell' on what seemed to his rescuer a trumpery charge, and impressed into the Army; 'I am resolved to prosecute this business to the very jaws of Government.' 'A widow-woman with three infants was taken up by constables. I remonstrated, I pleaded. I was everything that my powers could make me. . . . The constable relented; and when I asked him if he had a heart, he said—To be sure he had as well as another man, but that he was called out to business of this nature twenty times in a night. The woman's crime was stealing a penny loaf. She is, however, drunken, and nothing that I or anyone can do can save her from ultimate ruin and starvation.' Yet these very wretches would gape in loutish admiration at the equipages rolling to some grand function at the Viceroy's Lodge. 'I shudder to think that for the very roof that covers me, for the bed whereon I lie I am indebted to the selfishness of man.' But the remedy, he fears, is in the far future: 'I shall address myself no more to the illiterate. I will look to events in which it will be impossible

---

[1] Book IV, chapter ii, section 3: 'Of Political Associations' (ed. 1793). There are, of course, many passages on the harm done by forcing the pace of reformation: e.g., especially, VI. i.

that I can share, and make myself the cause of an effect which will take place ages after I have mouldered in the dust.'

He discovered, moreover, not only that his hopes might waver, but that his principles were dubious. Throughout the Irish enterprise he corresponded with Godwin, and his candid monitor discoursed to him as Burke himself might have done. 'So far as I can yet penetrate into your character, I conceive it to exhibit an extraordinary assemblage of lovely qualities, not without considerable defects. The defects do, and always have arisen chiefly from this source, that you are still very young, and that in certain essential respects you do not sufficiently perceive that you are so.' Else why did he hasten into print, and in the guise of a teacher dispense his ignorance? Because, Shelley answered in effect, I advance and clear my thought by writing, and because my health is poor, and the time before me may be short. But, came the rejoinder, why perform these exercises in public, and why not remember that a young man's health changes, and usually for the better? 'One principle that I find is wanting in you, and in all our too fervent and impetuous reformers, is the thought that almost every institution and form of society is good in its place and in the period of time to which it belongs. How many beautiful and admirable effects grew out of Popery and the monastic institutions, . . . in the period when they were all in their genuine health and vigour. . . . What excellent effects do we reap, even at this day, from the feudal system and from chivalry.' In particular, the Association was dangerous. Association was at that time a pungent word: it reeked of the Jacobin Club, and the principle it stood for had been violently put down when in the year 1800 the Corresponding Societies were declared illegal. What was more, associations had been all but prohibited in *Political Justice*, and the neophyte was contending with the pontiff. What, he asked, had Godwin's book effected? Was man's estate any better in 1812 than in 1793? Was it tolerable, in face of the misery in Dublin, to sit and speculate till the light should lighten every mind, including those no better than oysters? Was he not right in his *Proposals* to aim at a union not for thinking only, but for acting, and acting peaceably? No, Godwin replied, Associations could not lead to liberty, vitiated as they were by incendiary passion. That way lay bloodshed, in Ireland especially; nor was

Shelley less unwise in extreme discouragement than in heedless hope:

'The seed is sown and the soil for a long time seems ungrateful.' But 'the happiest operations are going on quietly and unobserved', and the consummation is often sudden and joyful. 'You find little difference between the men of these islands and of Europe now and twenty years ago. If you looked more keenly into these things, you would perceive that the alteration in Europe in the last twenty years has been immense, however inapparent. "In the hour that ye think not the Son of Man cometh." '

Shelley wavered, retracted his Association, and received a blessing in terms that might have alarmed him, had he known his man: 'Now I can look on you not as a meteor, ephemeral, but as a lasting friend, who, in the course of nature, may contribute to the comforts of my closing days.' But, as Godwin perceived, he was 'only half converted'. He suspected that in this question neither he nor his philosopher had gone home, and still doubted whether in political action we must think unanimously before we move, and the man of Reason were not waiting for a miracle after all.

Without his knowing it, the eyes of Government had been upon him.[1] On 18 March he stowed the remaining copies of his two pamphlets, the copies of the *Declaration of Rights* and the broadsheet of the verses on the Devil, with a letter from Harriet to 'Portia' (as the Shelleys called their friend) in a large deal box, and dispatched it by the Holyhead Packet to 'Miss Hitchener at Hurstpierpoint'. But he paid for the carriage as far only as Holyhead, and expected that the box would be forwarded from there to the consignee, and the extra charges paid upon delivery. This was not done, however. For some days the luggage lay at Holyhead with no one to answer for it, till the Surveyor of Customs, Pierce Thomas by name, searched it for excisable articles, and discovered the letter and the printed documents. He reported his discovery to Mr. William D. Fellowes, an official of the Post Office, who thereupon forwarded to Francis Freeling, Secretary to the Post Office, a copy of the *Proposals* and one of the *Declaration of Rights*, and cited the letter where it speaks of the *Declaration* as 'inflammatory matter' which should be 'dispersed' in Sussex, and posted up

---

[1] See MacCarthy's *Early Life*, pp. 308–22, where the documents are cited fully.

on farm buildings. Freeling forwarded Fellowes's letter with the documents to the Earl of Chichester, one of the two Postmasters-General, and Chichester answered him from Stanmer Park in Sussex on 5 April that he had made inquiries; that Shelley, son of the member for the Rape of Bramber, was 'by all accounts a most extraordinary man', who had 'married a servant or some person of very low birth', and that Miss Hitchener was school-mistress at Hurst, and daughter of a publican and former smuggler in the neighbourhood. She was 'well spoken of', but he would have her watched for any connexion she might have with Shelley. Meanwhile, on 30 March, Thomas the Excise-man had sent to Richard Ryder, Secretary of State, copies of one of the pamphlets and the *Declaration*, with a transcript of Harriet's letter. The box, he said, remained in his custody; should he send it to London and withhold it from the addressee? Ryder sent Thomas's letter, with the transcript of Harriet's, and presumably the pamphlet, to the Secretary's office in Dublin, and on 8 April, by which date Shelley had left Ireland, the Secretary returned them to London in an envelope inscribed simply 'with his compliments'. There the matter ended for the while, but not for ever. The box and its contents were evidently forwarded at last to 'Portia', who must have brought them with her when she joined the Shelleys at Lynmouth in August of the same year; and there the unlucky consignment was to set on foot a much more serious trouble.

# VIII

## FROM PILLAR TO POST

### 1. NANTGWILLT: 14 APRIL–25 JUNE 1812

LEAVING Dublin on 4 April 1812, the Shelleys and Eliza Westbrook, with Daniel Healey, arrived at Holyhead after a voyage of thirty-six hours against the wind, and were landed in pouring rain and pitch darkness on a rocky beach at 2 in the morning, to clamber a mile and a half to the inn by the light of the sailors' lanterns.[1] Wales had been long marked down for the next philanthropic exploit, the next area of the Association, from which it should extend to England and 'quietly revolutionize the country'; and Merionethshire, whose magnificent scenery Godwin had depicted in his tale of *Fleetwood*, was the county of their choice. And their hearts were still set upon that countryside, though now the Association was not to be. But from the 7th to the 14th of April they had to traverse a half or more of the Principality in search of a tenantable house. One incident of the quest was a thirty hours' passage in an open boat from Barmouth to Aberystwith; and the fatigue of these seven days of wandering threw Harriet into a serious illness. A house, of which the larger part could be taken over as furnished lodgings, was eventually discovered six miles from Rhayader and within two of Cwm Elan, the summer residence of the Groves, where Shelley had spent the rememberable days preceding his marriage. It was called Nantgwillt, or 'Wild Brook', and stood in a narrow valley down which the Clearwen ran to meet the Elan, 'a spot of singular beauty', says Peacock who subsequently explored it. The occupier, who was also the owner, a retired sea captain of the name of Hooper, had been declared a bankrupt, and wanted to lease his house and farm and sell his stock and furniture. It was a roomy dwelling, with 130 acres of arable

---

[1] Medwin (*Life*, revised, p. 115) has a wild story which probably travesties what he had heard of the outward journey in February. 'His departure from Ireland was occasioned, as he told me, by a hint from the police, and he in haste took refuge in the Isle of Man—that extra-judicial place. . . .' On leaving Douglas in 'the month of November' for some port in Wales, he 'embarked in a small trading vessel which had only three hands on board'. There was a dreadful gale, and 'the skipper attributed to Shelley's exertions so much [of] the safety of the vessel that he refused on landing to accept his fare'.

land and 70 of woodland or hillside belonging to it, the whole
available at £98 a year, which it might be hoped that the farm-
ing of the land would more than pay, or subletting reduce by
perhaps four-fifths.  On 14 April the three travellers and their
Irish servant moved in; and on the 24th Shelley wrote asking
his father to lend or stand surety for £500, that he might make
the purchases, take up the lease and become a farmer, and so
qualify himself in a 'quiet and gentlemanly' manner to be the
heir to a great estate.  On the day following he desired the
elder Medwin to assist him for the same purpose to the amount
of £600 or £700.  But in each case the petition was declined;
and on or before 6 June, Nantgwillt had to be vacated.

Shelley took to that farm-house with all his heart and continued long afterwards to covet it.  'Our dear Nantgwillt', as
he and Harriet called it in retrospect, with the 'mountains and
rocks forming a barrier round the quiet valley, which the tumult
of the world may never overleap', and 'the guileless habits of
the Welsh'.  The house would accommodate the 'amiable
beings' whom he wished to have about him, and make 'an
asylum for distressed virtue'; the largest room should be
furnished as a library, and be used 'for the benefit of the
human race'.  An outdoor being, a lover of running waters, he
could wander in the glens, and use the streams, as he had done
in the previous year, to sail his toy boat, running along the bank
with a pole in his hand to push it clear of rocks and shallows.
The memory of the mental desolation with which in the previous summer the scenes before him had seemed to be in league
touched him to a lively fondness for Harriet, ill and tired, as
for a time she was, in his strenuous service.  It was now that
in *The Retrospect* and now or a little later in a poem of many
lines addressed to her[1] that he gave thanks for the 'warm,
tranquil, spirit-healing' love between them, reconciling passion
and virtue, impervious to the cold touch of Custom or Time.
Relieved of the coil in Ireland, he had time to attend to himself
and to resolve upon weeding his nature of what he regarded
as its worst faults—its impatience and bitterness and propensity to despair, its deficiency in 'mild and equal benevolence'.[2]
Since reading *Political Justice* his thoughts had been 'painful,

[1] *To Harriet*: 'It is not blasphemy to hope that Heaven', dated 1812.
[2] To Godwin, 3 June and 11 June 1812.

anxious, and vivid, more inclined to action and less to theory';
now, over the *Système de la Nature*, he felt that if his opposition
to Christianity was becoming less of a 'fever', it was more
determined, more of 'a perfect and full conviction'.

Two things derogated from this promise of tranquillity. One,
the eternal want of pence. The Irish expedition and the printing of the tracts and the legal business over Nantgwillt had been
dear, and he had reckoned in vain to publish the 'minor poems'
that he had in hand at Keswick and the 'Moral and Metaphysical Essays', written in the previous summer, at prices that
would reimburse him, and spoil the rich for the advantage of
the poor. There was also the romance of *Hubert Cauvin*, which
he had expected to finish before the move to Ireland and
intended to print cheaply. But of these projects the story was
lost or discarded so that not a shred in print or manuscript
survives, and the Essays and the collection of poems were left
behind with the Dublin printers, R. and J. Stockdale, who,
after printing a part of one or both of these works and asking
in vain to be so far paid, refused eventually either to return the
manuscripts or to complete the business in hand. Early in
June Shelley was wondering when the book of his poems would
come; and later in the month was for sending his man Healey
over to Dublin to learn directly how the matter stood. When
later he moved to Lynmouth the news came that the Stockdales
were impounding his documents and until late in the autumn
he agitated to retrieve them. Would Lawless go and get them?
Or Catherine Nugent? 'I am afraid', writes Harriet to her
friend Catherine, 'you will be obliged to do a little manoevre . . .
you can say you wish to look at them [the "poems and other
pieces"] and then you may be able to steal them away; . . . I
leave it all to you, knowing you will do your best.'[1] Whether the
ransom was paid or not, the Stockdales released what they had
in pawn in December 1812, and what the nature of these
writings was and what became of them are matters for a later
page. At Nantgwillt, therefore, nothing came of these literary
designs in aid of a lean purse.

But a greater trouble was the absence of Elizabeth Hitchener
and the 'high mental yearning' for her that he had poured out
in the many letters from Dublin continually reporting how he

[1] Harriet Shelley to Catherine Nugent from London, 1812, no precise date.

fared and what was in his mind. She had declined to act immediately on the proposal made in January that she should resign her school and for the rest of her life become his pensioner and an inmate of his home. She could not join him in Ireland, but would visit him in the summer in Wales, and reserve her decision on his plan for her. He now insisted on it. And in all the letters about it, from Ireland or from Wales, the *falsetto*, audible from the beginning of their correspondence, persists. They harp on her genius. Were they together, she would organize his schemes of action or devise her own, and would share with him not only the inexpressible joy of communion, but the joy of awakening a noble nation from its lethargy of bondage. 'O thou ocean, whose multitudinous billows ever lash Erin's green isle . . . roll on, and on every wave shall die one of those moments that part my friend and me': some of the mouthing that begins with these words he afterwards versified for *Queen Mab*. In truth he had to mouth that he might deceive himself. He was trying to run two loves at once, no mind in the one and no body in the other, and to fend from his consciousness the inference that if both were wanted neither would suffice. As to his wedded wife, in *The Retrospect* and the lines *To Harriet* he could put by and put out the sense that he needed much more than her lulling affection. And in the letters to the other he could quench in tall language what he inwardly knew—that she carried no femininity for him. And now nothing could dissuade him from this foolish experiment. On Harriet's part there was no demur; sucked in, as it were, by the wind of his will, she entreated her 'dear sister' to come and be one of them and form and mend her mind. 'Portia' herself, however, was disposed for some time to look before she leaped, until remonstrances that were almost reproaches bore her scruples down. Between souls like theirs what was money but a slave, or obligation but a fancy? But could he not himself reside at Hurst, and spare her the uprooting? That was countered by the charm of Nantgwillt; there at the end of June he should expect her, and her father with her, who could amuse his declining years by running the farm. But again, she would be looked on as his mistress; already Hurstpierpoint had heard of the plan and all the neighbourhood were condemning it, even Captain Pilfold and, with especial acrimony, Mrs. Pilfold.

Finally, her father had forbidden it outright and the worry had made her ill. Shelley was flamingly angry: he twice wrote to Mr. Hitchener in conscious rectitude and severe rebuke; he sent his uncle a letter that 'would make his soul start back to see it'; and he envisaged his aunt as 'prepared to hold out the right hand in affection and with the left tear your heart-strings'. By the beginning of June 'Portia' had determined to brave the storm and become an 'eternal inmate' of Nantgwillt. 'One fortnight more', he writes on the 2nd of that month, 'and we meet. . . . I have much to talk to you of, Innate Passions, God, Christianity, etc. . . . I think I can prove to you that our God is the same.' But before the 11th she had hoisted signals of distress: if she were to get free he must come and fetch her; and a week later he and Harriet resolved to do so, albeit on a failing purse. 'It is playing a momentous game. It demands coolness and resolution. Calm yourself, collect yourself, my dearest friend. How little ought your mighty soul to be shaken by the whisper of a worldling!' But presently she recovered heart; no derring-do was necessary; and in a letter to Godwin from Lynmouth, dated 5 July, Shelley told him that she was soon to pass through London and asked him to see her. At last his 'star of peace', as he had called her, beckoned from ahead.

After leaving Nantgwillt the wanderers were invited by the Groves to Cwm Elan, where they waited over a fortnight for quarter-day and a new supply of money. By this time his several vexations had affected Shelley's health, and in hope of mending it he applied for passports to Italy. Meanwhile, until the passports should come, he would move to the sea-side, and preferably to Ilfracombe; and when—or if—they came, he found himself, we may suppose, too poor to use them. Towards the end of June he and his party left Cwm Elan; looked in at Chepstow, where Godwin had recommended a cottage; found the cottage 'half built and by no means large enough'; set forward for Ilfracombe; were arrested on the way by the charm of Lynmouth, and made there their journey's end.

## 2. *A Letter to Lord Ellenborough*

By this time Shelley was composing, in a tract some twenty pages long, an argument for the liberty of the press which is clearly more ardent, though not less unorderly writing than the

Dublin publications. It was occasioned by the trial of the book-seller Eaton, on the 6th of March 1812, before Lord Chief Justice Ellenborough for blasphemous libel, consisting in the publication of the third part of Paine's *Age of Reason*. After the hearing the defendant was committed to Newgate, and on the 15th of May brought up for judgement, when the Court con-demned him to be imprisoned for eighteen months and to stand once in the pillory for two hours. This was one case beside four others of legal persecution on religious or political grounds: Peter Finnerty in 1810 and John and Leigh Hunt in 1813 imprisoned for seditious libel, William Hone indicted on the same accusation, but acquitted by the jury in 1817, and Richard Carlile, severely sentenced in 1819 for this same 'blasphemy' of publishing works by Paine, all of them moving Shelley to ardent indignation and the active assistance of the victims.

Daniel Isaac Eaton kept his shop, which he called 'The Ratiocinatory, or Magazine for Truth and Good Sense', in Ave Maria Lane, and disseminated free opinions on religion and government, not only as a publisher, but as a writer or translator also. He had been in trouble by his propaganda six times already and once at least had suffered in property and person. He was now aged sixty, infirm in body and extremely poor, and eked out what he might earn by his trade with 'a recipe from America for the manufacture of a certain soap, a cure for scorbutic eruptions'.[1] That he was an honest man there is no reason to doubt; that he was a man of strife—pertinacious, imperturbable, crammed with examples, ready at fence, and slyly ironic—the records of the trial prove. For once there was one in the dock who could stand up to Ellenborough. And Edward Law, Lord Ellenborough, was at this time in his hey-day, perhaps the most formidable and masterly personage in a generation of great lawyers, as learned as Eldon, but direct and rapid where Eldon 'wound in like a serpent', and rough and stern where the other was courtesy itself. A great admirer of Dr. Johnson, he would imitate him not only in the stateliness of his speech, but as often in its collected force. ('You may read your story in the eyes of the gentlemen around you.' 'I will not endure this industry of coughing.') An entirely upright judge

[1] From his plea for mitigation of sentence. See the record in *State Trials*, xxxi. 927–58.

according to his lights, he inherited the feudal sentiments and the traditional faith from his ancestry of Cumbrian 'statesmen' and seasoned them with the same honesty and austerity. Eaton was in for it.[1]

In 1812 Christianity was the law of the land in the form both of Statute and of Common Law. A statute of 1698 had enacted that anyone brought up as a Christian who should in any manner whatever deny the doctrine of the Trinity or the divine authority of the Scriptures should be disqualified from all offices and on a second offence be imprisoned for three years. But this law had fallen into entire desuetude, and in 1813 was repealed. From motives of humanity, as the Court declared, Eaton was prosecuted at Common Law, which might visit blasphemous libel more lightly than the statute, namely, by fine and imprisonment for less than three years without hard labour. Moreover blasphemy was understood as denying the Christian faith scoffingly or irreverently or insulting the person of Christ or the Scriptures, and it was disputed among the authorities, old and new, whether infidelity gravely and decently expressed was a misdemeanour at all.[2] To this question the Attorney General, Vicary Gibbs, who appeared for the Crown, had a decided answer. It was true, he said, that learned men were wont to examine critically parts of the Scriptures or the creeds, but the law imposed a limit on scepticism. 'So far as is compatible with public safety I am the first man to maintain that no clog should be placed on the freedom of the press. . . . Let the discussion of controverted points be fairly admitted; but let no man dare to put the axe to the root of the tree.' And in his summing up the Lord Chief Justice endorsed that view: 'To deny the truth of the book on which our faith depends has never been permitted.' Still, to make assurance sure, Counsel for the Crown adduced a sentence of Paine's which could pass for indubitable blasphemy; Paine had not only argued that the Bible and the miracles and the divinity of Christ were fables, but he had written that 'he who believes in the story of Christ is an infidel to God'. Paine's publisher, then, was punishable; writer or publisher, it was no matter. For the rest, the Attorney General laid himself out to raise alarm. Assuming that Chris-

---

[1] *Twelve Eminent Judges*, by William C. Townsend, 1846, i. 299–346.
[2] Halsbury, *The Laws of England*, ix. 530 f.

tianity was the same thing as religion itself, he set forth the consequences of losing it. What of those gentlemen of the jury who were advanced in years, and, if they had led unsullied lives, were expecting a heavenly reward? No one who knew human nature could doubt that, but for the fear of more than temporal punishment, indescribable mischief would break loose. How would the jury take it if the morals of their dearest relatives and the honesty of their domestics were undone? What would happen in that Court if oaths were taken on a discredited book, and if his Lordship had not 'imbibed from our holy religion such pure sentiments of truth and justice'? In fine, society would fall to pieces if Eaton were to have his way and there were no requital for 'so foul a crime'.

Eaton, who conducted his own defence, had determined to improve the occasion. He read out a long essay of his own to prove that the God of the Jews was not the God of the Christians and therefore the begotten of the one not the begotten of the other. It reprobated the wars and slaughters of the Old Testament, and the account of history-making in Esdras xiv, and it argued, with a great parade of learning, for the spuriousness of the Gospels. Ellenborough almost rent his clothes: 'Defendant, I must inform you that this is not to be made use of as an opportunity for you to revile the Christian religion, and if you persist in aspersing it, I will not only silence you, but I will animadvert on your conduct as an offence of the grossest kind against the dignity of the Court.' Again and again the judge commanded him to omit 'what it was painful to him and every Christian present to hear'. But Eaton argued that it was pertinent to his defence and refused to continue pleading if he might not read; and in the end his obstinacy conquered, and the Court was silenced and gave ear. Not a word in the summing up, or afterwards in the passing of the sentence on the considerations put forward on that occasion with notable force by the prisoner's Counsel, of the value of the free inquiring mind. 'The love of God is free', said Counsel, 'or it is not love at all.' If, as is likely, Shelley read this drama as given in *The Examiner*, he would feel a consolatory pleasure in the final scene. Eaton was placed in the pillory opposite Newgate at noon on 26 May. 'No sooner was he brought out from prison than he was greeted by the crowd with a cheer of approbation, which was repeated every ten minutes during the scene, and he was re-conducted to prison amid the waving of hats and cheering of the assembly. During the period of his punishment not a single voice or arm was raised against him.'[1]

'What do you think of Eaton's trial and sentence?' writes Shelley to Godwin on 11 June. 'I mean not to insinuate that this poor bookseller has any characteristics in common with Socrates or Jesus Christ; still, the spirit which pillories and imprisons him is the same as that which brought them to an untimely end.' He had already drawn the outline of an Address to the public on the issues of the case, and it must have taken shape as the *Letter* before or soon after he arrived at Lynmouth; for on 29 July he wrote from there to Thomas Hookham that he had dispatched to him twenty-five printed copies, not for sale, as he had once intended, but for gratuitous distribution, which would be less dangerous. The pamphlet was printed by the chief bookseller of Barnstaple, a Mr. Syle, Shelley coming in occasionally to correct the proofs. A thousand copies had been ordered and all or many of them struck off when, on 19 August, Daniel Healey was arrested for posting the Dublin broadsides on the walls of the neighbourhood, and Healey's master was in hot water. Syle looked into the *Letter to Lord Ellenborough*, and forthwith destroyed all the copies on hand and pressed the author to send back as many as had been delivered to him. But Shelley had sent Hookham an additional fifty on the day before, and posted a number of others to friends and notables, so that none were left. To-day, the copy in the Bodleian library, presented to Lady Shelley by Hookham or Leigh Hunt, is the only one extant.[2]

Shelley is not entirely fair to Lord Ellenborough. He up-

---

[1] *The Examiner*, No. 231, 31 May; see on the trial No. 219, 8 March; No. 227, 3 May; No. 228, 10 May. Crabbe Robinson describes in his *Diary* the scene at the pillory and Eaton there seated with 'round grinning face', quoted in Peck's *Shelley*, i. 266.

[2] The facts about Syle and the printing of the *Letter* were discovered by Mac-Carthy (*Early Life*, pp. 344 ff.) in *Sketches of the Literary History of Barnstaple*, by John Roberts Chanter, Barnstaple, 1866, pp. 55, 56. Something which it shares with popular oratory once earned for the *Letter* a brief success in America. An abridged edition of the abridged reprint in the *Shelley Memorials* appeared as one of the 'Truth Seeker Tracts' in New York in 1879, on an occasion similar to the condemnation of Eaton, and had an 'immense sale in the United States and Canada' (Buxton Forman, *Shelley Library*, pp. 33, 34).

braids him with reason enough for allowing or assisting the
Attorney General to exacerbate the jury. But he charges him
principally with not refusing to apply the law, and that he
could hardly have done without defaulting as a judge and
without becoming someone else. Nor, apart from a few things
said, but not much laid to heart, has Shelley conceived more
justly and deeply than he was wont to do of the traditional
theology. Apart from what may be described as an undigested
postscript, he looks on the religion of the country as purely
stuff and nonsense. Belief and unbelief, he says, and it is a
favourite saying of his about this time, are involuntary: plain
truth compels us; and Eaton was under the compulsion of plain
truth. Nor, as he goes on to argue, was there any substance
in the moral outcry over Paine's Works, and for this reason:
morality is based on the nature of things; no God made or has
any power to alter it; no religion, therefore, has aught to do
with it. Not that the *Letter* is all along so crude. There is nothing
blind or light in what it says of 'the crime of inquiry', the
futility of persecution, the enmity of these persecutors to the
English tradition and to the teaching of Christ.

It is not, however, as a contribution to the theory of freedom
that the *Letter* has its worth for us, but as a milestone on Shelley's
way and a gleam of his spirit. Here is the bud or early bloom of
persistent thoughts of his, and here he catches that aspect of the
contemporary world that loomed before him more and more.
Ellenborough and Gibbs, furious obscurantism exasperating
unreasonable law, were men of the epoch, and while such as
they remained in power there would be no sweeter and kinder
time. Eaton was a saviour of society in his slight degree. All
that Shelley used to put into the word 'Christianity' and all the
meaning of 'atheism' on his lips were once more contrasted as a
dead and a living faith, the pestilence of to-day and the salvation
of to-morrow; and not for the first time, but more clearly than
ever he saw his age as a Valley of Decision where the dignities
of our nature were at stake, and for a time at least it might go
hard with them. 'I do not warn you', he writes, 'to beware lest
your profession as a Christian should make you forget that you
are a man; but I warn you against festinating that period which,
under the present coercive system, is too rapidly maturing, when
the seats of justice shall be the seats of venality and slavishness,

and the cells of Newgate become the abode of all that is honourable and true.' But he concludes in a fresh line of thought. Interpreting his text and putting one thing to another, the reader can make out the beginnings of a theory of religious progress. Reason is great, and the time will come when (to construe his text rather than paraphrase it) the men of all the religions shall discover under each perishing embodiment a common soul of truth, and love one another. From time to time through the great reformers the body is more or less purified by the soul. And for the first of several times in his writings he names together Christ and Socrates as the supreme among the cleansing influences and the discerners of the eternal element. Here again, with what it says, or tries to say, of the unity, under deciduous manifestations, of the spiritual life, and with that choice of masters, the *Letter to Lord Ellenborough* presents in a weak and inchoate form ideas that some time later on were of the staple of his thinking.

### 3. At Lynmouth, from the end of June to the end of August 1812

They took lodgings at Lynmouth in a rudely furnished cottage embowered in myrtles and roses, in front the sea and stony shore, behind them hills and valleys 'of indescribable fertility and grandeur', and the Valley of Rocks near by. And to Shelley's deeper contentment in the middle of July 'Portia' or 'Bessie' arrived. She was evidently excited at the first contact with those on whom she now depended; and indeed in no long time between her and the other women the ground began to part and the fiction to dissolve. Three weeks after her arrival Harriet describes to Catherine Nugent the tall thin figure with the dark hair; 'she talks a great deal', says the letter, '—if you like great talkers she will suit you'; 'busy writing for the good of mankind, laughs and talks and writes all day'. A week later her mood was quite the contrary. A book called *Pieces of Irish History* had depressed her, she would avenge Ireland with a volume of extracts, and Percy would print an appeal for subscribers. 'She possesses too much feeling for her own happiness', writes Harriet. '*You* do not let your feelings get the better of your reason. If you do, I am extremely sorry.'

If there were signs of the oncoming disagreement, Shelley

would not perceive them. He was too happy: in the scenes around him, in Harriet and the appeals and 'quick and warm returns' of their love,[1] and in this long-awaited 'sister' and messenger of deep things. He must have lived as joyously in the nine weeks at Lynmouth as ever before or after, not only with that part of him that disported in the blowing of soap-bubbles, but with the severer part. Ireland was much in his mind; in the middle of August he wrote to the radical publisher, Thomas Hookham, proposing a reprint of the History of that country that had so much affected Miss Hitchener, as well as a reprint in London of his own two Irish pamphlets in a single volume. He came upon absorbing books and fresh ideas, like the picture of ideal matriarchy in Lawrence's *Empire of the Nairs*; and he carried on or went beyond the purposes conceived at Nantgwillt, with 'several works, some unfinished, others yet only in contemplation, principally in the form of poems or essays'.[2] He had more matter, that is to say, to be added to the poems and essays held to ransom by his Dublin printers. He was still captivated by the *Système de la Nature*, so much so that he set himself to English it;[3] and Dowden refers to this period two long poems in the Esdaile Note-book, *The Voyage* (three hundred lines in the verse of *Thalaba*) and the rhymed and regular *Retrospect of Times of Old*, both about the wrongs of society and those who inflict or suffer or contend with them. Further, it was at Lynmouth, if not previously at Nantgwillt or even earlier, that he began composing *Queen Mab*. Not by Leagues and Societies, since Godwin forbade them, but by random impregnation he would diffuse truth; and while *Queen Mab* had yet to be written, there was seed worth sowing in his *Declaration of Rights* and his *Devil's Walk*, of which Miss Hitchener had brought the copies with her, little suspecting what had happened to them in the hands of Customs Officers and Secretaries of State.

Of the child-like operations that now ensued we learn mainly from three or four documents among the records of the Home Office.[4] On 20 August, on directions from the Mayor of Barn-

---

[1] From the fragment of a sonnet dated 1 Aug. 1812. The long poem *To Harriet* cited in the section on Nantgwillt may well have been written at Lynmouth, as Dowden supposes.

[2] To Thomas Hookham, 29 July.          [3] To Thomas Hookham, 18 Aug.

[4] Subsequent biographers have drawn for the story of the residence at Lynmouth on an article by W. M. Rossetti, entitled 'Shelley in 1812–13', *Fortnightly Review*,

staple, Henry Drake, Town Clerk, wrote to the Home Secretary, then Lord Sidmouth, that on the previous day 'a Man was observed distributing and posting papers about the Town, entitled *Declaration of Rights*, who said that on his road from Linton to Barnstaple he met a gentleman dressed in black, whom he had never seen before', and the gentleman gave him papers (the *Declaration* and *The Devil's Walk*, attached for the Secretary's inspection) and five shillings to distribute them. They were without the printer's name, and on that account the man was fined £200, and, the money not forthcoming, consigned to prison for six months. His name was Daniel Hill (or Healey); he was servant to a Mr. Shelley, a visitor at Lynmouth; and Drake suspected that Mr. Shelley (on whom and his companions he added a few notes) was the author of the papers; more especially as he had often been seen to go out in a boat, and on one occasion to wade into the sea, and drop bottles with seditious writing in them, as had been discovered when one of these vessels drifted to shore. The seditious matter in these bottles, though the Mayor and the Town Clerk did not know it, was *The Devil's Walk*. At almost the same time—on 22 August— Richard Jones, Postmaster at Barnstaple, wrote to Francis Freeling at the General Post Office of the case of Daniel Hill, enclosing a copy of the *Declaration*; and Freeling was once again in council with his official superior, Lord Chichester, over a document which they had seen once before and its extraordinary author. They laid the matter before Sidmouth (to whom Shelley's name would be not unknown, if he had glanced at the Ellenborough pamphlet, sent to him a week or two previously by post); and it was resolved, upon legal advice, not to prosecute the young agitator, nor to approach his parents, who, as Chichester remarked, had suffered by his conduct enough already, but to have him watched and further reported on. For this purpose, on 8 September the Barnstaple Town Clerk made a journey to Lynmouth, and on the next day forwarded to London more gleanings about Shelley, proving him the writer of one at least of the incriminating papers. (Evidently he had not been told that the authorities at the Home Office knew who the author was already.) Shelley, he reported, who was 'rather thin and

Jan. 1871. Of the Home Office documents there quoted Drake's first report and most of his second are given in a corrected form in Peck's *Shelley*.

very young, his appearance almost that of a boy', had often been observed on the beach in company with a Female Servant (supposed a Foreigner) to push out to sea some small boxes', and one of the boxes, 'carefully covered with Bladder and well resined and waxed', with 'a little upright stick fastened to it at each end, and a little Sail; besides some Lead at the Bottom', had been picked up and opened and found to contain the *Declaration of Rights*. Of another of the young man's methods of wafting disaffection the lawyer did not learn: that is to say by small truth-carrying balloons, launched into the winds, glowing in the sun, and speeded by a sonnet, as the bottles also were.

On learning of his man's arrest Shelley at once came forward, visited him in jail, begged for his discharge, and afterwards paid weekly for comforts and privileges for him while the sentence ran. But for Mr. Syle, his Barnstaple printer, who now discovered what he had printed and delivered as *A Letter to Lord Ellenborough*, he had no comfort but that he could tell him that in some at least of the copies sent away he had used a pair of scissors to excise his name. Presently Lynmouth, no less than Barnstaple, was 'regarding him'—in Drake's words again—'with a suspicious eye from the Circumstances of his very extensive Correspondence, and many of his Packages and Letters being addressed to Sir Francis Burdett'. 'I also learnt at Lynmouth that Mr. Shelley had with him large chests, which were so heavy that scarcely three men could lift them, which were supposed to contain papers.' Soon after Hill's arrest Shelley, it would seem, discovered that he was watched, and abruptly departed, he and his family, to Ilfracombe, after borrowing ready money from his landlady, and paying her bill with a draft on Lawless, his friend in Dublin.[1] When on 8 September Drake came over to Lynmouth, the Shelleys had been gone ten days; and following them to Ilfracombe, he found, and so reported, that they had taken ship for Swansea. There, 'in great distress and difficulty' they turned up at the house of Captain Gronow, an Etonian contemporary,[2] so loath to tell him why they had come that Gronow could only conjecture 'an *affaire de cœur*'. Shelley had

---

[1] The draft was not honoured (see note *ante*, p. 137). On 19 Nov. Shelley sent Mrs. Hooper, the landlady, £20 with a promise of £10 to follow and expunge the debt.

[2] From his *Reminiscences and Recollections* (ed. 1900, i. 155); reminiscent of Shelley at Eton.

planned to winter in the Vale of Llangollen, but his old interest in Carnarvonshire drew him farther, and the story now moves on to Tremadoc and another skein of troubles. Not for the last time might he think of himself and those with him as not much happier than so many gipsies harried by the police as a vexatious and insanitary lot. For a testimony against North Devon he shook the dust from his feet in a parting sonnet; but could he have penetrated the Home Office he would have enjoyed a crumb of comfort. On 14 September, from the *Speedwell* Revenue Cutter off St. Ives, John Hopkins, Inspecting Commander of Revenue Cruisers, Western District, sent up to Lord Sidmouth a paper (the *Declaration*) with its envelope—paper tattered owing to dampness—'having found the same in a Sealed Wine Bottle, floating near the Entrance of Milford Haven on 10th Inst.' The Inspector had heard that a similar paper was taken up in a similar manner a few weeks before near Lynmouth by a Preventive Revenue Boat at Porlock, envelope pointing to 'a person of the name of Shelley living thereat'. So, if thought of sufficient importance, it might lead to 'a discovery of the Parties concerned in this novel mode of disseminating their pernicious opinions, and which appear to me intended to fall into the hands of the Sea-faring part of the People, many hundreds of which may thus reach that Class and do incalculable mischief among them'.[1]

On 18 September, three weeks after the flight, the oft-invited William Godwin knocked at the door where the Shelleys had been dwelling. Godwin had by now lost favour a little, at any rate with Harriet, by stretching his authority. He had pressed Shelley on leaving Wales to move to a house in Chepstow, which Shelley had considered too small, and reprehensions and apologies had followed. Then Miss Hitchener, having stayed for a night in Skinner Street on her way through London, had tales to tell of Godwin's overweening; and when the Shelleys had entreated that, in default of the great man himself, Fanny might come to them at Lynmouth—Mary Wollstonecraft's daughter Fanny—the answer had been that she could not be entrusted to strangers. But the disciple would have clean forgotten all these

[1] H.O. 42. 127. So far as I know this report from Hopkins has not hitherto appeared in print. I owe it to the kindness of Mrs. Barbara Hammond, who came across it in the course of her researches on other subjects in the Record Office.

things if he had seen his master stepping ashore from a ship's boat after a distressful voyage of fifty hours from the port of Bristol on purpose to see him. Even after being sea-sick, but 'not decisively', the philosopher bore calmly with the misadventure, and came away from Mrs. Hooper, the delightful landlady who 'loved the Shelleys', not only with a precise account of them, and particularly of their finances, but with 'good news', as he wrote to his wife. 'The best news is that the woman says they will be in London in a fortnight. This quite comforts my heart.' It was a tangible comfort that he wanted, for he was at this time in sorer straits for money than usual, and 'there can be scarcely a doubt', says his biographer, 'that he and Mrs. Godwin had already fixed on Shelley as their rescuer'.[1] Godwin had an art of borrowing. He would have been gracious to his hosts in manner and charming in talk, and would have alluded to his distresses only in flying hints: a light reconnaissance preparatory to the real attack.

## 4. At Tremadoc: September 1812

After leaving Ireland Shelley had been at a loose end. He had at first intended to plant his Association in Dublin, then in Wales (the likeliest ground, as he now considered), then in England. But Godwin had forbidden the plan, and to agitate by his bottles and balloons was among the few resources his preceptor had left him. Nevertheless, it was upon political agitation that his heart was set, and on writing only as a means to it. 'I once thought to study these [political] affairs', he said at the end of his life, 'and write or act in them. I am glad that my good genius said *refrain*.'[2] But the genius was a long while saying so: his thoughts in this autumn were still upon the world and its great controversy; and the famous saying of Archimedes that he set before *Queen Mab*—'Give me leverage and I'll move the world'—was pertinent to himself: he wanted a leverage, something to do and the means of doing it. Meanwhile under the Welsh hills he could think and write in peace: and with no other purpose he went to Tremadoc because there the scenery pleased him and a good house chanced to be available. Having arrived, he found at his door the opportunity of action in a new form,

---

[1] *The Life of William Godwin*, by Ford K. Brown, n.d., p. 266.
[2] To Horace Smith, 29 June 1822.

that divided his energies with the propaganda in verse and prose, and put him on another adventure in knight-errantry.

William Alexander Madocks, after whom Tremadoc is named, a Fellow of All Souls and for eighteen years Member of Parliament for Boston on the Whig side, was a person of large views, with a public spirit and a good fortune, but with no great fund of providence or persistence, *un bon commenceur*. In 1798, at the age of twenty-four, he bought the estate of Tan-yr-Allt (Under the Hill) on the border of Merioneth and Carnarvon, looking down on the estuary of the Glaslyn and an area known as Traeth Mawr (the Great Sand) which the sea covered at high tide for several miles inland. In 1800 he began to drain and recover 2,000 acres of the marsh of Penmorfa, adjacent to Traeth Mawr; and after 1807 started the embankment across the sands between Port Aberglaslyn and Gest Point, by which a further 3,000 acres were reclaimed. When completed in 1811, the great dam carried a road and connected the two counties. It was thrown out at the same time from each of the opposite shores, and the race of the waters through the narrowing gap at ebb of tide is memorably described by Peacock in a page of *Headlong Hall*. On the site of Penmorfa the founder put up his little brand-new town, with a church, a market-place, a Town Hall and a Square, and from his own villa on a natural platform at the foot of a stretch of towering wood-covered rock surveyed his achievement. A few might feel with Peacock or his interlocutors that in all this utility there were things to regret: the social consequences of the new industries in Tremadoc and the impairment of a wonderful scene. As the spectator might view it, standing on the embankment with his back to the sea, 'vast rocks and precipices, intersected with little torrents, formed the barrier on the left; on the right, the triple summit of Moëlwyn reared its majestic boundary; in the depth was that sea of mountains, the wild and stormy outline of the Snowdonian chain, with the giant Wyddfa towering in the midst. The mountainframe remains unchanged, unchangeable; but the liquid mirror it enclosed is gone.'

The triumph over Nature was communally celebrated in August 1811, when among other gaieties an ox was roasted and eaten by the workmen on the causeway, whom the munificent benefactor had clothed in uniforms; but on 14 February 1812, a storm made a breach in the centre of the dam, and though the labourers and landowners of the district came with all speed to the rescue, the wall against the sea and the whole town with it were in danger. Madocks was at this time away in England, with no money to spare; but his agent, John Williams, first his gardener, then the foreman and supervisor of the great undertaking—'a sober man and a pillar of the Independent Chapel'— took the situation in hand, and with the aid of several eminent Welshmen appealed for a public subscription to mend the embankment in time. The appeal, though by no means understated, made but little headway; the mending languished; and it was under these circumstances that Shelley came in with a flaming zeal for it. On some date towards the middle of September, as is most likely, he had taken Madocks's untenanted villa, and soon after his arrival, presumably on quarter-day, presented Williams with a hundred or possibly five hundred pounds, and by means of this gift (whichever was the amount) the work was pushed on, for a short while at any rate, 'with renovated activity and spirit'. More than that, he promised his utmost endeavour to bring subscribers in. At a meeting of distinguished friends of the embankment at Beaumaris on 28 September, his 'providential interference' was warmly acknowledged, his health was drunk, and he made a speech. He said that the embankment was one of the noblest works of human power; it was an exhibition of human nature as it appears in its noblest and most natural shape—beneficence: it saved, not destroyed. 'Cast a look round these islands, through the perspective of these times, behold famine driving millions to madness, and own how excellent, how glorious is the work which will give no less than three thousand souls a means of competence.' And then the speaker pledged himself 'to spend the last shilling of his fortune and devote the last breath of his life to that great, that glorious cause'. Six weeks later he wrote to Williams that, while unable to do a great deal at present, he trusted to effect something 'grand and decisive' on his coming of age, and would desert the enterprise 'but with his life'.[1]

---

[1] In this section I have relied mainly on the article on Madocks in the *D.N.B.*; on an article by R. W. King, entitled 'Shelley and the Tremadoc Embankment', in the *Welsh Outlook* for June 1930; and on *Eminent Welshmen*, by Robert Williams, 1852. Dowden's account is somewhat erroneous. The Julian Shelley (vii. 326 f.) reprints (from the *North Wales Gazette*, Thursday, 1 Oct. 1812) a report of the

A few days after the meeting at Beaumaris, partly to raise money for the causeway and partly to see Godwin, he and his three companions set out for London, where they arrived on 4 October. There was another advantage in the journey—the getting rid more easily of Elizabeth Hitchener, whose presence was verging on the intolerable. It was not only that Eliza Westbrook was at war with her from jealousy; but 'we were entirely deceived', writes Harriet, 'as to her republicanism and everything else she pretended to be'; moreover, 'she built all her hopes on being able to separate me from my dearly loved Percy, and had the artfulness to say that Percy was really in love with her'. All the circumstances considered, these were pardonable offences; but real faults of temper and behaviour are laid to her charge in the intemperate abuse that Shelley flung at her when all was over between them—'our tormentor and schoolmistress'; 'an artful, superficial, ugly, hermaphroditical beast of a woman'; 'a woman of desperate views and dreadful passions, but of cool and undeviating revenge'; 'a brown demon'. The hearthungry lady had been cheated for a time of her real opinions and her sound senses, as well as the means she lived by; and it is little wonder that, finding herself the fool of a comedy, she became guilty of a certain venom. We know that after her dismissal at the end of the London visit she wrote to Williams and to Pilfold with false and malignant aspersions on Shelley and his wife and his wife's sister. And there is some evidence that, in the two or three weeks of her stay at Tan-yr-Allt, she made mischief there. One Robert Leeson, of Morfa Lodge, whatever position in life he filled, was a man of influence in the place. Dowden describes him as 'an eminently loyal and disagreeable Englishman', and Williams's widow, writing in 1860, as 'an envious unfeeling sort of man, not very particular what he said of anyone'. The Shelleys, who had heard of him in that character, would have nothing to do with him, and he, almost as soon as they appeared, smelt out their political or other heresies and vowed to have them out of the town. If the evidence borne by

proceedings at Beaumaris and a list of the subscribers, where Shelley's name is entered for £100. But in *Shelley Memorials*, p. 43, his subscription is said to have been £500. Williams's speech at Beaumaris would seem to imply that the sum was fairly large: 'From the providential interference of a friend he had been able to put in employ so many men as, in the event of his meeting with public encouragement, would fortify the Embankment against any apprehended damage!'

Mrs. Williams and cited by Dowden is sound, on some occasion before she left Tremadoc Miss Hitchener talked with this Leeson and told him of one of Shelley's pamphlets 'containing matter dangerous to the State' and of the speech in Dublin. And when Shelley, hearing, no doubt, that his recent utterances were a scandal to his neighbours and had been represented to them as incendiary, went and demanded of his enemy who the informant had been, Leeson, after first naming Williams, presently retracted that assertion and named Miss Hitchener. But neither was Williams as careful as he ought to have been; it was from him that the 'loyal Englishman' obtained a copy of one of the pamphlets, and sent it to the Home Office, where they must have been weary by now of Shelley's name.[1] At the time, therefore, of the expedition to London there was a seed of trouble germinating in the public opinion of Tremadoc and a domestic tempest labouring up the sky.

## 5. In London: 4 October–12 November 1812

Godwin, after the age of fifty, was a short, thick-set, thick-legged man, with a fair complexion, a bald and very large head, and normally a placid manner. 'Characterless nose, ditto chin', wrote Carlyle after seeing him, then an old man; but Northcote's portrait renders the look of a daring and severe intelligence that Shelley often noted with a qualm of contrition for liking him less and less. He dressed like a dissenting minister, only the suit was far behind the times, carelessly put on, and as a rule wearing bare. His demeanour had always something in it a little underbred, and his talk, except in congenial company, was dull. 'He had less of the appearance of a man of genius', wrote Hazlitt, 'than anyone who has given such decided and ample proofs of it.' He tells us in his notes upon himself that he 'was cold and uninviting' from timidity. This timidity, which in scenes of violence disabled him and made him tremble, and

---

[1] On 5 Mar. 1813, a week after the flight from Tanyrallt, Leeson, who had a spite against the agent, wrote to Shelley, then at Bangor, telling him not only that the pamphlet came from Williams, but that it came with the remark that here was 'matter dangerous to the State' by a man who 'was in the practice of haranguing 500 people at once when in Ireland'. Shelley then wrote from Bangor soon after 5 Mar. the letter in which he upbraids Williams for deceiving him, but says also that, while he is sure that Williams gave Leeson the pamphlet, he does not believe that, in giving it, he uttered those slanderous remarks.

M

which unfitted him to be alone 'in a circle of strangers, in an inn, almost in a shop', embattled itself in vanity, dogmatism, and 'a harshness that his heart disowned'. It wanted Charles Lamb to appreciate his affectation, 'since your coxcombs are always agreeable'. With friends or admirers, on the other hand, he was 'as easy as an old glove'. With small experience of actual life, and no store of images or instances from it, he was nevertheless a rich talker, who in his soft and pleasant voice would gossip, as Hazlitt wrote, 'in a fine vein about old authors'; and you perceived 'by your host's talk, as by the taste of seasoned wine, that he had a *cellarage* in his understanding'.

41 Skinner Street, close by the corner of what are now Holborn Viaduct and Snow Hill, contained on the ground floor the shop of the Juvenile Library, and on the first floor the living-rooms of Godwin's family. On a higher floor still was 'a little study, shaped like a quadrant, with windows in the arc, a fireplace in one radius, and in the other a shelf full of old books; with Opie's portrait of Mary Wollstonecraft and Northcote's portrait of the philosopher himself on the walls'.[1] Here in the two upper stories Godwin exercised his unfailing virtues of literary diligence and domestic amiability, while his wife was the manager of the shop. With that buxom, good-looking, clever, vulgar, ill-tempered, and domineering woman this history will not have much to do; but from now onwards she operates in the background. She had sterling virtues and a hard task; and if she plagued her husband with her quarrelsomeness and 'baby sullenness', and the bond between them was more than once near breaking, yet he bore her a real affection, and depended too much on her firmer judgement and stronger will to regret, as many of his friends did, that he had married her. If Francis Place, speaking from much experience, called her a devil, and laid the ruin of the Library at her door; if she moved Charles Lamb to malice and Shelley in her company 'languished into hate'; if because of her some of her husband's oldest friends came to see him rarely or not at all: she was capable of friendships and in some eyes her merits countervailed her faults. Unfortunately, with regard to Shelley, her inferior qualities are those that count. In the industry of borrowing from him she was her husband's abettor, equally callous and disingenuous,

[1] Ford K. Brown, op. cit.

equally unthankful. She concerns us more, however, as a mother and stepmother, with a family of five children, three of whom were deeply implicated in Shelley's life. There were the two children of Mary Wollstonecraft: Fanny, her daughter by Gilbert Imlay, born in April 1794, and Mary Godwin, born at the cost of the mother's life on 30 August 1797; then, Mrs. Godwin's two children by her first marriage, Mary Jane (afterwards called Claire) and Charles Clairmont, born respectively in April 1798 and in June 1795; and finally William, the only child of her marriage with Godwin, born to them in 1803. To all of these, except perhaps to William, she made the home in Skinner Street uninviting, and eventually unendurable. Of this domestic underside the Shelleys in the autumn of 1812 would be unaware. Mary returned from a visit to Dundee on 10 November, and they saw her only once on the evening of the 11th; Jane, except for two nights, was away from home; Charles was in Edinburgh, in Constable's office; and William all day at school. But Fanny was at home, 'very plain, but very sensible', drudging in the house, returning Godwin's kindness to her with an anxious care for him, and his wife's unkindness in the spirit of a saint.

Fancy may conceive with what feelings Shelley first spoke with this child of Tragedy and took Godwin's hand. For a while his fond faith that time would have produced 'no soul-chilling alteration' in his Master's nature, was sustained. Godwin was exceedingly friendly, talked in a 'pleasing manner' on matter and spirit, atheism, utility and truth, the clergy, church government, German literature and thought[1]—and reminded Harriet of the bust of Socrates. And Mrs. Godwin seemed to them a 'magnanimous woman', with a 'very great sweetness' in her face, contending with many troubles, especially with the need of capital and shortages of ready money. But the glossy appearances would not wear. To Harriet at least, by the end of these London days, the distinction between the man in Skinner Street and the author of *Political Justice* had come clear. The man in Skinner Street was 'old and unimpassioned', 'filled with prejudices', wanted Percy to turn Whig, indicated to his young friends how young they were, and expected homage. So unpleasant was he at last, and his wife 'so extremely disagreeable',

---

[1] The list of subjects is taken by Dowden (i. 304) from Godwin's Diary.

that when the Shelleys came to London in the early summer of the next year, they were no more eager to frequent his
house.

For a compensation, Shelley made new friendships and
repaired an old one. Two of the dramatis personae who were
presently to perform their parts appear in these days in a brief
preliminary manner. One was John Frank Newton, who is
probably alluded to in Hazlitt's essay *On People with One Idea*.
He had been cured of diseases through the vegetable diet,
supported by distilled water, that William Lambe, a London
physician, advocated in books and pamphlets in the first thirty
years of the century; and in 1812, in his forty-third year, was a
zealot of the meatless school.[1] In 1811 Newton had published
his abundantly documented *Return to Nature, or A Defence of the
Vegetable Regimen*,[2] and in his house in Chester Street his children,
thanks to the 'natural' food and the influence of light and air on
their naked bodies, advertised to all comers the efficacy of the
system. These were the troop that one day in the summer of
1813 ran in complete nudity to meet Shelley at the front door,
and, seeing Hogg in his company, raced screaming up the
stairs, that 'presented the appearance of Jacob's ladder'. 'From
the window of the nursery at the top of the house they had seen
the beloved Shelley; me, the killjoy, they had not observed.'
Shelley, in fact, went straight to the heart of the Newtons. He
was already a vegetarian of six months' standing,[3] one of the

---

[1] See *The Ethics of Diet, a Catena of Authorities Deprecatory to the Practice of Flesh-
eating*, by Howard Williams, 1883. Newton gave an account of his own case and a
particular account of the treatment of his children in the concluding pages of one
of Lambe's Reports on the effect of the 'Peculiar Regimen' on cancer. Professor
Koszul, in an appendix to *La Jeunesse*, reproduces from the *London Liberal* of 1823
(a short-lived journal set on foot as an answer to the *Liberal* of Byron and Leigh
Hunt) a report of an imaginary dinner in Apr. 1814 at which sixty vegetarians
are supposed to assemble to celebrate the success of a three years' experiment. The
note on diet in *Queen Mab* announced that 'hopes are entertained that in April,
1814, a statement will be given that sixty persons, all having lived more than three
years on vegetables and pure water, are then *in perfect health*'. Newton is President
of the feast, Shelley Vice-President, and both make speeches, which are well done
in the style of Peacock, who in *Headlong Hall* had made some play with Newton in
the figure of Mr. Escot. I suspect Peacock of the authorship. See *William Lambe,
M.D.*, by H. Saxe Wyndham, published by the Vegetarian Society, 1940.

[2] *The Return to Nature, or A Defence of the Vegetable Regimen, with some account of an
experiment made during the last three or four years in the Author's Family.* The dedicatory
letter to William Lambe, M.D., is dated Apr. 1811.

[3] In the letter from Dublin to Elizabeth Hitchener of 14 Mar. 1812, he tells her

twenty-five in all England, and was now to adopt in his Note to *Queen Mab* on food and drink the main content of *The Return to Nature*: all about the garden of Eden and the myth of Prometheus as a vegetarian allegory, and the herbivorous structure of our bodies, and the capital dogma that all human depravity has originated in the eating of flesh and the drinking of fermented liquors. The two men were personally somewhat similar. There is a glimpse in Hogg of Newton surprised by his visitors over some experiment upon water, his clothes 'barred and brindled' with chemical smear. Peacock tells of the enthusiast encountering the landlord of an inn whose sign was four horseshoes. Four: the number of divisions in the zodiac of Dendera. Why four? 'Why, sir, I suppose because a horse has four legs.' 'Did you ever see such a fool?' said Newton, 'bouncing away'.

If Peacock's humour would be thrown away upon Newton, it could fall to more purpose upon Shelley for the good of his soul; and he came in for a wholesome and a bountiful influence when the Hookhams introduced him at this period to their new poet.[1] In 1811 Edward and Thomas Hookham had started a publishing business at their father's famous Library in Old Bond Street, and among their first issues were Peacock's early poems, *The Genius of the Thames*, *Palmyra*, *The Philosophy of Melancholy*, and the Chevalier Lawrence's *Empire of the Nairs*. Shelley had already put down the enlightened Hookhams as his future publishers, and in the summer had corresponded with Thomas on friendly terms. Peacock, at this time Edward Hookham's nearest friend, was almost a denizen of the British Museum, Reading Room and galleries, if he were not roaming some wild countryside. He was now aged twenty-seven, and, as was said of the youthful Tennyson, 'a kind of young Hyperion' with strength and joyousness written on his face. With no train-

he has been upon the vegetable regimen a fortnight. Dr. Anster in his reminiscences in the *North British Review* (1847) mentions this diet in Dublin, which Shelley seems then to have grounded on a belief in metempsychosis.

[1] In the biographical preface to the *Works*, in three volumes, ed. Henry Cole, 1875, p. xxxiii, Edith Nicolls, Peacock's grand-daughter, says that the two men met in 1812 at Nantgwillt, and a statement of Peacock's own in his memoirs of Shelley refers the meeting to 1812, 'just before he went to Tanyrallt'. But Shelley's references to the author of *The Genius of the Thames* in his letter from Lynmouth of 18 Aug. do not consist with a personal acquaintance, and Peacock's statement, when examined, does consist with a first meeting in the autumn in London. See *The Life of Thomas Love Peacock*, by Carl van Doren, pp. 54–6.

ing in exact and formal scholarship, he employed his many years of leisure on an amateur erudition, with a preference for peaceful wisdom and elegant wit. He gave his mind to Homer, Sophocles, Aristophanes; to Virgil, Horace, Petronius; to Pulci, Ariosto, Rabelais, Voltaire; and not so much to Lucretius or Juvenal or Dante. Chaucer and Shakespeare were old friends; but he 'preferred Milton's prose to his poetry', and 'the dramatists of the Restoration shared his interest with the wits and poets of the age of Anne'.[1] He considered, moreover, that 'life is too short to learn German', but not too short for secondary studies in archaeology and mythology, philology, classical art and modern painting, many tracts of history, and the lore of medieval England and medieval Wales. In his evolution as an author 1812 is a turning-point. He had concluded his early poetry 'of the prize-poem order', and was to prove four years afterwards by *Headlong Hall* that his true vein would be social satire, and not romantic melancholy. Towards him Shelley's feelings were, and were bound to be, admiration with a rebate; as when in the early volume of verse, sent him by the Hookhams, he had found at the end of *Palmyra* on the fashion of this world passing away 'the finest piece of poetry I ever read', and quarrelled with the paean to sea-trade and empire in *The Genius of the Thames*. But of all his early friends and companions he found in this one the wealthiest mind and the largest personality.

It appears that Shelley did not know before the end of the sojourn in London that Hogg had come to town in the spring to keep terms at the Middle Temple and to be indentured to a special pleader. One day in early November 'a very wild-looking man' invaded the lawyer's chambers and was with difficulty persuaded that the pupil had departed to his lodgings; and at those lodgings about ten o'clock on the following evening, 'I was roused', says the biography, 'by a violent knocking at the street door, as if the watchman was giving the alarm of fire; someone ran furiously upstairs, the door flew open, and Bysshe rushed into the middle of the room'. There was a great talk, and on at least two evenings Hogg dined in the family circle at the St. James's Coffee-house. With Shelley the Irish question was still to the fore; on his table were several books of Irish history, and Harriet put into his hands 'a large sheet of

[1] Carl van Doren, op. cit., pp. 18–26.

thick paper, printed on one side only, and with an engraving on
the top, much like an Oxford Almanack'. It was a report of the
trial of Robert Emmet, and in the illustration the unfortunate
youth was standing at the bar and pleading. 'The sooner such
rascals were hanged', said Hogg, 'the better.' Harriet, full of
the sentiment of '98, and of the Irish melodies she was at that
time learning, misliked the observation, and Shelley would not
talk of Ireland, and when his friend inspected one of the histories, drew it gently from his hand. The small incident
signified. Like water, the friendship found its level under the
initial pitch, and no resurgences of Shelley's admiration could
enduringly raise it. At the meeting in London both felt the
coming change; and when Shelley left for Wales Hogg pursued him with apprehensive letters. Shelley answered that he
quarrelled only with opinions badly motivated, as his friend's
surely were not; that he was no cold reasoner as his friend supposed him, and that he preferred a cultured aristocracy to a
vulgar democracy. 'Perhaps he may still be my friend', he
wrote in the Journal two years later, 'in spite of the radical
differences of sympathy between us.'

He had done well on the London visit at 'keeping friendship
in repair'; he ended it with a blessed disencumbrance. For
nearly the whole of the six weeks Miss Hitchener had remained
of the party. In one of his memorable pages Hogg has depicted
the last scenes of the comedy, himself by chance an actor in them.
It had been at last arranged that, on Sunday, 8 November, the
lady was to go. That morning Hogg called at the hotel; and
in the afternoon, Shelley detained by an engagement, and
Harriet by a headache, was 'condemned to walk with the two
spinsters':

'Accordingly', writes Mephistopheles, 'I was turned over to
them; and, with the brown demon on my right arm and the black
diamond on my left, we went forth into St. James's Park, and
walked there and in the neighbouring parks for a long time, a
very long time. "These were my jewels", as Cornelia proudly
exclaimed. In the beginning the dark rivals quarrelled with one
another across me, to whom, however, they were both exceedingly
civil. The lovely Eliza attacked the foe with haughty contempt;
the bearded preceptress defended herself, and offended her enemy
with meek contumacy. I never saw Eliza so much alive before or

since. I never knew her come out so decidedly. For some time there was hit for hit delivered on both sides with calm, soft acrimony, but by degrees the jangling abated, and the angel on my left relapsed into her normal condition of languor. I then turned to the angel on my right, and interrogated her about the Rights of Women, respectfully requesting to be informed what they were.'

After dinner that evening a coach carried Miss Hitchener away for good and all. The dinner was 'tranquil'; nay, over tea the parting guest started once more on the Rights of Women, till 'Bysshe quitted his chair, and stood before her, looking enthusiastic'. She said farewell, 'freely, quietly, and civilly'; but in spite of Shelley's promise of a compensatory grant of £100 a year till she were once more the mistress of a livelihood, she persisted for some time afterwards in her bitterness, 'her reputation gone', as she said, 'her health ruined, her peace of mind destroyed'. Perhaps no portion of the grant was even once accepted.[1] She resumed her profession, and in later life at her own school at Edmonton was a successful and beloved teacher.[2] 'My astonishment at my fatuity was never so great', wrote Shelley, looking back on the whole erratic episode.

He was to have dined with Godwin on 13 November, but did not appear. Instead he and his were on the road to Oxford and bound for Wales, no time taken to bid his friends good-bye. In a letter to Fanny, who was hurt by the unkindness, he wrote of the qualms which this behaviour had cost him, and of a 'galling and unappealable necessity' for it; but what the necessity was remains obscure.

### 6. Tremadoc again: the middle of November 1812– 27 February 1813

Not long after his return Shelley was weary of Tremadoc. All classes seemed to be steeped in prejudice. Even Mrs. Madocks, who was staying somewhere in the neighbourhood, spoke of Mr. Peacock, in his solitary cottage at Tan-y-bwlch in the year 1810, 'hiding his head like a murderer—*but he was worse than that*, he was an atheist'. The zealotry of saints matched

---

[1] Or perhaps one instalment; as might be inferred from Shelley's language to Hogg in the letter of 3 Dec.
[2] Dowden, i. 315.

with the despotism of aristocrats, and the villainy of lawyers, and the serfdom of the poor—these, to the onlookers at Tany-rallt, were the aspects of a backward society with no redeeming dignities. The squalid poverty around him moved Shelley to frequent deeds of mercy; in after years Madocks would often dilate, says Medwin, on this 'friend of the unfriended poor' visiting their stricken homes and supplying them with food or clothes or fuel; and the pain of the revelation in the course of these activities broke out in solemn verses *To Cambria*,[1] adjuring her to hear the voices of her hills and permit these woes and wrongs no more. By the middle of January the Embankment itself had become, in Harriet's eyes at least, a blot upon the landscape that had brought about nothing but a sandy marsh and the complacency of its builder. Of him, Madocks, there was presently no good thing to say; he never paid his bills; you might see his unpaid labourers working their barren lands in the moonlit nights; and his dwelling bore the traces of 'folly and extravagance'. Moreover, it may have occurred even to Shelley that, whatever the cost of the embankment, the returns, in the shape of new rents, would be no trifle in the projector's pocket. So commented, no doubt, the Duke of Norfolk and the other gentlemen of Sussex, whom during the sojourn in London he had asked in vain for aid. Calling in Williams's company at the houses of the gentry, and busy in the Agent's office, sometimes from morning to night, at dispatching the appeals for money,[2] he more and more lost heart under the ill success of his pursuit and under the sense that, as he once confided to Hogg, he had 'thoughtlessly engaged in it'.

Again, as in Ireland, he had leaped into a baffling element: not this time the inveterate prejudices of two nations at fever heat, but a small town or province, threatened with industrial ruin by the faults of a grandiose schemer and the shyness of the well-to-do. To set the crooked straight, and make the motives pure and single in situations like these was a hope too close to despair, but the draggled wings were soon away again to occasions in which right and wrong were, as it seemed, in no

---

[1] Verses from the Esdaile Note-book, Dowden, i. 317–18.

[2] Two of these letters survive (Julian Edition, nos. xciii, xciv). They are to one John Evans, of Carnarvon, who had promised and not performed, and are couched in direct and austere terms.

tangle and in no doubt, and good might be done forthwith. Nothing drained his purse more instantly than a case of martyrdom or the destitution of martyrs. In the January of 1813 fourteen Luddites were executed at York; he immediately proffered money for their orphan children. And all his loyalties were in arms when on the 9th of December 1812 the two editors of *The Examiner* were charged before Lord Ellenborough with a libel on the Prince Regent. *The Examiner*, a weekly paper, issued on Sundays, had begun its course in January 1808, and gone since then from strength to strength, battering the Tory government and the public system from the angle of culture, as Cobbett did from the angle of the plain man, and including in its purview religion, manners, and the arts. The sturdy and resolute philanthropist and reformer, John Hunt, was the prime mover of the enterprise, and contributed his practical judgement and managerial ability, and in joint editorship with him his younger brother Leigh bore the chief burden of the writing, with his boyish audacity and gay reasonableness, his extensive reading and fine but uncertain taste, and his easy and animated pen. Youth and independence were the notes of the venture: John Hunt in 1808 being thirty-three, Leigh his junior by nine years, and most of the other collaborators young men; and as in the artistic sphere they owed no service to any man or men, so in politics they were tied to none, though many of their aims were those also of the Radicals or the Whigs. In that period of our history they were doomed to martyrdom. After twice resolving, and dropping the resolve, to prosecute them at law, the Government in February 1811 put the two editors on trial for an article on military flogging, and lost the case. But another opportunity soon came. When early in 1811 the Prince of Wales became Regent, he added to the multitude of his haters his old friends the Whigs, whose company and whose principles he now forsook, and among the Whigs those especially who set most store by Catholic Emancipation. The fall of his stock among the Irishmen was signally demonstrated at the annual Dinner in London on St. Patrick's Day 1812, when the diners hissed his name and shouted down his friend Sheridan, when he rose to defend him. Thereupon, in the Tory journals a flood of retaliatory adulation, and in *The Examiner* of 22 March the swordplay that set the law on foot. What person unacquainted with the true state of the case, the writer asked, would imagine, on reading the Tory eulogies,

> 'that this *Glory of the People* was the subject of millions of shrugs and reproaches! . . . That this *Breather of Eloquence* could not say a few decent extempore words! . . . That this *Conqueror of Hearts* was a disappointer of hopes! That this *Exciter of Desire* . . . this *Adonis in Loveliness* was a corpulent gentleman of fifty! In short, that this . . . *honourable* . . . and *immortal Prince* was a violator of his word, a libertine over head and ears in debt and disgrace, a despiser of domestic ties, the companion of gamblers and demireps, a man who has just closed half a century without one single claim on the gratitude of his country or the respect of posterity!'

At the trial lengthily reported in *The Examiner* on 13 and 20 December, the skill and caution of the lawyers were put to it, for the counsel on the one side could hardly say those words were false, nor on the other pronounce them true. If the Jury could not know an outrageous libel when they saw one, the Attorney General would prefer not to argue with them. Was it right, asked Brougham for the defence, to visit severely what a shy young scholar had written about vices at Court not knowing the sort of places that Courts are? This time, however, the Crown had a strong legal case; the verdict was 'guilty'; and, after a delay of some weeks, on 3 February sentence was delivered. Each of the brothers was to be imprisoned in a separate jail for two years, to pay a fine of £500, and on release to find security of £500 for good behaviour during five years, or remain in prison. Shelley, to whom the Regent was a picture of evil itself,[1] fretted over the reports of the trial at all the indirectness and time-servingness, and the sentence shocked him. He wrote 'boiling' to Thomas Hookham, enclosing £20, and urging him to set a subscription on foot that the martyrs might not 'pine' unaided 'in a dungeon'; and on further thoughts wrote straight to Leigh Hunt with 'a princely offer'. Hunt, remembering a

---

[1] The prince is mordantly satirized in *The Devil's Walk* as an object of the Devil's particular satisfaction:

> Fat as that Prince's maudlin brain,
> Which, addled by some gilded toy,
> Tired, gives his sweetmeat, and again
> Cries for it like a humoured boy—
> For he is fat, &c.

In *Peter Bell the Third* the Devil and the Prince are evidently the same person.

youth who had called on him a few times two years before with
an undisposable poem—a gentlemanly youth with an earnest
gaze, who quoted the Greek dramatists—declined the offer,
whatever it was, but made a note of it. Of 'pining' in the jail in
Horsemonger Lane 'far from all that may make life desired' he
was in no danger: what with his elegant rooms, his flowery
pleasance, his select companies, his *Examiners* or *Story of Rimini*
continually in hand, his family to live and play with, and all out
of earshot of the other prisoners and their clanking chains. But
there is no more admirable chapter in Leigh Hunt's life than
this in which his blithe courage made abundance of his consola-
tions and would suffer no one else to be any the poorer by his
mischance.

Although at this period of his life the scholar, the metaphysi-
cian, and the poet in Shelley had still to draw level with the
friend of man, there was never a time when they were, any of
them, less than restive, or when one part of him gave no aid to
the others. At Tanyrallt, after the colloquies in London, he
laid in equipment for new ventures into the fields of truth. Of
the books ordered from his booksellers in some quantity,[1] one or
two—Monboddo's *Origin of Language,* Horne Tooke's *Diversions
of Purley*—tell of a passing infection by one of Peacock's hobbies;
and Trotter on 'Drunkenness' and 'The Nervous Temperament'
of the physiological bent then prevailing with him. Of the books
of poetry, some, presumably, were new altogether, and others
in the place of old copies: Aeschylus and Euripides (all the
texts in Greek, prose or verse, to be faced, if possible, with
Latin or English translations); Spenser, Shakespeare, Cowley;
Darwin's *Zoonomia* and *Temple of Nature*; and Wordsworth,
Southey, and Coleridge. There is a substantial list in the subject which, as he said, his heart hankered after: Plato, Seneca,
Epicurus, and Marcus Aurelius; Spinoza (the *Tractatus Theo-
logico-Politicus* and the *Opera Posthuma*), Berkeley, and Kant (in a
Latin version). And it is all in the course of his mind at this
period that, with Plato and Spinoza, he should also 'hanker' for
the works of the French Illuminati or their allies; he asks for
the writings of Cabanis, Diderot, Condorcet, and the works of

---

[1] There are two substantial lists, one of orders from the Hookhams on 17 Dec.,
given for the first time in full in the Julian Edition (cxvi), and the other and larger
from Clio Rickman on 24 Dec.

Paine; and thinks of acquiring the *Encyclopaedia*. But most of the orders point to a new line of reading. Godwin had soon perceived the ignorance of History at the root of Shelley's headiness, and in one of his letters to Dublin preached to him that every form of social life had had its value in its time. And in the summer a small skirmish had been fought between them on the Ancients and the Moderns and the essay in *The Enquirer* on classical studies and the Greek and Roman virtues. The Greeks and Romans, Shelley wrote, were 'fit for nothing but the perpetuation of the noxious race of heroes'; their poets and moralists setting honour above goodness.[1] Did classical learning civilize the soul of Johnson? 'Reason sits arbiter between us', he pleaded, considering who he dared to differ from; but gave way at last, with regard both to the Ancients and to his own intellectual need, under the impression of a long letter from Godwin in the middle of December. Accordingly the books on history dominate in his lists: the classic triad of Gibbon, Robertson, and Hume; all the chief historians in Greek and Latin, including Polybius, with more or less important auxiliaries. 'I am determined', he tells Hookham, 'to apply myself to a study which is hateful and disgusting to my very soul, but which is, above all studies, necessary for him who would be listened to as a mender of antiquated abuses, I mean that record of crimes and abuses, History.' Yet on History, otherwise understood, much of his mind and much of his poetry were ultimately to rest.

These were preparations for the years to come; for the present his pen was running fast and his heart inditing. The bitter cold of that winter, sensible enough within the walls of Tanyrallt, fell upon Napoleon's troops in Russia. They had left Moscow on 19 October, and the remnant crossed the Niemen on 13 December, while the younger prophets of Liberty looked on in mingled sorrow and gratulation. In after years Shelley came to think tragically of him

> Whose grasp had left the giant world so weak
> That every pigmy kicked it as it lay;

but his youthful severity stripped the falling despot of any but a 'vulgar ambition' and a 'commonplace talent', and 'excepting Lord Castlereagh, contemned and abhorred no one more

[1] To Godwin, 29 July.

vehemently'.[1] It was the dying of what had been at one time
the Good Cause and the agony of the foundering army that
filled him with 'horror and regret', and what he felt on those
events, and the standing misery in the lanes of Dublin, and the
truth strangled in Courts of Law flowed all together into the
impulse to set down his reading of the world. As usual, he had
by-works on hand, boluses for the public mind: his 'Biblical
Extracts' for the purge of superstition, would the Hookhams
publish them;[2] and his own particular National Anthem,
ordered from the same firm, probably as a broadsheet.[3] And he
was eager to publish at last the Minor Poems, revised and
augmented, no doubt, since the Stockdales let go of them, in a
separate volume, as at first intended, or along with *Queen Mab*,
as afterwards preferred; till here again, it would seem, the publishers fought shy and the script returned to its author, to rest
eventually with the Esdaile family, his only surviving descendants. But it was not enough to 'breathe hatred of government and religion' in minor pieces; he must set his mind
in full array. If the lesser poems represent, as Dowden puts it,
'the history of his imagination from his days at Oxford to the
days at Tremadoc', *Queen Mab* and its Notes, incorporating, in
part no doubt, the content of the long-laboured 'Metaphysical
Essays', are a register and a summary of the same period of his
thought. Indeed, there is reason to suppose that he was as long
in writing it. For he, or others on his authority, several times
asserted that he wrote it 'in early youth', or 'at the age of eighteen',[4] referring, as Dowden well suggests, to the lost poem of

---

[1] To Hogg, 27 Dec. 1812.

[2] Harriet's letter to T. Hookham, 31 Jan. 1813, shows that at that date Shelley
expected some copies in print. So far as is known they were not printed.

[3] To T. Hookham, Julian Edition cciv. Written, no doubt, on the lines of his
*New Version of the National Anthem of 1819*; either lost or never printed.

[4] 'When very young' (to J. Gisborne, 16 June 1821); 'in early youth' (to Charles
Ollier, 11 June 1821); 'at the age of eighteen' (in a letter to the Editor of the
*Examiner* dissociating himself from Clark's reprint, 22 June 1821, and Mrs.
Shelley, Notes, 1839); 'partly written at the early age of eighteen, and printed
before he was twenty-one' (Trelawny, *Records*, i. 82, 83). In presenting a copy to a
Mr. Waller in Nov. 1817, Shelley wrote that 'after six years of added experience'
he was more than ever devoted to its doctrines. 'It was written and printed by
Mr. Shelley when he was only nineteen' (Wetherell's brief in the Chancery suit
*Westbrook v. Shelley*). Medwin (revised *Life*, p. 62) chooses to understand Shelley's
'at the age of eighteen' to mean 1809 and continues: 'Though begun, it [*Queen Mab*]
was not completed till 1812'; which is wrong as to dates, but may be right as to a
beginning and a resuming. The fact that Shelley introduced a passage of *Queen*

his college days, the *Essay on the Existing State of Things*,[1] which must have run, partially at any rate, on similar lines. However that may be, on 18 August 1812 he sent to Thomas Hookham from Lynmouth 'by way of specimen all that I have written of a little poem begun since my arrival in England'—since leaving Ireland, that is—'of which the Past, the Present, and the Future are the grand and comprehensive topics'. Besides the specimen, he had matter, he said, for six more cantos, and in the next mention of the design—on 26 January—expected to finish the whole, consisting of ten cantos, by March. By 7 February he had 'finished the rough sketch', and by the 19th of the same month had used the file so well that the poem was completed (in nine cantos) and transcribed. But in that case the resemblance was so much that he could think of the earlier poem as an earlier draft, and so little that at another time he could date the inception from the spring of 1812. Then, some way on into March 1813, it was dispatched to the Hookhams with a promise to send the 'Notes' after it, and in May the printing had begun.

Intense pursuits and austere sensibilities kept Shelley an entire stranger to the society of the place, except for some happy intercourse with the family of the Solicitor General for the County, the Nanneys of Gwynfryn, seven miles away. Moreover, for all his good deeds, there were always those who looked askance at him, what with his dangerous reputation, and his unpaid bills, and Leeson's tongue. But it was apparently a rougher and an angrier man than Leeson that drove him eventually from the town. Here, however, the historical evidence leads to no certainty, the authorities differ, and it has to be judged or wagered on as much as we know of the case that Shelley was in fact murderously assaulted on the night of the 26th of February 1813.

Our chief informant of the occurrences of that night is Harriet, who in a letter of 11 March described to Thomas Hookham what she saw and heard and what Shelley and his man told her. She does not say, and it does not seem that any of the fighting (if any there was) took place before her eyes. But at each of the two alarms she was quickly upon the spot; and

*Mab* ix (on giant Time) into a letter to Miss Hitchener of 14 Feb. 1812, writing it in the form of prose, argues that he had it before him in verse.

[1] See p. 53.

she writes in unquestionable sincerity. As for Shelley, his letters say little of the subject, for he was too unnerved to endure it. Some late and derivative evidence comes from the lady who seven years afterwards married the Agent Williams, and in 1860, some time after her husband's death, wrote down what she remembered of his talk about Shelley. Peacock passed through Tremadoc in the summer of the year, and informs us in his *Memoirs* of a few particulars gathered in the town. Lastly, in the year 1860 a local sheep-farmer gave information by which it is just possible the whole affair is unriddled.

Supposing a real assailant, and supplementing and at one point correcting Harriet by Mrs. Williams, we can be fairly sure how the matter went. On that day, 26 February, Shelley was somehow aware that mischief was intended him, and had two loaded pistols near at hand when, between the hours of ten and eleven, he went to bed. By good luck Healey (or Hill), having served his sentence at Barnstaple, had arrived at the house a few hours previously. At eleven or so, though the night was stormy and rainy, Shelley heard a noise from 'one of the parlours', and, taking his pistols, descended to this room, otherwise called the billiard-room, and followed retreating footsteps to the office, a small apartment communicating with it and leading out to the shrubbery by a glass door. There a man with a gun or pistol, in the act of departing by the glass door, turned and fired at him, but missed. Shelley took aim with one of his pistols, but it flashed in the pan; whereupon the man knocked him down, but fell with him, and they grappled on the floor. 'Bysshe', continues Harriet, 'then fired his second pistol, which he thought wounded him in the shoulder, as he uttered a shriek and got up, when he said these words: "By God, I will be revenged! I will murder your wife; I will ravish your sister! By God, I will be revenged!" He then fled.'

By this time the rest of the household were hurrying downstairs, where they gathered in the 'parlour' (i.e. billiard-room), a room looking on to the lawn and a great beech-tree. There they sat up together for two hours, until Shelley told the women to retire, and leave the watch to Daniel and himself. Three hours later, that is at four in the morning, Harriet heard another shot. 'I immediately ran downstairs', she writes, 'when I perceived that Bysshe's flannel gown had been shot through, and the window curtain. Bysshe had sent Daniel to see what hour it was, when he heard a noise at the window. He went there, in that direction, and a man thrust his arm through an open panel of the glass,[1] and fired at him. Thank Heaven! the ball went through his gown, and he remained unhurt. Mr. S. happened to stand sideways; had he stood fronting, the ball must have killed him.' 'The ball of the assassin's pistols (he fired at me twice)', writes Shelley, 'penetrated my nightgown and pierced the wainscot.'[2] Thereupon, while the assailant followed his shot into the room, Shelley fired, missed, shattering a part of the window,[3] then attacked him with an old sword belonging to the house. 'The assassin attempted to get the sword from him, and just as he was pulling it away Dan rushed into the room, when he made his escape.' It is here that an incident took place of which the account by Mrs. Williams may not be in every particular true. Shelley was by now excited to the visionary pitch. He 'bounced out upon the lawn', says Mrs. Williams, 'and saw or thought he saw the face of his enemy against the beech tree, so hideous that he took it for that of a ghost or devil'. A few hours after, in conversation with Williams, he drew its outline on a firescreen and then, in his horror, tried to burn it. The screen was afterwards lost; but a supposed copy of the fantastic vision, as Shelley limned it there, survives.[4]

All Tremadoc put down the story, with Williams, as a fancy, or, with Leeson, as a lie, by means of which the liar might run from his debts. Jeaffreson is sure it was a lie; Hogg and Peacock, not doubting their friend's honesty, remember his proneness to waking nightmares and obstinate illusions. What Hogg describes as 'a very careful investigation' by local persons was thought to prove that the bullet through the wainscot had been

[1] A window must have been easy to open from outside. By it the invader came in and went out.

[2] To Hookham, 6 Mar. In declaring that the assassin fired twice Shelley means, presumably, once in the office, and a second time in the parlour.

[3] Harriet says that Shelley's pistol again failed to go off; but Mrs. Williams's assertion that it did go off and that the bullet shattered the window is supported by Shelley's undated letter to Williams, evidently from Gwynfryn: 'Mr. Nanney requests that you will order that some boards should be nailed against the broken window of Tanyrallt.'

[4] The screen was in Mrs. Williams's possession, and then in Lady Shelley's, at whose house Garnett once saw it. The copy was taken by a Miss Fanny Holland and came into Garnett's hands.

fired towards the window and not from it. (But however this fact may be explained, if we are to take it on trust,[1] it will not dispose of the bullet-holes in Shelley's gown, attested by Harriet, and the struggle with the sword, attested, as it will have been, by Daniel.) Other biographers or memoirists, unable to resist Harriet's testimony, disperse in all directions after the malefactor: he was, as the Shelleys themselves assumed, Leeson, or an agent of his; he was Daniel Hill, with scores to pay off, nipping into the garden; he was a jail-bird from Barnstaple, whom Hill had put up to it; he was Hitchener, indignant at his daughter's wrongs and the retardation of her stipend. Until yesterday it was thought we had at last unearthed the secret. In an article entitled 'A Strange Adventure of Shelley's' in *The Century Magazine* for October 1905, Miss Margaret L. Croft recorded a statement by a Miss Greaves, who in the middle of the last century lived at Tanyrallt. She informed her that Robin Pant Evan or Ifan, a rough, ugly, quarrelsome fellow, used to tell the members of her family that he was at the time of the incident the tenant of the pasturage and farmstead on the summit of the steep rock at the back of Tanyrallt. On one occasion in the year 1862 he professed that it was he and some neighbours who had made the attack on Shelley. He said that Shelley used to climb to his pasture by the Roman steps in the face of the rock, and (with his pistols presumably) 'more than once put an end to the life of a sheep affected by the scab or some other disease'. Whether these acts of mercy were made good to him Robin did not say; but in any case he and two other shepherds agreed together to give the meddler such a fright as would immediately expel him. He described how he fired a shot into the office, 'not meaning to murder anyone', how Shelley fired or missed fire, how they wrestled, and he (Robin) escaped. He acted his 'bursting out of the bush, to frighten Mr. Shelley'. Miss Greaves's sister to whom he gave his story remembered 'Old Robin' in his excited narration 'jumping about and brandishing a great hooked stick', and felt no doubt that in the wild event he might well have passed for the very Devil. But Shelley's latest biographer has now produced the evidence of a death certificate that in 1813 this Robin Pant Evan was an

---

[1] Peacock did not himself examine the room. Had he done so he would have said he had.

infant of the age of three.[1] Yet even so, he may have gloried in an action borrowed from someone else. The shooting of the sheep is not an incident easily invented. If Harriet's evidence can be trusted, the assailant knew about Shelley and about his family and came to avenge some real or fancied wrong. And Peacock tells us that the ground about the tree was found on the next morning to be much trampled, as by several accomplices.[2] Moreover, if Robin's story, with another actor in his part, has something to recommend it in the evidence and in itself, it would give us also, if it were so far true, the cause of the effect. For, by all that is natural, only an actuality would have impressed the sufferers as that night's terror did. Harriet has written for herself. Eliza Westbrook to the end of her days spoke of the outrage as 'a frightful fact'. Shelley was not transiently convinced. In after years he put down his internal malady to the furious grapple in Tanyrallt and would sometimes fancy that the ruffian was after him.

On the next few days he was altogether unnerved. There was now no thought but of flight; and late on the 27th Shelley and his household took refuge with the Nanneys at Gwynfryn. In great need of money and in fear of his creditors in the town, he had one resource: John Lawless was his debtor. And so, with the aid of £20, which he had sent to Hookham for Leigh Hunt, and Hookham sent back to him in the nick of time, he made by Bangor and Holyhead for Dublin, and on the 9th of March arrived with his company at his friend's in Cuffe Street, again a fugitive and a beggar.[3]

## 7. IRELAND AGAIN: 9 MARCH–2 APRIL 1813

Of Shelley's second visit to Ireland little is known, and it lasted for less than a month. He arrived in Dublin recovered from the excitement at Tanyrallt, but 'so poor', as he wrote to Williams, 'that, unless we find some friend, I know not what we

[1] See White, i. 650, notes. He avers that the man's real surname was Williams, that he was the son of the postmaster of Tremadoc and called Pant Evan or 'Ifan' after the name of his farm. This farm he inherited in 1832 from his maternal grandfather. According to his death certificate he died in 1878, aged 68.

[2] It is not necessary to suppose with Jeaffreson that Shelley wanted this beaten ground to support his lie and rolled himself around the tree accordingly.

[3] He left the Great Embankment to Williams to care for, eventually with complete success.

shall do'. Lawless, who a little later went to a debtor's prison, was in no case to help him, and in his dealings with him even fell short, actually or seemingly, of his reputation for honesty.[1] But in some way or other means were found for living and even for travelling. Harassed as he had been, Dublin was not the place, nor perhaps the exuberant Lawless the man for him, and in something like a fortnight he and his household were lodging in a cottage on an island at Killarney, with a pile of books to help him for the Notes to *Queen Mab*. The beauty of the place deeply impressed him; years afterwards the memory of the lake and the arbutus islands threw even Como into the shade; and hereafter a lakeside cottage under the shelter of trees was one of the pictures of his dreams.[2] But boating in the treacherous winds was perilous; the cottage was uncomfortable; and in another ten days or so, on news received from Dublin, he had once more flitted. Hogg was in the city, urgently invited to join him there, but uninformed of his going away. The sardonic man had journeyed all the way through a series of keenly appreciated discomforts, and now kicked his heels where nothing found favour with him, except for Lawless's affability, and what he heard on all hands in praise of Shelley, and what the women said of Shelley's locks of dark brown hair and 'intellectual and inspired countenance'. After a week or more of this loitering he left for home, and twenty-four hours later, on 31 March, Shelley and Harriet came in by the mail from Cork, having left Eliza at Killarney with Daniel Hill and the books, and travelled night and day. After delaying two days more in order to raise money, they took the boat on the 2nd of April and were in London on the 5th.

This has been a long chapter with a broken surface, but a single trend. With the first Irish episode it covers a distinct period, in which Shelley tries his hand at action, and at the same time fills up his first idea of what is wrong with men and what is right for them. It ends with *Queen Mab*, the digest and the garner of his early speculations. By the end of the period he has taken his bitter experience to heart: action is not to be his sphere, and he will avoid it hereafter as the burnt child shuns the

[1] See Letters from Harriet to Catherine Nugent.
[2] *Rosalind and Helen*, 1245 f.; *Revolt of Islam*, IV. ii, iii.

fire. The more eager is he to launch his political poetry, didactic and apocalyptic. He was to grow out of the intellectualism
of this period. But that change was to follow on profound and
passionate experience long drawn out, in which 'the genius and
the mortal instruments were in council' and the whole man
'suffered the nature of an insurrection'. That ordeal was by
now near at hand. While he was absorbed in his political or
philanthropical enterprises, the excitement of his activities all
but sufficed him, and he asked of the comrade at his side nothing
more than she could give. But when in the field of men's
affairs he ran against the mystery of evil, and came away sadder
and wiser, with time upon his hands, he was thrown for inspiration on his own means, and the means nearest at hand, and just
where they should have abounded, found them poor. Gradually
he discovered the ordinariness of his element, and that, spiritually
and intellectually, he did all the carrying in the house. And
at the same time the two women began to weary of high
flights, and to think of their new gentility and an appropriate
style of living. By the spring of 1813 Shelley knew only that he
could not bear Eliza Westbrook. He had left her at Killarney,
and when he saw Hogg in London, 'exulted with a malicious
pleasure that he had fairly planted her at last . . . '. (But the
Ineluctable was quickly on the scene again.) On the other
hand, between Bysshe and Harriet there was as yet no trouble,
nor thought of any. She was now advanced in pregnancy, and
consequently, after coming to London, Shelley tried again to
conciliate his father and get his affairs into better trim, the
Duke of Norfolk again intervening, and the mother and sisters
at Field Place lending their eager aid. A letter is extant[1] in
which Timothy answers his New Year wishes in terms so con-
ciliatory that the reader is once more sensible of bungling on
either side. 'I am willing', Bysshe wrote to the Duke, 'to con-
cede anything that does not involve a compromise of that self-
esteem without which life would be a burthen and a disgrace.'
But again the father hardened his heart and repeated his old
demands. 'I cannot prevail upon myself', Bysshe had written
some weeks previously, 'to care much about it [i.e. conciliation]:
Harriet is very happy as we are, and I am very happy. I
question if intimacy with our relations would add at all to our

[1] Julian Shelley, ix. 39, note.

tranquillity. . . .' That may have been Harriet's view as well, but perhaps the idea of Field Place had more charm for her than he thought. Fanny Godwin watched her in London, and described her to Shelley as 'a fine lady', which annoyed him. 'The ease and simplicity of her habits', he writes, 'the unassuming plainness of her address, the uncalculated connection of her thought and speech have ever formed in my eyes her greatest charms; and none of these are compatible with fashionable life or the attempted assumption of its vulgar and noisy *éclat*.' Yet Fanny had the sharper eyes, aided by the still and steady affection she bore him. And, as in the acutest tragedies, he trod care-free on the edge of a disaster for which he had only himself to blame.

# IX

# MINOR POEMS AND *QUEEN MAB*

## 1. MINOR POEMS

THE Minor Poems of this period are contained for the most part in the Esdaile Note-book. Among the pieces in that manuscript Hogg published five, and Rossetti four of the earlier and inferior, and Bertram Dobell one of much finer workmanship, *The Soliloquy of the Wandering Jew*. Of the other maturer pieces Dowden printed in his biography some fragments and a few sonnets, the lines 'on leaving London for Wales', and the two longer addresses to Harriet, one from Cwm Elan (*The Retrospect*) and the other probably from Lynmouth. We must judge the remainder of the collection by Dowden's account of it.[1] He divides it into classes: impressions of natural sights or scenes, some of them moralized; the poems to Harriet; and poems on the state of society, its enemies, saviours, martyrs (such as Robert Emmet), its evils past or present, and the good to come. *The Retrospect of Times of Old* is a disquisition in rhymed verse, 'having much in common with the earlier part of *Queen Mab*'; but in a few instances the poet tries his awkward wings in the element of fiction, on the model of Wordsworth's stories of poor men and women under the iniquity of their conditions. In *Henry and Louisa* the hero follows the army to Egypt in the mad pursuit of glory, and his mistress, following him to the field, makes away with her own life over his dead body. The fragment *A Tale of Society as it is: from Facts, 1811*, touches the cruelties of the press-gang, military service, and the workhouse. A yet more poignant feature of 'society as it is' had thrown Shelley at Oxford into a 'three weeks' entrancement', during which he poured out a number of poems 'To Mary' or 'To the Lover of Mary', four of them contained in the Note-book. Mary, who was personally known to Hogg, had loved and lost, and in losing had suffered some piteous wrong of which there is no account; but it may be that the calamity narrated in the stanzaic poem of *Zeinab and Kathema* is in one point similar to hers. Zeinab is 'a maiden of Cashmire, borne away from her native home by Christian guile and rapine'. Kathema, her betrothed, follows

---

[1] i. 345–9.

her to England; after long search finds her body hanging in chains from a gibbet on a heath; scales the gibbet, and hangs himself at her side. She had been ruined, flung upon the streets, goaded into crime, and destroyed by senseless law. Another kind of art is attempted in *The Voyage*, a fragment in irregular unrhymed verse, some three hundred lines long; it describes 'a company of voyagers with their various passions and imaginings': ardent youth, mean and crafty age, and again the victim of the press-gang in the person of an unhappy sailor. Not much has been lost by the inaccessibility of these poems; but they prove that Shelley, as time goes on, is writing better verse, and his imagination not succumbing to its intellectual load. And, as Dowden has reported, much of it is imitative, and smacks of its examples in Wordsworth, in Campbell, and in Scott.

## 2. *QUEEN MAB*: SOURCES

But, intent as he was on a theory of the course of things, he chose for his larger unburdening a mode of didactic poetry nameable as the Vision, of which the classic instance is the discourse of Michael with Adam, in *Paradise Lost*. More immediately, he looked to a document of the faith of the Revolution that had gone into many languages since its appearance in 1791, the principal work of the traveller and *savant* Constantin Volney: *Les Ruines*. Here, in an invocation to ruins and waste places, Volney declares that these have been from the beginning the announcers of men's future equality, the teachers of the secrets of life; and relates how one evening, when meditating sadly among the ruins of Palmyra on the blind Fate that swept the kingdoms to their fall, he was aware of a Phantom or Spirit that demanded of him why man should weary Heaven with complaining of his history when the reasonable laws that shape it are ever in his sight. Did not those ruins tell of the changeless laws that God appointed to the world? The Traveller beseeches the Spirit to interpret to him the scroll of Time, and at a touch of its hand his soul is carried out of the body to a station whence this earth looks no bigger than the moon as we see it, though his sharpened eyes can still discern the rivers, mountains, and towns. The Genius then discourses on truth: on the universal harmony, on the powers and passions of man, and the pain that warns him of evil, and the pleasure that sweetens his good.

These sure and simple monitors, pleasure and pain, led him on in the infancy of the race to society and to civilization, till greed and power and ignorance brought in the misery that now prevails—wars and tyrannies and, last and worst, religions; for, as there were none but tyrants on earth, so man expected none but such in heaven. At this point the signs of a war appear on earth below, a war between Turk and Russian, Crescent and Cross. The Traveller is distressed: 'I see', he cries, 'the world divided between twenty religions. What man or nation can help us in this confusion, the source of so much woe?' In reply, the Genius tells him what the coming century has in store: a nation downing its tyrants, a national inquiry into the grounds of conduct, a great assize where the priests defend their creeds, and after much debate a manifesto by the sages of the land. All religions, these sages aver, are a vain endeavour to know the unknowable, whereas only learning of the ways of Nature will guide the individual and conserve the state.[1] One more plank from the flotsam of his vast reading, and Shelley has the frame of his argument. He would, like Volney, display the fortunes of mankind; but his discoursing Spirit should be not only a prophet of the coming age, but a power towards it, a Guardian or 'Daemon of the World', as he later renamed her, a little lower than divinity or much the same thing.[2] 'Time dare not give reality to that whose being I annul.'[3] She is to see man's future in his conscience,[4] and to work upon him to blend his fancies with intuitions of truth.[5] And her auditor is not man, but deep-conceiving woman with the ken of the lover and the saint. These requirements called up a memory of the Indian story of *The Palace of Fortune* which Sir William Jones had done into English in heroic verse.[6] In this story young

---

[1] See the article in *Englische Studien*, xxii. 9–40, by L. Kellner: 'Shelley's *Queen Mab* und Volney's *Les Ruines*.'

[2] The word 'Daemon' is a Platonic word, and stands for an order of beings immortal and divine, but dwelling on Earth and engaging in the affairs of man. In the *Symposium* Love is one of them. They play a great part in Shelley's poetry, these intermediary powers.

[3] i. 167–85.          [4] vii. 49–63.          [5] viii. 46–8.

[6] See the article by E. Koeppel in *Englische Studien*, xxviii. 43–53. Sir William Jones's *Poems, consisting chiefly of Translations from the Asiatick Languages*, appeared in 1772, and were reprinted in 1777 and 1800, and again in the tenth volume of the *Works* in 1807. In 1810 they were included in Chalmers's *English Poets*, vol. xviii. The *Works* were among the books that Shelley ordered at Tanyrallt.

Maia, roving in the spring in the musky shades of Tibet, complains that no admirers approach her in her solitude and no hope of one day living in a splendid style. At a flash of light the clouds divide, and a queen or goddess rides towards her on a golden chariot drawn through the air by a team of peacocks. She lifts Maia, overcome with sleep, into the chariot; the peacocks ply their wings; and the car and its load are carried to a wonderland in the sky, a gorgeous garden and a lustrous palace, in the hall of which the queen ascends her throne. She announces herself to Maia, now awakened, as Fortuna, the mistress of the rolling earth, which is dimly visible in the great distance with all its seas and hills; hers it is to 'rule the thoughts of men', to hear their prayers, and 'some to grant, and some to waste in air'. She has called Maia, who is a favourite of hers, to school her to moderate wishes and a governed will, and this she does in a way that the reader may discover in the poem if he will. The queen is a queen of 'fairies', with a train of fairies to attend her and a wand to conjure with. Shelley has given her, or her counterpart in his poem, another and higher function, and her English name.

### 3. *QUEEN MAB*: THE ARGUMENT

*Queen Mab*, no less than *Les Ruines*, is a prophecy of things to come in the light of a new religion. After the preamble, where the spirit of Ianthe, the maiden of peerless beauty and stainless soul, is rapt from the body as it lies sleeping in her lover's gaze, and is wafted in the Fairy's car to a skyey palace, whence all the firmament is on view, and all the actions of men on earth, the poem begins with Palmyra, the Pyramids, the Temple at Salem, Greece, Rome, and the forgotten cities of Mexico and Peru, each of them speaking of the life that is by virtue and the death by pampered vice. So wills the Spirit of Nature that animates all things to the smallest, and builds and wastes for ever (i, ii). Then—in a larger survey than Volney's, to make room for elements from Godwin and others—the poem goes on to the grand calamities, one by one. First the King, with his callous luxury and lacerating conscience, with his train of guards and courtiers: Nature deals with them as she deals with men alone of her creatures, she casts them out from peace. Yet in men also, unconscious of it though they be, the Spirit of Nature lives and moves unto the day when the frame of things shall own no flaw (iii). Then come War and the soldier, pressed or hired. But neither is this an eternal malady. It came not of human nature but of kings, priests, and ministers of state; and will not stand before that Power that fills the worm with spirit, thought, and love. For, though the bane of human kind is fast upon it even before birth, yet Soul, good and pure in itself, but tainted by body, will one day defeat that infection, and the man that shall be immeasurably surpass the man that is (iv). Next in the train of Evil are Commerce, Riches and Poverty, Power and Fame. These are the upas-shade over virtue and genius; they are the tyrant's lures, the drugs of the vulgar or the easy mind; so that love, conscience, life itself are bought and sold. There is that in the make of things, however, that wars upon them all, that visits the virtuous with pleasure, and the selfish with pain, and brings hither the new and blessed age (v). But who or what can set the change in motion? 'Men eminent in virtue will start up', and with their words slay Falsehood, the ally of Lust, and first of falsehoods, root of men's ills, taint of all their thoughts, from its rude infancy to the frenzies of its age—Religion. Already it is dying in contempt. How different from the God of the Christian Inquisition is that omnipresent unfading Life, that Necessity, that operates in health and disease, in happiness and in woe, that moves, guides, foresees each atom on its course, each flicker of light, each passion and purpose. For it is no heeder of praise and prayer, no lover, or hater, or favourer. It is unaffected by the joy or pain that thrill its passive instruments. Its temple is the whole wide world. There is no God—no Creator of the world; infinity without and infinity within deny Him. And here once more in Shelley Ahasuerus treads the stage, accusing Christ himself of the vengeful spirit that had its long day in the history of his Church (vi, vii). Lastly, the fruits of Necessity: the new age, the new line of the earth's axis and the bland and fruitful clime from the Sahara to the poles, the love of all creatures, man or animal, to each other, the surcease of poison in the herb and hatred in the heart, and the unison of Reason and Passion. O glorious prize of blindly working Will, when even Time shall be vanquished by intensest sensation, when nought shall mar the beauty of Youth or Age, nor 'dull and selfish chastity' hold up the course

of love. Then palace, fane, and prison shall moulder by the
way, and death itself, now terrorless, lead the passing soul to
'happy regions of eternal hope'. This, then, was the *viaticum*
for Ianthe to take with her, favoured mortal, worthy of the
boon, whose re-embodied soul will awake to the light of Henry's
eyes (viii, ix).

## 4. *QUEEN MAB*: THE EDITIONS

That being its tenor, Shelley's philosophical poem was in its
day by far the most marketable of his works. For eight years
it lay obscure in the private edition of the summer of 1813—
'Printed for P. B. Shelley, 23 Chapel Street, Grosvenor Square'
—for of the 250 copies only 70 had been distributed by the end
of that time.[1] But in 1821 William Clark, a London bookseller,
much annoyed the poet and heavily armed his enemies by
pirating the poem and the Notes in the first public issue; for
which, notwithstanding its timorous omissions, he was promptly
brought to trial by the Society for the Suppression of Vice, and
escaped imprisonment only by surrendering the stock in hand.
In the same year the work was published in New York (if the
imprint was not a fake), and thereafter, down to 1852, twelve
editions, including two more American, followed besides the
reprint in Mary Shelley's collection of the poems in four volumes
in 1839 and in one in 1840. The little book was anathema
indeed to the more static elements in the religious and the
political worlds, but dear to the 'advanced', whose reason or
sentiment it had gathered in and tipped with the fire of youth.
As early as 1815 the *Theological Enquirer*, a journal 'open to all
parties', contained in an epistolary form, in four of the eight
numbers to which it ran, a laudatory review and large citations
(Shelley himself being almost certainly in collusion) and con-

---

[1] In the *Republican* for 17 Dec. 1822, Richard Carlile announced that he had
purchased the remaining 180, and offered them for sale 'to those friends of Mr.
Shelley, or others, who may prize an original copy'. I draw for this paragraph
mainly on the fascinating section in Buxton Forman's *Shelley Library*, pp. 35–58.
See further: Mrs. Julian Marshall, *Life and Letters of M. W. Shelley*, ii. 289; *Letters
of Edward John Trelawny*, ed. Buxton Forman, pp. 209–10, 263–4; *Edward Moxon,
Publisher of Poets*, by Harold G. Merriam, Columbia University Press, 1939, pp.
101–3, 115, 117; *Speech for the Defence in the Prosecution of the Queen v. Moxon*, by
T. N. Talfourd, 1841, and *Reports of State Trials*, New Series, ed. Wallis, 1892,
pp. 694 ff.; and the whole section on *Queen Mab* in Professor White's *The
Unextinguished Hearth*, pp. 45–104.

cluded with an Ode to the poet.[1] It was almost a sacred book to the followers of Robert Owen, who counted Shelley among their Saints, so that one of them, Medwin tells us, found in the Shiloh of the Bible a dark hint of his coming. John Brooks, their publisher, who twice reprinted it, long suppressed the copy in which the author had remoulded and reprinted the first two cantos into *The Daemon of the World*, for not the hand that wrote it might be suffered to tamper with it.[2] Richard Carlile, again, the bravest of the brave who waged the war for a really free press, loved the book, without endorsing all that it pronounced, and after vainly urging Shelley to let him reprint it in 1819, sent it forth for a challenge and a stimulus in four editions from 1822 to 1832, as from his own business or from his wife's.[3] It was he who in 1826 lowered its price to half a

[1] See White's note, op. cit., pp. 45–6. He supposes the contributor and author of the Ode, signing 'F', to be one of the three Fergusons then prominent in public life, and favours General Sir Ronald Crawford Ferguson, a Member of Parliament, and a constant champion of civil and religious liberty, to whom Shelley presented a copy of his *Proposal for putting Reform to the Vote*. The Ode is reproduced by the Editor of the 'first American edition' of 1821 (perhaps not American at all, but made in England with a false imprint after the suppression of Clark's) and is there signed R. C. F.; while a prose extract from the review in the *Enquirer* appears in the Preface. The Editor of this first American *Queen Mab* (if American it was), who signs himself 'A Pantheist', says that he obtained a copy of the private edition from Shelley himself while on a visit to England in 1815. The inference is that F. and R. C. F. and 'A Pantheist' may be identical. F. declares, suspiciously, that the celebrated Kotzebue, whom he visited in Berlin in the summer of 1814, had given him a copy, speaking of the poem with great admiration, and supposing it too bold to be read in England. It was on sale in Berlin, however, and F. had purchased six copies.

[2] Medwin, revised *Life*, pp. 98–100. He once saw the book on sale at a table in the ante-room of the Owenite Chapel in Charlotte Street, and on the same occasion set Owen himself talking of it, and especially of the part about matrimony, with high praise. Brooks reprinted several other works by Shelley, including *The Revolt of Islam*. Shelley used two copies for the revision of *Queen Mab*, the corrections being nearly the same in each. The first copy, in which he revised the first two cantos, is in the Ashley Library in the British Museum (*Catalogue*, vol. v, p. 58); the other, with the revision of the last two cantos as well, came into the hands of Buxton Forman who, in his edition of the collected poems in 1876, printed 'Part II', the revised text of the two last cantos, as a complement to that of the first two, which Shelley included in the *Alastor* volume of 1815 as *The Daemon of the World*. Subsequent editors have made use of this acquisition, and printed 'Part II'.

[3] He says in the *Republican* for 1 Feb. 1822 that in 1819 he had made an effort to obtain Shelley's consent to its publication in *The Temple of Reason* without 'coinciding' with some of the Author's 'metaphysical opinions' or with his opinions on marriage, and he had printed the entire text so as to 'give no encouragement to the hypocrites and villains who would stifle all discussion' (quoted in *The Unextinguished Hearth*, pp. 95–7). 'Carlile, like Bunyan, was a tinker. He came to London when a young man, and followed his trade for several years. He had not

crown, and made it a messenger to poor men under the harrow of 'The Bleak Age'; for the price continued low, and there must be many a copy like that discovered by Forman of an undated issue, 'extremely dirty' and evidently 'used by some person or persons whose way of life did not admit of much nicety'. Not all the editors were undaunted by the widespread reprobation that in 1817 by the mouth of the Lord Chancellor deprived the author of *Queen Mab* of the custody of his children, and in 1821 broke in fury on his head. Clark, in a certain number of his copies, had cut out aggressive words or verses, and in 1830 an edition appeared 'free from all the objectionable passages', amounting to the Notes and 800 lines of the poem. Even Mary Shelley in her first edition in 1839 stooped reluctantly to that expedient, excising much of the Notes, much of canto six, and all of canto seven, and so offending many of her readers and Trelawny exceedingly. But Edward Moxon, her publisher, had warned her, it would seem,[1] that 'certain passages would injure the copyright of all the four volumes', and not groundlessly, for when in the new edition of 1840 the omitted matter had been restored, he found himself on 23 June 1841 in the Court of Queen's Bench under the charge that, 'being an evil-disposed and wicked person', he had 'uttered a libel of the

Bunyan's genius, but he had his courage, and braved imprisonment and endured it with as much heroism. In days when gentlemen were transported for having in their possession Paine's *Age of Reason,* Carlile published editions of his works. He was imprisoned himself altogether nine years and three months—his wife was imprisoned also—more than one hundred and fifty of his shopmen were at various times imprisoned. He wrote heretical books, delivered lectures, and by his pen, his speech, and in his person maintained the conflict until he established a free press . . .' (George Jacob Holyoake, *Sixty Years of an Agitator's Life,* i. 189–90).

[1] There is an insoluble contradiction between Mary Shelley's assertions in her Journal and in a letter to Leigh Hunt of 12 Dec. 1838 (printed by Ingpen in the Julian Edition of the Letters) that she resisted Moxon's appeal for omissions, the omission of canto six in particular, and 'wished she had resisted to the last', and assertions by Trelawny. In a letter to the *Athenaeum* of 3 Aug. 1878, Trelawny stated that, breakfasting one day at Sir William Molesworth's at Pencarron together with Charles Buller and others, he talked of Mrs. Shelley's suppressions in *Queen Mab*; which being condemned by the whole company, a letter of protest over his signature and Molesworth's was sent to the publisher. Soon afterwards he met Moxon in a London street, who said: 'Mr. Trelawny, you have done me great injustice and given me great pain. I did not edit Shelley's works; I had no control; I am merely the publisher. Pressure has been put upon me, but at whatever cost I am determined to have a complete edition of that true poet's works.' Trelawny then suggests that Moxon showed Mary the letter of protest, and that that induced her to restore the text in 1840.

Christian religion, the Holy Scriptures, and Almighty God'. But the issue was in Shelley's favour. Indeed, the charge was really a sham; for the prosecutor, so far from being an enemy, was the Owenite Henry Hetherington, proprietor of the unstamped *Poor Man's Guardian* and hero of the long war for the cheap newspaper, who, while a suit was pending against him for aspersions on the Old Testament in a publication of his— *Haslam's Letters to the Clergy*—took this way of trying whether there were one law of blasphemy for the small bookseller and another for the great. Moreover, there was a new temper even in the Courts. The judge, Lord Denman, while definitely adverse, thought that influences like those of the poem were better combated by reason; and the defendant, pronounced guilty, was not called up for judgement. The prosecuting counsel eulogized the genius of Shelley and deprecated that kind of trial; and Talfourd for the defence delivered an eloquent lecture on the 'atheism' as a passing phase and much misnamed, and on 'chaotic thought not yet subsided into harmony' in 'this perturbed, imperfect, but glorious being'.

This sustained influence was due in a degree only to the art of the poem. It was characteristic of Shelley to change the heroic couplet of Jones's story to blank verse in the disquisition and the free measure of *Thalaba* in the description, for elasticity and for pliancy; but the special music of his maturer writing is to seek. He has already a sufficient and a plenteous language, clear and fluent, instinctively well-chosen, and elevated at need: but not yet the perfect mirror of his spiritual subtlety. The appeal of the poem comes from what is true and impressive in its argument, from its knightly championship, from the tone of the 'glad confident morning' in which it was written. 'Villainous trash', he called it, writing in 1821, and much of it is heady enough. But in 1817 he had thought otherwise, and more justly. 'It was a sincere overflowing of the heart and mind', he wrote, 'and that at a period when they are uncorrupted and pure'; adding that its doctrines only gained upon him, as time went on, by their 'beauty and grandeur'.

## 5. A METAPHYSICAL POET

Shelley was a keen and a constant reasoner, but intuition or, as he sometimes called it, feeling was his greater light. He would assail with mettlesome logic propositions that had no hold on either his understanding or his heart; but the heart, in a conflict between them, would drive the discursive reason from the field, or keep it at any rate at bay. And more and more he discounted it and the writers who excelled in it, and in whom he had himself at times rejoiced. Walking on the terrace at Gibbon's home in Lausanne in the summer of 1816, he would pluck no leaves from the old acacia, as in pious memory Byron did, 'fearing', he says, 'to outrage the greater and more sacred name of Rousseau', and declining homage to 'a cold and unimpassioned spirit'. But in the letters of 1811 this temper is already pronounced, and the two powers at odds with each other, as they were in a measure to the end. 'Analytical reasoning', he says, 'induces gloom', and leaves a man 'pursuing virtue without the weakest stimulus'. 'This is the tree of which it is dangerous to eat, but which I have fed upon to satiety.' 'Reason can never either account for or prove the truth of feeling. . . . Reason tells me that death is the boundary of the life of man; yet I feel, I believe the direct contrary. There is an inward sense that has persuaded me of this. Those who *really feel* the being of a God have the best right to believe it. They may indeed pity those who do not; they may pity me: but until I feel it, I must be content with the substitute, Reason.' Mary Shelley tells us that her husband at times wondered if he had not been meant for a philosopher instead of a poet. He need never have done so. His philosophy ministered to his longings, twining and conforming with them, but he never achieves nor even desiderates a formal consistency. Accordingly, the metaphysical speculations are in intimate touch with the poetry; they go before and come after it; they are its fruit and its food. It behoves us, therefore, taking the letters of 1811 and 1812 and the verse and prose of *Queen Mab* as the outcrop of one intellectual period, to follow him in his exploration and make out the tangle or conflict, for nothing less it is, of ideas thrown out and thrown together in his divinations and desires.

# X
## SHELLEY AND GODWIN
### 1. An Inchoate Metaphysic

SHELLEY is supposed to address Godwin in verses about a tempest-scorning eagle, and in exalted terms he always thought of him, or rather of his mind. He saw in him, much as Lucretius did in his chosen Master, one of the saviours of the race, who, as Wordsworth phrased it, had 'set the hopes of man for ever in a clearer element'. In *Political Justice*, as he believed, the great turn in the human story begun in France was established in argument and bound, as it were, on the time to come. For, as *The Prelude* has it again, the marvellous expectations were, or seemed to be, logically made fast in 'a clear synthesis built up aloft', where every prophecy was a sure and certain inference and Reason a 'prime enchantress'—Reason, from the ground of a serene faith in human nature and the tendency of things, and in face of sombre realities fairly confronted. For the book is full of a sedate but extensive pity. A battle-field, a massacre, a prison gang, the toiler in his famished home, the more garish fruits of society as it is, are not oftener in the writer's vision than languor, vice, disease, and stunted joy and power. Wherever civilized man lived, as Godwin saw him, he withered, and death was 'the slightest of his evils'. There is a point at which, considering the rule of prey in Nature and of suffering in all life, and the degradation and disablement inscribed on the faces of men, he can ask whether 'Improvement or Vicissitude' is the law of the world.[1] But he is sure after all of the answer: sure that Nature, by means of influences from the enlightened few (who are always the fountains of our good), sooner or later, slowly to begin with, but then, perhaps, 'with inconceivable rapidity', will pour salvation upon all men,[2] and that the human mind,

---

[1] IV. xi. I use the third edition (1798). Shelley preferred the first, but he must, then, have known one or both of the others, and most likely both.

[2] Godwin is consistently cautious as to the pace of the coming age. It is the tendency of the intellect to go forward and of truth to spread, and mind, once awakened, will not go back (I. vi). Moreover, the present age is 'an age of innovation'. There will be a 'stage of slowness' and 'stages of folly and mistake', and then, very likely, a spate of renovation (VIII. vi). But he says too that it will take a long time and 'the slow incessant pressure of reason' to overcome 'the present puerility of the human mind' (VIII. iv).

O

which has hitherto lain passive to the imprint of bad institutions, of bad opinions and accordant ways of life, will presently seize the initiative, and cast its fetters from it.

This saving movement will not begin, it seems, in the good people. They will have it from Nature, and Nature, as at times he seems to consider, has a mind. In many of the 'illuminated' minds of that epoch the lifted horizons, the new faith in a law of progress were the fruit of a metaphysic, or of what is the same thing, the endeavour to avoid one. Even in Holbach the great word Nature continually suggests much more than the sum of things and their operations or the rule of fitness and soundness in them; it would seem to cover an inexplicit surmise or suppressed inference of a universal will, blind but mainly good. Godwin has made more progress to a theology. He had been a clergyman and a strain of religious feeling emerges at times in his theory, as when he says that intercourse with 'the author of nature' lifts us over temptations and fills us with 'sacred confidence'. But in another vein of thinking he seems to contemplate a principle that does not stand to us as one individual to others, but moves in all our selves, thinks in our thoughts, and determines therefore what we do. 'Man', he writes, 'is in no case, strictly speaking, the beginning of any event or series of events that takes place in the universe, but only the vehicle through which certain antecedents operate.' This universal power—if that is what he means—acts in a way that reason approves, or in a way in which reason recognizes itself, though an inimical or obstructive element in the forces at play impedes and troubles it. And Godwin now talks of the ideal rightness and righteousness implied in its proceedings, not yet entirely made good, but more and more tending to be so, and now apparently of the final perfection not coming about only, but foreseen and willed. It is sometimes hard to say whether he is thinking of movement or mind in terms of validity or in terms of will. It is Reason as well as Nature and Truth; it is 'immutable' and 'irresistible'; it is holy, for vice and crime cannot spring from it, and governors and governments are clogs upon it; the laws of man are sound only as they interpret its 'decrees'; and after 'gradual luminosity' and 'sudden eruption' it will so shine into our souls that we can now conceive but faintly of its 'unfathomed power'. Call it Necessity and you express the dependable issue of virtuous doings from virtuous minds, and the sure and certain triumph of a sound gospel, and you get yourself ardour and tranquillity at the same time.[1] But if the Power be so resistless, how came evil to contend with it? How came the sovereign mind imposed upon and the Stygian brood of priests and princes? Of this problem Godwin is hardly even aware; but Shelley, with far more metaphysic in him, ponders it ever and again. The master had lighted on a disciple who had deeper intuitions and was soon to be a scholar who was immensely versed in literature and on whom his overbearing influence was sure to wane.

## 2. ETHICS

From other inspirations determining and fulfilling this abortive metaphysic, as well as from the romances of *Thalaba* and *Kehama*, Shelley came by the hope or dream of a divine Mind or Will in and through the elect of men and women dispelling the world's long night. But he drew from Godwin moreover a body of dogma and a view of the social realities to fill that outline. It was Godwin who first apprised him how grievously the masses of men spend their lives bound and maimed in body and soul. He had defined moreover the state of things to wish for, and in so doing had given with extraordinary daring and system the extreme enunciation of the truths and half-truths and ravishing fallacies of his school. Here was the sovereign individual in a comity of sovereigns, inwardly illumined,

[1] What is left more or less vague in *Political Justice* Godwin definitely admits in the account of his religious opinions bequeathed to Mary Shelley, and suppressed by her and others until 1873, when it appeared, not as *The Genius of Christianity Unveiled*, the title originally intended, but as *Essays never before Published*. A handy report of it will be found in Mr. H. N. Brailsford's *Shelley, Godwin and their Circle*, pp. 179 ff. It trenchantly attacks the doctrines of Calvin, especially that of eternal punishment, and takes the agnostic line as to an Author of Nature. (This would appear to involve a change of mind since the writing of *Political Justice*, when he used deistic language, as well as language not inconsonant with the tenet of an *anima mundi*. But to the end of his days he sometimes spoke or wrote as an ordinary believer.) On the other hand he avows a faith in 'a principle, whatever it is, which acts everywhere around me', and 'in the vast sum of instances works for good and operates beneficially for us'. 'We have here a secure alliance, a friend that, so far as the system of things extends, will never desert us, unhearing, inaccessible to importunity, uncapricious, without passions, without favour, affection, or partiality. . . .' No doubt, this metaphysic would be proffered to Shelley in conversation in the autumn of 1812; and indeed it directly recalls the passage in *Queen Mab* on 'The Spirit of Nature, Necessity' at vi. 197 ff.

master of every passion, free, as far as may be, of every tie, addicted to the common happiness, and innocent not of power only but of property as well. The political consequences of this conception Shelley fervently accepted in a general way and as a remote ideal. And they carried with them an ethic of pure reason in which an unfaltering altruism is the effectual form of self-pleasing, so serenely certain, so heroical that it lit for Shelley the lamp of the moral passion. To that doctrine he had owed, as he told Godwin, the birth of his 'power, feeling, thought', and his call to the service of men. Even when he came to feel how much it wanted, and to put Christ and his theocentric teaching in supreme authority,[1] its note of measureless giving accorded with the higher inspiration. 'Political Justice', he wrote in his review of Mandeville, 'is the first moral system explicitly founded on the negativeness of rights and the positiveness of duties.' 'We have in reality', says the Book, 'nothing that is our own. There will be no disease, no anguish, no melancholy, and no resentment, but every man will seek with ineffable ardour the good of all.'

Yet teacher and pupil were far from consentaneous. Whatever Godwin meant by Nature, he never clearly defines. As he came to perceive, his book had set too little by 'the empire of feeling'. Feeling or passion in his view of it is mostly a cheat and a snare. If I may save either Fénelon or his valet from the burning house, and the valet is my father, I am fairly sure to be fuddled with affection and let the great man die. If the passions were as strong and as determinant as men think them, the hope of progress would be vain. In fact, however, and in spite of seeming, our voluntary actions never directly proceed from them, but are determined by 'opinion'. When we choose to act, a desire or, as he prefers to call it, an 'idea' of what is good, or more than one, presents itself to 'the judgement of the understanding'. The judgement says 'this is good', and action follows. The passion or feeling which is present in the 'idea' may invade, and so weaken the understanding, but cannot do its office and take its place. Nor as a poison or a spell is passion to be greatly feared, even in its fiercest hour. The lover in the arms of his

---

[1] As in the *Essay on Christianity* in 1816, or thereabout. On the date of its composition see A. H. Koszul, *Shelley's Prose in the Bodleian Library*, pp. 9–11.

beloved is checked and chilled at the thought of his horse that was stolen from the meadow. Between us and the empire of reason the lions can be caught and chained. Thus Godwin; as if the desire or felt want or 'idea', as he calls it, having pleaded to the 'understanding', ceased to participate and stood down for reason to speak and the action to ensue; as if the action, before it is taken, must cease to be desired.[1] And if it be asked why he made so light of the element of passion, the answer is simply that his humanity was incomplete.

For the same reason the end that he sets to life will not answer to all our nature needs and is. It would give us inducement, but not the longing of the soul. The end he sets is pleasure or 'agreeable sensation'. Having done his best to disparage the feelings and oust them from the will, he goes on to resuscitate and raise them up on high as the aim and reward of living. Pleasure is the end; but at the same time we shall aim immediately, if we are wise, at the pleasure of others, which is the true constituent of our own. In the wise man the love of his own agreeable sensations is 'the later or after-coming motive', the 'disinterested motive' is 'the present and direct'. For no one is as happy as the man of active benevolence and universal sympathy who enters imaginatively into all the good that men possess and all that lies in store for them. It is equally true, then, that the virtuous man, aiming at 'utility' or general happiness, 'sits loose to life' and all its baits and charms, and also that 'virtue is on no other account valuable than as it is the instrument of the most exquisite pleasure'. Pleasure *as* the good or pleasure *in* the good: the old vexed theme demanded a keener dialectic and a deeper introspection than Godwin had to give.

Shelley also has a 'way', which he defines in the last lines of *Prometheus Unbound*. It leads to the four excellences of Gentleness (or charity), Virtue (or self-control), Wisdom, and Endurance, and it teaches to suffer, to forgive, and to hope,

> till hope creates
> From its own wreck the thing it contemplates.

[1] No account is here taken of what is said in *Political Justice*, iv. ix, of 'the mechanism of the human mind', as it is clear that Shelley passed it by. It would hardly have enlightened him on a latent problem of his own, the escape from Hume's *principia*. He had heard of Kant, and wished to read him, in Born's translation, but ended by ridiculing what he had failed to take in hand (*Peter Bell the Third*, vi. xiii).

It is a war with evil passions in order to live and live well. So only may man be 'good, great, and joyous, beautiful, and free'. But intenser blessedness lies beyond it, in the 'visitations of divinity', fits, or spells, or seasons of extraordinary power and joy, too fugitive, but in good souls clustering to a robe of glory in the days of youth, and leaving to age a legacy of unfailing peace. They are the happiest with whom the rapture comes oftenest and stays longest, and the far-off goal of our nature is to have and hold it evermore. The discipline is for the days when our light is low and for the phase of Time we live in, and we must resume it even in the golden years to come if evil shall have broken loose. We use it on divided wills, where reason fights with passion, love with lust, and charity with revenge. But when all is better than well, 'reason and passion will cease to combat' and 'leave the moral world without a law'.[1] For reason, as he once told Hogg, is passion pure and good; 'the assemblage of our better feelings', or 'passion considered under a certain mode of its operation',[2] law and truth in one and the same moment seen and loved.

Are we to take it, then, that our strenuous morality is a task to be deplored, and that we must look for the life indeed in the trances of spiritual power, in the poet, or the lover, or any soul of that degree? And do we receive the trances or do we earn them? Are they straight from heaven, or the casual incandescence of a labouring flame? Or is it a glory of our own beginning divinely completed? He loves to imagine divine grace flooding every heart, good or bad, but sometimes lessens the miracle. The soul, he says in the *Essay on Christianity*, is a lyre suspended in an atmosphere that 'visits with its breath our silent chords at will'. But, as he insists throughout that Essay, we and our dispositions invite and induce these interludes, and only as a man is pure in heart can he 'see God'. 'Those who have seen God have, in the period of their more perfect nature, been harmonized by their own will to so exquisite consentaneity of power as to give forth divinest melody when the breath of universal being sweeps over their frame.' Prometheus must forgive his enemy before the life of life can come to him.

From this point, however, ambiguity sets in. When the inspiration has come, does it take over and carry us? Or do we

---

[1] *Queen Mab*, viii. 23; ix. 40 ff.    [2] 7 Feb. 1813.

remain militant all but unawares? And will the day dawn, not upon us, but upon men after us, when the rapture will abide, no longer an episode, but a mode of being? At any rate in the 'beautiful idealisms' of his poetry Shelley aspires for the men of the future to undividedness, reason merged with passion for ever and a day. In *Prometheus Unbound* our worser selves fly away like films or fall to the ground like masks. At the visitation of the divinity we become 'its passive slaves'.[1] Like a boat on a racing stream the perfected soul shall speed onward through its earthly life.[2] When it comes upon him that in this mortal span dividedness is not to be put by, he strikes the plangent note of his nostalgia. But this 'idealism' of Man translated to a sort of Godhead, much as it attracts him, is not invariable. It sways between a longing and a dream, and his afterthoughts cross or chasten it. Shelley has in fact stirred up the question that is still on foot:[3] whether, when perfection comes here or hereafter, we shall lose our moral personalities by ceasing to strive. But he has given us words to the contrary. In the hey-day to come even on this our planet we shall still feel the burden of our finitude— 'chance and death and mutability'—though easier;[4] and the other lives that await us after this are 'regions of eternal hope'.[5] Prometheus passes from his defiance of evil to the other militancy of the artist and the man of science. It is true he writes of the *afflatus* in the poet's mind as 'already on the wane' when he turns to write his verse, and flaming in the moral impulse, and flagging in the common task. But what he neglects to insist on and is prone to forget he knows at times well enough: namely, that 'the breath of universal being' still blows when in art or morals we take pains; and, conversely, that it is never the office of the Spirit to dissolve or absorb our selves and our shaping wills. We shall be kindled, but not lost; we shall have gone from strength to strength (*appetitus inhiantis fit amor fruentis*); and we shall continue to endeavour and aspire.

[1] *Essay on Christianity.*

[2] *Prometheus Unbound*, II. v. 72 ff. These stanzas can mean only the course of the new and deified and painless life, wafted by the waters and winds of music or inspiring beauty from infancy to age.

[3] It is fully discussed in Prof. A. E. Taylor's *Faith of a Moralist*, ch. ix, 'The Goal of the Moral Life', which answers the dilemma incisively put in Bradley's *Appearance and Reality*, ch. xxv, 'Goodness'.

[4] *Prometheus Unbound*, IV. 200.        [5] *Queen Mab*, ix. 163.

This, then, is the end of living for Shelley: the divine possession, of which we can never know the fullness in this life, 'the
invisible and unattainable point to which Love tends'. So much
of it as we may experience imparts pleasure in the highest
degree, and we may use that word, if we will, of the Influence
itself:

Nature, or God, or Love, or Pleasure.[1]

In a lucid piece of writing in his *Speculations on Morals* he gives
us his conception of how the entirely selfish appetite of the new-
born child is gradually mixed with the desire of pleasing or not
displeasing others and may change into the pursuit of 'the
highest pleasure of the greatest number of sensitive beings',
theirs and his own in one. So far he is in Godwin's tracks; but
the essays of the same period—say, 1816—extend this aim to
'the fountain-fire of all goodness', the Spirit that clasps all
things 'like a surrounding atmosphere'.[2] It is 'the fire for which
all thirst', that according to the mirror in each man's soul 'burns
bright or dim', or is confounded with false splendours, such as
the glare that dims the sun and maddens the crowd in the
weird and sombre procession in *The Triumph of Life*. In 1813
this impassioned and theocentric doctrine has not arrived, but
it begins to appear in the fragmentary romance of *The Assassins*,
written in the summer of the next year. The Assassins in their
sequestered valley were as all men should be, uncontaminated,
vessels of 'a sacred fire'. 'To love, to be beloved became (to each
of them) the famine of his nature, which the wide circle of the
universe appeared too narrow to satiate.' But they could not
live for ever above ordinariness. Even so, 'that cause which had
ceased to act as an overwhelming excitement was still the
unperceived law of their lives and the sustenance of their
nature.' We pass, in short, from reason in Godwin to inspiration
in Shelley; from benevolence as a means to love as an end, and
love unbounded by the world; from pleasure as an end to
pleasure unseparated from the infinite and supreme Good.

3. TOUCHSTONES

Shelley proceeds, then, from the assumption of a Universal
Will which is also the object of Man's love and the mover of his

---

[1] *Revolt of Islam*, v, Song, ii. 9.                    [2] *Essay on Christianity.*

actions. And this assumption Godwin cannot definitely attain, and ought in logic to have disallowed. For how can reason be divine if it is not the self-same power, one and many, but divided and dissipated in all the minds there are, and every man his own preceptor and guide? Shelley, in his predominant mood, is at the other pole. For with him Reason or Love, or whatever he may call it, is a fusing fire where the individual is all but lost. The one abstraction faces the other. One by one the topics of *Political Justice* betray this difference as the two pens deal with them; and we shall be exploring Shelley's mind if we select three instances.

### (a) Punishment

We must argue with the criminal, says Godwin, and apprise him of his error. His error, not his guilt: for if Necessity be a fact, 'the assassin is as irresponsible as his dagger'. 'Punishment, unless for reform, is particularly absurd. Shall I inflict calamity upon a man for the reason only that he has already inflicted calamity upon himself?' And so on: vice 'a distemper' and punishment a medicine. All this Shelley has reproduced in his Note on Necessity and in his poem; but he lays the emphasis where Godwin hardly touches, on the punishment by conscience. There is the worst distemper and religion's dint:

> Thine is the hand whose piety would soothe
> The thorny pillow of unhappy crime
> Watching its wanderings as a friend's disease.

It is not for corroding that he deprecates Conscience, but for hurting at all. He would have it speak only in the voice of incitement, and never in the voice of blame. And so he continued to think. 'Blush not', says Cythna to the men who saved her from the sea

> for what may to thyself impart
> Stains of inevitable crime; the doom
> Is this which has, or may, or must become
> Thine and all humankind's.

This idea of crime as only compassionable has not fared well under criticism. If crime be error, it certainly should not be punished. And it will be mere error if a man can aim only at pleasurable sensations. If my error annoys others, they will take steps to improve my reckoning in some illuminative way. If I am under laws, civil and moral, my crime is disobedience, and a law implies a sanction. If I am responsible, I am punishable, whether in the court of conscience or a court of law. Nor must you say, if you will have a moral world,

> I wish no living thing to suffer pain,

for pain will be inevitable. It is inherent in a lustful will at feud with a lawful, a particular with a universal. And Shelley in his interim morality for our probation here and now accepts this fact. But under the numinous overpowering that is yet to come we shall pass our time in 'passion's golden purity', passion and reason a perfect unity 'beyond the evil and the good'. It comes to the same thing whichever you do: leave a man to his pleasurable sensations or absorb him into something else, tie him up in separateness, or melt him in universality. Neither way is he human enough to deserve punishment.

### (b) Marriage

In the first and boldest edition of his book in 1793 Godwin declared that 'the abolition of marriage would be attended with no evils', and that, as men grow wiser, inconstancy will evoke no tears, for 'we shall all consider the sexual intercourse as a very trivial object'. 'Reasonable men will propagate their species because it is right that the species should be propagated', and 'it cannot be definitively affirmed whether or not it will be known in such a state of society who is the father of each individual child'. But in the later amendment of this chapter, marriage is retained as 'a salutary and respectable institution', provided that divorce shall be easily effected at either party's will. Moreover, infidelities are reprobated if 'the periods of absence be of no long duration'. Not that the wedded wife need fancy she is slighted. 'It is by no means indispensable that the female to whom each man attaches himself in that matter should appear the most excellent and deserving of the sex.'

The body and the soul that Godwin put asunder Shelley joined. For him the bodily union of the lovers was the seal of the spiritual, or else a sin. What to the radiant poet of *Epipsychidion* were the sordid counsels of carnal appeasement and conscientious venery? At the same time the passion was in its nature, as he put it, 'indisciplinable', and the worst of sins to deny its will. Both of them agreed that vows of constancy and, still more, the legal fetters were idle. But, over and above that, the regimentation according to Godwin made too much of that which is trivial, and according to Shelley put vile duress on that which is holy. Each of them would have his freedom in his own way. Godwin refuses the tie; and the lovers in Shelley, while love lasts, are a single person, a unity without a difference, like streams confused. To Godwin's mind there can hardly be two, and yet one, and to Shelley's there can hardly be one, and yet two.

### (c) Freedom and Force

Godwin's ideal community is a collection of free, equal, and like-minded persons, too reasonable to need a government, though there are common arrangements to which they all consent. They do what they like, and no one interferes with anyone. No class, grade, or function distinguishes some from others; politically considered, they differ no more than ninepins. Being completely reasonable, they never eventually disagree; for if first opinions vary, they can be argued till the truth prevails. Freedom is perfected in a political consent with no compulsion, and finally no demur. All this being impossible, however, less visionary thinkers were bound to reckon with the dissenter, even the unruly one, and to bring in force. *On le forcera d'être libre*, says Rousseau, and so installs a General Will and a magistracy to impose it. The will of the abstract individual passes at a hand's turn into the abstract universal of 'the general will', and Girondist and Jacobin quoted the same Bible. This easy road from thorough individualism to thorough collectivism Godwin never travelled; he will not admit authority. But what of Shelley? Will he also wait for the waverer and argue on and on with the wicked? We have seen how Godwin was afraid of him in Ireland, afraid of his passion and his desire of a mass movement. And Godwin was right. The disciple was indeed in two minds as to the rule of governing by the spiritual arm alone and as to the collateral rule of not resisting evil by any kind of force. He detests war; he will have no retributive punishment; and in the *Essay on Christianity* writes in fervid eloquence of the interdiction laid by Christ on all requital and revenge. Prometheus wins his victory by learning not to hate his foe, and in the *Mask of Anarchy* the people of England are to stand up passively to the dragonnades. In these cases Demogorgon and Hope are to do the fighting; and yet what hands have they but hands of flesh and blood? And this fact Shelley frequently recognizes. The praise of unlimited forgiveness as taught by Christ leads on at once to the praise of the 'holy patriots' who killed Julius Caesar. The Ode to Naples is an incantation to the Spirit of Love to turn all implements of Death on the Austrians as they march upon the city. 'The religion of an Assassin imposed other virtues than endurance.... The perverse and vile and vicious—what were they? Shapes of some unholy vision, moulded by the Spirit of Evil, which the sword of the merciful destroyer should sweep from this beautiful world.' From premisses like these it would be an easy way, were his passion to call for it, to political Jacobinism. The two abstractions of the revolutionary creed might have lain down together in the mind of Shelley as they had in the mind of Rousseau. The men and women of his ideal world fleet the time by twos and threes in dells and woods entirely free. Yet it has been said of him that in an English revolution he might have become an actor like the young St. Just, ardent, apostolic, abetting a terrible government for the love of humankind.[1]

## 4. THE ONE AND THE MANY

Godwinism was his first haven, and he began from the outset adjusting it to his own instincts and spiritually underpinning it. From the outset he took in material from very dissimilar sources to join to it, and the more as time presented him with problems far beyond its scope. But its prophecy of the days to come and its unbounded philanthropy blended harmoniously with the other theme of the soul's desire. Almost all his principal poems are in one of two classes: *Queen Mab*, *The Revolt of Islam*, *Prometheus*, *Hellas* on the conflict in the State; *Alastor*, *Epipsychidion*, *Adonais*, *The Triumph of Life* on the conflict in the

---

[1] 'At Naples the constitutional party has declared to the Austrian Minister that, if the Emperor should make war upon them, their first action would be to put to death *all* the members of the royal family—a necessary and most just measure, when the forces of the combatants as well as the merit of their respective causes are so unequal. That kings should be everywhere the hostages for liberty were admirable.' To Mary Shelley, 1 Sept. 1820.

soul, though there is plenteous over-flowing from one theme to the other. Here political freedom, finally sure and certain, and the way in which men should live; there evil, love's 'hidden want', the soul a prisoner, her consolation, her release. Godwin was the source of the first chapter, and Plato of the second. Godwin gave him politics and ethics; Plato the Beauty that 'clasps and fills the world'. But to bring these chapters into agreement Godwin must be modified. 'The negativeness of rights and the positiveness of duties' and the unlimited ability of the once enlightened reason: these were epoch-making revelations and would for ever stand. But the 'empire of feeling' or intuition must be brought in to correct the imperception of a dismembering intellectualism and to put on the roof and crown of Shelley's edifice: that is to say, the 'rhythm' or order imposed on men's natures and societies and the whole frame of things by 'the one Spirit's plastic stress' and a goal or centre of men's purposes beyond this sphere of time. Shelley's progress in the years of his greatest power was on those lines.

# XI

## THE RIGHTS OF WOMEN AND THE LAW OF MARRIAGE

### 1. ROUSSEAU

OVER the whole romantic movement the genius of Rousseau 'broods like a cloud', and Shelley is steeped in it. He owed Godwin a system of exciting ideas; he found in Rousseau that and more: not only a potent reasoner and writer, but a reader of the heart of man, a poet, a profoundly kindred soul on whose tragedy he might look and fear. In many a page of the confessional or imaginative writings he must have fancied that he saw his own face:

'When I see or hear of any act of injustice, my heart kindles with rage as if the effect of it recoiled upon myself. . . . I have often put myself in a perspiration, pursuing or stoning a cock, a cow, a dog, or any animal which I saw tormenting another merely because it felt itself the stronger.'

'The first, the greatest, the most powerful, the most irrepressible of all my needs was entirely in my heart; it was the need of a companionship as intimate as was possible, it was for that purpose especially that I needed a woman rather than a man. This want was such that the most intimate corporeal union had been unable to satisfy it; I should have wanted two souls in the same body; without that I was always conscious of a void.'

'Seeing nothing in existence which was worthy of my enthusiasm, I sought nourishment for it in an ideal world, which my fertile imagination soon peopled with beings after my own heart . . . heavenly alike in their beauties and virtues; trusting, tender and loyal friends, such as I never found in this world below.'

'This disposition [to solitude], apparently so gloomy and mis-anthropic, is really due to a too affectionate, too loving, and too tender heart.'

'I have never been fitted for civil society, when all is embarrass-ment, obligation, and duty. My independent temper makes me incapable of the subjections necessary to him who would live with men.'[1]

---

[1] This and the preceding quotations are from the *Confessions*, Everyman Edition, J. M. Dent & Sons, Ltd.

'The gold of the broom and the purple of the heather smote my eyes with a richness that touched my heart; the majesty of the trees that covered me with their shade, the astonishing variety of the plants and flowers—these held my spirit with a continual alternation between study and wonderment. . . . Soon I lifted my thoughts from the face of the earth to all the beings of Nature, to the universal system of things, to the incomprehensible Being who encompasses all. Then, my mind lost in that immensity, I was not thinking; I felt with a kind of voluptuousness that I was over-whelmed by the weight of that Universe. . . . I would have liked to soar out into the Infinite . . . I cried out in the excitement of my transports: "O great Being! O great Being!" '[1]

This, then, among the influences on Shelley is elemental and unmeasurable. Early and late in strong attraction or in sharp recoil he pronounces on the enchanter. The French language, he once declared, were better left unlearned, 'did not the great name of Rousseau redeem it'.[2] Nay, we are told that 'Rousseau is perhaps the philosopher among the moderns who in the structure of his feelings and understanding resembles most nearly the mysterious sage of Judea', and that his writings have the advantage of the gospels in 'connected and systematic enthusiasm'.[3] He is, thinks Shelley, one of the great poets of love. *La Nouvelle Héloïse*, instinct with 'supremest genius and more than human sensibility',[4] is 'one of the trophies planted in the human heart of the sublimest victory over sensuality and force'.[5] All the more tragic therefore was the fall from the beauty of the dream to the 'strange defeatures' of the dreamer's life. As early as 1812 there is a cross-current in Shelley's thoughts of him; for in the second of the Irish pamphlets he is said to have 'given a licence to feelings that only incapacitate and contract the heart'. And in the last and greatest of Shelley's works, *The Triumph of Life*, the maenadic dancers fall at last by the way, deformed and spent, and among them Rousseau, heavy-hearted and grotesquely withered, interprets the pageant to the bystander. It is a vision of tyrannous desire and the devastation thereby of men's lives, and he, the victim of his sensations, has

[1] Letter to Malesherbes, 26 Jan. 1762; *A Citizen of Geneva*, by Charles William Hendel, Oxford, 1937, pp. 213–14.
[2] To an unidentified correspondent, a lady, in the spring of 1812.
[3] Section on Equality, written perhaps in 1816 or 1817.
[4] To Peacock, 6 July 1816.          [5] *Defence of Poetry*, 1821.

paid the price of 'that sweet and bitter cup drunk to the lees'.

> See the great bards of elder time who quelled
> The passions which they sung, as by their strain
> May well be known: their living melody
> Tempers its own contagion to the vein
> Of those who are infected with it—I
> Have suffered what I wrote, or viler pain!
> And so my words have seeds of misery
> Even as the deeds of others. . . .

From this aspersion *La Nouvelle Héloïse* is surely not exempted, for Shelley could sometimes think as changefully of letters as he often did of men. He was himself not always clear of the morbid vein to which that once so potent tale belongs, or he would never have ranked it with the great love-poems of the world. It was far easier, however, to see the moral taint or rather failure in the idyll of the fifth book of *Émile* and the discourse on the sexes introducing it. For here was the classical exposition of those 'facts of Nature' which, taken in the general mind for the truth and the whole truth, had bogged the wheels of progress, as Shelley considered, much more than other causes. The woman's one function, it is argued, is to bear and rear children, and 'mediate between the father and the child'. Nature, which disapproves of any long interval between one pregnancy and another, has 'made her for man's delight', and armed her with the arts and means to allure her mate and the tenderness and devotedness to keep the home. While, therefore, the man is 'strong and active', the woman must be 'weak and passive'. Not that she must have no mind. Among her allurements is wit as well as grace, and she should have an education to improve it; but one that is 'planned in relation to the man'. For 'to be pleasing in man's sight, to earn his respect, to train him in childhood, to tend him in manhood, to counsel and console him and make his life happy—these are the duties of woman for ever'. And all this reinforced on other occasions by 'Fabricius in his thatched hut' and his good wife and many children. In the *lex amandi* delivered to Émile the understanding and the sensibility of the tale of Julie had failed of their kindly fruits. The withered and withering spellbinder of Shelley's fearful Vision had not framed himself to the adventure of civilization. The moral indolence that he himself confessed to, the *âme paresseuse* so intimately mated with the *âme ardente*,[1] had told upon his thought and made him a defaulter from his own ideal of equality and the high demands of love.

## 2. THE ISSUE

This was with Shelley the besetting issue. For him the upholding and uplifting power in men and their societies is Love (or Imagination), whose language is poetry or any kind of beauty. And where can it be in purest energy but in societies such as Petrarch wrote and Raphael painted for? That was an age surpassing even the splendour of Greece, where woman was enthralled and unhonoured, and the free man lived on the labour of the slave.[2] A new day dawned when the teaching of Christ, radiant from his words, combined with the Germanic sentiment that flowered in chivalry and liberated the serf and the woman:

'The abolition of personal slavery is the basis of the highest political hope that it can enter into the mind of man to conceive. The freedom of women produced the poetry of sexual love. Love became a religion, the idols of whose worship were ever present. . . . The familiar appearance and proceedings of life became wonderful and heavenly, and a paradise was created as out of the wrecks of Eden.'

In this world Petrarch wrought his spells:

'It is impossible to feel them without becoming a portion of that beauty which we contemplate. It were superfluous to explain how the gentleness and the elevation of mind connected with these sacred emotions can render men more amiable, more generous and wise, and lift them out of the dull vapours of the little world of self.'[3]

In course of time Shelley evolved a complete theory of the mission of Woman and her relation to Man. It makes out a difference of intellectual faculty and spiritual function, which is exceeded and made away with, as it would seem, in the transparent unity induced by the intensest passion. In the busi-

---

[1] See 'Rousseau and his Romantic Experience', by Professor L. A. Bisson, in the *Modern Language Review*, Jan. 1942.
[2] *Essay on the Literature, the Arts and the Manners of the Athenians.*
[3] *A Defence of Poetry*, 1821.

ness of the day and the conflict of political forces man is the effective leader; it is Laon who calls up and guides the movement and in his poems indites the idea, while Cythna absorbs, cherishes, and fosters it in the hearts of men. She is a type that modern revolutions have made familiar, the woman in the heart of the storm, at the head of the crowd, diffusing the joy of devotion. But of the truth which Laon shapes in verse and brings to bear upon the world she has a deeper hold. She is instinctively wiser. It is she whom Demogorgon summons to his cave to learn what he has to teach. She excels in the triune virtue of Faith, Hope, and Charity as is implied in the triad of Panthea, Ione, and Asia. She knows that without love the strong things fail, that sins must be forgiven,[1] that the guiltiest are in sorest need:

> Some said he was a man of blood and peril,
> And steeped in bitter infamy to the lips.
> More need was there I should be innocent,
> More need that I should be most true and kind,
> And much more need that there should be found one
> To share remorse and scorn and solitude,
> And all the ills that wait on those who do
> The tasks of ruin in the world of life.[2]

Towards the man she is not only an answering and vivifying intelligence, but she has more than he of the 'peace in believing'. From *Queen Mab* to *Hellas* she waits and watches in unwavering hope for the good Cause, either in her mortal form, or translated, like Asia and the Lady of Atlas, to the rank of the intermediary between Men and Gods, the δαίμων of the Platonic mythology, but there imagined of the other sex. In the myth that opens his epic, she is the beloved of the Morning Star, which is Hope, and nurse of the world's life; for when the snake, the Spirit of Good, is wounded by the eagle, the Evil Spirit, it nestles in her bosom, and she talks to it in their private language. Beauty the signature of the soul, the bent to heal and save, intuition, and the will secure: of these in Dante's poetry and in Shelley's is the glory of Woman.

All this is germinal in *Queen Mab* in the forms of Ianthe and the Fairy herself and in the account in the last Cantos of the

---

[1] *Revolt of Islam*, VIII. xix–xxii.
[2] *Fragment of an Unfinished Drama,* 113 ff.

great emancipation.[1] And the conclusion is there which in 1817 is the heart of Cythna's argument: 'Can man be free if woman be a slave?'[2] Can he afford what he then loses?[3] Tyrant at home, must he not behave as one abroad? Are not, then, the rights of women the first thing Freedom asks? For her glorious days, depending on liberty, were few. In Italy the Medici and their like soon ended them. Here in England liberty, of which she had the benefit, lasted longer under political forms inherently adverse to it. But since the Commonwealth, and since other dates elsewhere in Europe, a compromise has come about between the forces of progress and reaction—we have had our oligarchy and our Church, the sworn foes of the creative and the inquisitive spirit. At last it is ending, this gloaming, thanks to the children of the inflowing light and the longing of the human spirit for days like the best it ever knew.[4]

### 3. MARY WOLLSTONECRAFT

Shelley had read the long answer to the offending portion of *Émile*, Mary Wollstonecraft's *Vindication of the Rights of Women*, by the spring of 1812;[5] and it had impressed or implanted his conviction of the force and the priority of women's claims and the advantage to men themselves of 'rounding Cape Turk'.[6] Woman her own governor, man's equal friend, sharing his school with him and the life of the mind; politically and economically free, with a part to play in professional and commercial life, and even in Parliament;[7] above all, the mother

[1] *Queen Mab*, ix. 76–92.      [2] *The Revolt of Islam*, II. xliii.

[3] See ibid., II. xxxvi, on the waste of 'grace and power'.

[4] I have put together, using a measure of interpretation, the substance of *A Philosophical View of Reform* with what there is of historical retrospect in *A Defence of Poetry*.

[5] Writing to J. H. Lawrence on 17 Aug. 1812, he says that before the spring of that year he had 'no doubt of the evils of marriage—Mrs. Wollstonecraft reasons too well for that'. In fact, she approves of marriage, though she does say much of the unhappiness of woman, helpless as she was educated to become, under its yoke.

[6] 'If a woman have the misfortune of knowing anything, she should conceal it' (*Northanger Abbey*).

[7] The *Vindication* lays by far the greater stress on education; but it claims for women a share in some of the professions and in commerce, and in one or two passages 'hints' at the full measure of political enfranchisement; as more particularly in a passage in chapter ix: 'I may excite laughter by dropping a hint, which I mean to pursue some future time, for I really think that women ought to have representatives, instead of being arbitrarily governed without having any direct

and fosterer of society: these affirmations or hopes, or something approximate to them permeate the story of the apostle and martyr of his epic. And one of the factors of Shelley's own destiny was the picture conveyed to him by that sure-sighted, magnanimous, indignant book of the woman of mind and sense who renounces pleasure and fashion for what she owes to others and to herself, and companions her husband, and suckles her child. For the day came when, having that ideal at heart, he looked for such a one at his own side, and found her not; while at the same time on Mary Godwin, on whom her mother's eyes had rested but for a few hours, the 'radiance undefiled' of that parent life seemed to brood like a setting sun, or to strike through the 'tempest dark and wild of latter days'.[1] Yet the *Vindication* cannot have satisfied him. He would hardly approve of the somewhat other-worldly theology so often to the fore; or accede to what is cardinal in the treatise: the proposition, namely, that 'there is no sex in mind'. And he would be yet more disappointed by the fact that Mary Wollstonecraft, when she wrote this book, before her own crucial experience,[2] knew not what passion is. Passion, as she thinks of it, is a gale to be weathered; a fine madness, it may be, that matrimony will sober, matrimony, Nature's counsel and provident design. When two virtuous young persons marry, she writes, 'it would perhaps be happy if some circumstances checked their passion', as, for example, 'the memory of prior and stronger attachments'. For,

> 'friendship, the most sublime of all affections, is founded on principle and cemented by time. The very reverse may be said of love. In a great degree love and friendship cannot subsist in the same bosom. . . . The vain fears and fond jealousies, the winds which fan the flame of love, when judiciously or artfully tempered, are both incompatible with the tender confidence and sincere respect of friendship.'

To Shelley these would be blind words. With her disparagement of passion and her commendation of marriage throughout the book, he would think of Mary Wollstonecraft in her

share allowed them in the deliberations of government.' She complains elsewhere that women are 'denied all political privileges' (chapter xiii) and that their proper education is 'prevented by the very constitution of civil government' (chapter iv).

[1] Dedication of *The Revolt of Islam*, ll. 100–8.

[2] The *Vindication* was published in 1792: she was associated with Gilbert Imlay from 1793 to 1795.

fight for women as of one who had indeed delivered the prisoners prospectively from their cells, but had not unbolted the Great Gate.

## 4. THE EMPIRE OF THE NAIRS

But another hand had attempted to unbolt it, or rather to pull it down. In 1811 the Hookham brothers issued from their press in four volumes James Henry Lawrence's *Empire of the Nairs*,[1] a book which no revolutionary propaganda exceeded in audacity. It was formally a romance, with the purpose of depicting a high civilization without marriage, and dealt principally with the Nairs (a people living on the coast of Malabar, and described by Buchanan in his *Travels*), on account of the hegemony of women among them and the law and custom of free love. It ascribed to them other institutions than those upon record, as well as an imaginary empire in Hindostan and exemplary happiness. In this Utopia there is no matrimony, but the woman is free to choose and change her lover and to grant her person when and to whom she will, and not expected to declare who is the father of her child. She educates her children at the tenderest age, till the State consigns them to its own schools, which are common to boys and girls, and provide liberally for the body and the mind (thanks to Mary Wollstonecraft, who is cited and commended several times). Women alone may own and inherit real property, the men living on wages from the State as soldiers or workers, and offices or dignities special to men, like that of Emperor, devolve on the eldest sons of the eldest sisters or half-sisters. In an introductory essay, as well as everywhere in the book, Lawrence inveighs against marriage as a yoke; a blind plunge; a clog, as cruel as it is often futile, on the legitimate variability of passion; a tie of which only the Papists and the English have found no easy loosening. 'In a country where there were no wives there

[1] *The Empire of the Nairs or The Rights of Women, an Utopian Romance*, by James Lawrence, Author of *The Bosom Friend, Love, an Allegory*, &c. Lawrence published an essay on the system of the Nairs in Wieland's *Deutscher Merkur* in 1793. The romance was written in 1800, and in the following year published in German, on Schiller's recommendation, in the *Journal der Romane* under the title of 'Das Paradies der Liebe'. A French version appeared in 1803. In 1811 the English edition was ventured on to forestall an intended piracy. Its influence on Shelley has been noted by D. J. Macdonald in *Modern Language Notes*, xl, Apr. 1925, 246–9; and more extensively traced by Walter Graham in *P.M.L.A.* xl. 881–91.

would be no courtesans. . . . So long as Hymen continues a monopolist, Love will continue a smuggler.' There would be no forbidding, no selling of love, were we to live as the Nairs do: no enforced abstention, no young maiden or royal lady traded into loathsome wedlock. Could we in England rid ourselves of 'our preposterous estimation of chastity', how much less should we suffer from discord in families, from bad manners in men, from the rareness among women of an Aspasia or a Ninon de Lenclos. Nor would liberty bring licence, for there is a monkish and also a natural chastity, and, as a rule, he whom a woman binds by virtues and graces will keep to her. 'The Spanish lady and her cicisbeo are usually torn asunder by death alone.'

There would be no advantage in an outline of the huge and tedious story, that branches and branches again, flat in the style, wooden in the characters, and full to the brim of coldly imagined lubricity. For while Lawrence crams his page with the description of moral disorder in a vast flood and at a quite fantastic pitch, and has indeed a taste for it, he is nevertheless not a hearty pornographer, but a theorist rather who will prove a theory with dismaying and disarming evidence. England, the Continent, and Islam, from St. Petersburg to Cairo, from London to Kandahar: over all this region he pores and pries— deep in memoirs, books of travel, books of *causes célèbres*—into the consequences of the sexual passion, as he sees it abundantly mishandled. He is equally knowledgeable in the murders, duels, suicides, the enslavement, and the infidelity in the train of the law in England, so much inferior to other lands in the art of evading it; in the Mohammedan system and all it means of watch and ward; and in the horror of prostitution, East and West. On the other hand, even in England there are women 'superior to prejudice' who hold their own against the odds, who read the philosophers, and dare to be 'free'. Even in Sultans' harems there are those who kindle in their captive sisters the spirit of revolt and the demand to choose and change.[1] And among the glorious Nairs there was never a time when chastity, 'the most absurd of all prejudices', reared its head, or the law put limits to the illimitable. In Malabar brother and sister may become lovers without a scandal, and so it happens

[1] Roxana, vol. iv, book x.

in the story to a prince and princess of the Imperial House. True, there are constant friendships between their men and women, but 'constancy' is not 'fidelity', and never asks that it shall be. And the system occasions no jealousies, no strifes, not even heart-burnings, but only the finest and the suavest manners. Free, therefore, themselves of all the evils that come elsewhere of love, the Nairs look down on other peoples in wrath and pity. 'It would not surprise me', says one of them on a sojourn in England, 'if ye were to mark your women as ye mark your sheep.' They have an order of knighthood sworn to make war on the Mohammedans and to liberate their wives, and on two occasions, at Ispahan and at Kandahar, the knights break with that purpose into seraglios; after which, in the triumphant procession and at the feast in Calicut, the great Nair City, the emancipated women cannot believe their senses; the joy is too much for them, and the contrasts in the way of living on this side the Indus and on that.[1] The Nairs, in fine, have squared the circle: they 'allow every individual to give way to his inclinations without bad consequences to himself or society'. 'Let everything go the way of Nature. If constancy be natural, it will subsist of itself—if inconstancy, it cannot be pernicious—the law of Nature is the law of God.'

## 5. SHELLEY AND LAWRENCE

This book came into Shelley's hands in the spring of 1812, and thenceforward elements of the story supplied his imagination, and were embodied five years later in *The Revolt of Islam*: as in the incident of the women shipped for the harem and set free by the mariners, and Cythna, victim and vanquisher of the system of lust, diffusing her free spirit in the halls of the palace.[2] Later, in *Hellas*, the women of the Sultan's harem chant their superb choruses of undying hope. And Lawrence's readers would be well prepared for the original version of his epic in

---

[1] iii. 233 ff., and iv. 25, the women liberated at Kandahar.

[2] Cythna in the harem attracts the Sultan by the songs she sings to the lute. In his embraces she loses her reason, and is conveyed from the harem by an evil and evil-looking eunuch and 'a wretch made dumb by poison' to be immured in a sea cavern (VII. iv ff.). In Lawrence, Emma de Grey in the harem at Kandahar resists the Sultan, and is dungeoned on bread and water (iii. 246 ff.). She wins the favour of the Sultana by her skill on the harpsichord.

which the lovers are brother and sister.[1] More than that: the book had made him, as he stated, or overstated, in a letter to Lawrence, 'a perfect convert to its doctrines'. If the *Vindication of the Rights of Women* bore in on him that women's wrongs were the worst of our maladies, and there the surgery must begin, it was the survey in *The Empire of the Nairs* that displayed the suppuration wide and fierce, whether in Christian marriage or the cruel polygamy of the East. (The East, however, was the area of its greatest intensity, and a poem of liberated humanity would necessarily lay its scenes in Islam, and preferably in Istambul.) And the romance not only confirmed all that he had had in his mind about matrimony, but impressed on him for the first time the most poignant of the pleas against it, namely that it makes the prostitute, dooming to a life of devastating mischief and hopeless misery the victim of an overpowering force and monstrously requiting her for a venial or a nominal sin.[2]

He was, however, by no means 'a perfect convert'. As Lawrence thinks, the desire of the flesh is an imperious force whose victim can blame himself only for an unrewarding choice.[3] Shelley was addicted to *The Faerie Queene*, and not even Spenser more severely distinguishes love and lust. 'The author', he says in his review of Hogg's *Prince Alexy Haimatoff* in 1814,

> 'appears to deem the loveless intercourse of brutal appetite a venial offence against delicacy and virtue; he asserts that a transient connexion with a cultivated female may contribute to form the heart without essentially vitiating the sensibilities. It is our duty to protest against so pernicious and disgusting an opinion. No man can rise pure from the poisonous embraces of a prostitute, or sinless from the desolated hopes of a confiding heart.'

At the time of planning or writing *Queen Mab* he passed in his moodiness through a humour, not perhaps infrequent with him,

---

[1] In Lawrence, Firnos and Camilla, children of Agalva, the Emperor's sister, are lovers, though they do not discover their consanguinity until after their union. But it is no matter. At vol. i, p. 210, we are introduced to this type of marriage as prevailing in Persia.

[2] In the above-cited letter of 17 Aug. 1812, Shelley tells Lawrence that this had been for him the outstanding point in the indictment.

[3] Lawrence prefers a liaison with an educated woman to one with an uneducated, because there is more entertainment and refinement in it. And he is severe on those who carry on affairs with social inferiors.

of wishing away 'the detestable distinction of man and woman'.[1]
Yet again and again he writes of love in the present meaning as
a total commitment, soul and sense.[2] *Epipsychidion* in all literature is surely the sovereign utterance of this theme. As refinement advances, he writes, in his essay on the Athenians in 1818,
and might have written at any time,

> 'the satisfaction of the senses is no longer all that is sought in
> sexual connection. It soon becomes a very small part of that pro-
> found and complicated sentiment which we call love, which is
> rather the universal thirst for a communion not only of the senses,
> but of our whole nature. . . . The sexual impulse . . . serves . . . as
> a kind of type or expression of the other claims of love. Still, it is
> a claim . . . which our nature thirsts to satisfy.'

As Man becomes humaner physical beauty appeals to him by
moral characters, and Art and Nature speak to lovers with a
special power.[3] Nor has any other English poet written as
religiously of the joy of parenthood and the wonder of the fruit
fulfilling the wonder of the flower.

For a space, however, Shelley's 'bolder and purer ethics'
overlap on the opinions of the Nairs. For in respect of sexual
relations he would be simply irresponsible did he not stand for
one condition only, that is to say for love, not lust, on both sides.
Given love between them, men and women in an ideal society,
if not in ours, will do in this relation what they list, and that
without sin.[4] The desolated man in *Julian and Maddalo* was
faithful to the cruel lady:

> I have not, as some do, bought penitence
> With pleasure and a dark and sweet offence,
> For then, if love and tenderness and truth
> Had overlived hope's momentary youth,
> My creed should have redeemed me from repenting.[5]

The 'chastity' assailed in the text of *Queen Mab* and the relevant
Note[6] is not only the defrauding of the body through a 'monkish
superstition of the excellence of virginity', but true love sapped,
as he would say, by nothing other than timorousness.[7] (The

---

[1] He harps to Miss Hitchener of discarnate love. See above, p. 126, on his lost
novel, *Hubert Cauvin*.
[2] *The Revolt of Islam*, VI. xxviii–xxxvii; *Epipsychidion*, 513 ff.
[3] *Fragment on Beauty*, iii.    [4] Fragments of *Epipsychidion*, 6–26.
[5] ll. 3–8 ff.    [6] ix. 84 ff., and note on v. 189.    [7] *Queen Mab*, ix. 70 ff.

lover who loves his mistress but loves her honour more raises a difference where Shelley has acknowledged none.) And the story of the Nairs may have assisted the conviction so much at the root of his poetry, that love is in the nature of things 'indisciplinable' and in the end unhappy, a wanderer and a seeker, who 'knows he hath a home, yet scarce knows where'.

Shelley's intellectual history presents us with a collection of ideas which are almost all assembled at the first. They gain as time goes on in depth and substance, and are fraught with a larger passion. And certainly by 1816 and in the course of that year we can speak of a turn of mind, for by then he has made himself a mould of Platonic notions and the frequent use and sore need of it are new. Yet if we put to the sum of his earlier speculations not only what he wrote, but what he read and used afterwards, like a fund laid by, it may still be said of him that he 'grew like a tree', having loved Plato from his teens. So with his theory of love. The natures of Man and Woman, the rights of the body and the soul, the 'mingled identities', the 'stronger shadow of the divinity within him' discerned by the lover in the loved,[1] and with and for all that the 'indisciplinable wanderings of passion': here are the elements, all of them more or less declared in or before *Queen Mab*. Glance forward to *Alastor* and to the essay *On Love* in 1815,[2] and the *Hymn to Intellectual Beauty* in 1816, and then beyond that mark, and the theory fills out. The 'divinity within' is the 'epipsychidion', the 'soul within the soul' which is ever undefiled, a 'prototype' of moral beauty, 'a mirror that reflects only forms of purity and brightness'. This 'apex of the soul', as mystics have called it, 'describes a circle around its proper paradise which pain and sorrow and evil dare not overleap'. It is the moving and guiding principle in the poet, the lawgiver, and the lover: the poet images the truth or good it tells of in poetic terms, the lawgiver in laws, the lover in the person whom he loves. In his creative longing the lover sees or fashions[3] in her the 'stronger shadow' or 'anti-type' of the

---

[1] To Elizabeth Hitchener, 23 Nov. 1812.

[2] Unless the essay dates from a year or two years later.

[3] 'This object [ideal beauty] or its archetype for ever exists in the mind, which selects among those [visible objects] which resemble it that which most resembles it; and instinctively fills up the interstices of the imperfect image in the same manner as the imagination moulds and completes the shapes in clouds or in the fire . . .' (*Essay on the Athenians*).

beauty which in his inmost self is and is beheld. And then, as far as his mortality allows, he lacks nothing. Like the Idea of the old sonneteers she is not only 'the very soul of him', but the light of his soul, who 'veils under the radiant form of Woman' the glory

> That penetrates and clasps and fills the world.[1]

This high Platonic strain of *Alastor* and *Epipsychidion*[2] was the proper music of an experience that made him wonder if he had not been called at once to bear love's sorrows and plead its cause. The poet of *Epipsychidion* knew, after all, that he had 'sought in a mortal image the likeness of that which is perhaps eternal'; but the youth in *Alastor*, forbearing to seek, was caught, as it were, by an angered current and swept to his ruin; while smaller natures, the selfish and the torpid, are 'the unforeseeing multitudes who constitute, together with their own, the lasting misery and loneliness of the world'. The quest may be vain or fatal, and yet it is our life, and freedom with it. In the Note in *Queen Mab* he wants to smooth the way from an old morality to a new, arguing, for instance, as Lawrence had done, that under the free system constancy will not be rare. On this issue of practicability he was effectually assailed at the time, and is indeed sufficiently uncircumspect.[3] But he fares in

---

[1] That Shelley wrote *Epipsychidion* under the influence of Shakespeare's sonnets he has himself hinted in one of the fragments of the poem; and there are signs that he did so:

> And we will move possessing and possessed
> Wherever beauty on the earth's bare breast
> Lies like the shadow of thy soul.        (*Fragments*, 183 ff.)

[2] Shelley had no access to the Christian mystics. Presumably he arrived at the idea of the undefiled inner soul by putting together two passages of classical literature: (*a*) the passage in Lucretius, iii. 273–5, on the most recondite of the four elements of the *animus*, quoted *infra*, p. 234, together with the Lucretian phrase *adytum cordis*; and (*b*) the passage in Plato's *Republic*, x. 611 c, where the soul is compared with the sea-god Glaucus, his limbs broken by the waves and encrusted with weed and shell and stone: 'And the soul which we behold is in a similar condition. . . . But not there, Glaucon, not there must we look.' 'Where then?' 'At her love of Wisdom. Let us see whom she affects and what society and converse she seeks in virtue of her near kinship with the immortal and eternal and divine.'

[3] On the ground of expediency the Note on 'Even love is sold' was vigorously answered in a pamphlet entitled *Reply to the anti-matrimonial hypothesis and supposed atheism of Percy Bysshe Shelley as laid down in Queen Mab*, published in 1821 by William Clark, the pirate of the poem, and reprinted in *The Unextinguished Hearth*, pp. 62 ff. Professor White supposes the author to have been William Johnson Fox, one of the reformers of the 'thirties. The main contentions are that marriage, so far from enslaving the woman, safeguards her rights and protects her child; that without it

*Epipsychidion* by the royal road of poetry. His theme is the agony and ecstasy of the search and the glory of the hope. He declares the intractable need; let time meet it as it must and however it may. And this for him is the function of the highest poetry, as he argues in his *Defence*. Real poets like Lucan and Spenser may do well enough in celebrating accepted ethics; but the higher poet is a diviner of things to come. Enclose him in the present, and his genius, like a sword of lightning, consumes the scabbard.

the mercenary woman and the predatory man would have an easier run; and that something more than transitory passion would bind the lovers, some promise to be constant, actual or virtual, and the care of their offspring. Shelley in his own person bowed to circumstances and married; and the Note allows there will be moral obligations in the absence of legal ones, and when the physical attraction shall have passed. He would have said in reply to his critics that he was looking forward to an ideal society under economic equality; that 'passion' drives lust and greed away; and that any kind of bondage is an enemy to passion. For that reason he deprecates any promises. If asked, 'What would you do in a conflict of "passion" with "generosity", as you call it to an old love?' he might have answered, 'As things are, I should go by generosity, but in my ideal state, all the parties being enlightened, no such conflict would arise.'

# XII

# SHELLEY AND THE AGE

## 1. THE POLITICAL SITUATION

SHELLEY in 1813 was no admirer of Cobbett, though he subsequently became one. Nevertheless, his diagnosis of the state of society might have been copied from *The Political Register*. We have it in the fervent and discerning fifth Canto of *Queen Mab*, and eight years later in *A Philosophical View of Reform*. The *View of Reform* is naturally more knowledgeable, more precise, and offers a programme of remedies. But the prophetic generalities of 1813 are all in the direction of the analysis of 1821. The lust of riches and all that riches buy—so the analysis makes out—has cemented an alliance between the old feudal and mercantile aristocracy and the new body of bondholders and industrial magnates, who owe their capital to the two liberticide wars, that against the Colonies and that against France. The wars, launched upon us by the English patriciate, the constant enemies of freedom, resulted in the Debt, and so in paper money, and so in high prices, and so in the destitution and servitude of the labouring classes, including the horror of child slavery, and in the fierce unrest. For not only do their physical sufferings brutalize and exasperate the poor, but still more the sense of being chattels, the sense of dereliction even more than of wrong, and the want of all the higher pleasures, not to be made good by a religion that carries into the other world the unmercifulness of this, or offers a Paradise that 'like the flames of Milton's hell only makes their darkness visible'. Pay off the principal of the Debt, and tax the rich to pay it, disband the army, the instrument of an iron repression, and you kill the root of our miseries. Some inequality of wealth, it seems, there will have to be: the refinement of mind that comes of it is a great advantage; the modicum of humane and honourable sentiment in the older aristocracy was and is a great advantage. Let us at any rate cherish equality as an ideal and a natural right, and look on any breach of it as a necessary evil.[1] But the vast inequalities of the present system who can justify? And what advantage can we

---

[1] On equality and the duty of 'a strenuous tendency towards it' see the letter to Miss Hitchener of 25 July 1811.

attribute to the leisure and luxury of the new men and their swarming agents and dependants?

'These are a sort of pelting wretches in whose employment there is nothing to exercise even to their distortion the more majestic faculties of the soul. Though at the bottom it is all trick, there is something frank and magnificent in the chivalrous disdain of infamy connected with a gentleman. There is something to which—until you see through the base falsehood upon which all inequality is founded—it is difficult for the imagination to refuse its respect in the faithful and direct dealings of the substantial merchant. But in the habits and lives of the new aristocracy created out of an increase in public calamities . . . there is nothing to qualify our disapprobation. They eat and drink and sleep, and in the intervals of these things, performed with the most vexatious ceremony and accompaniments, they cringe and lie. They poison the literature of the age in which they live by requiring either the antitype of their own mediocrity in books, or such stupid and distorted and inharmonious idealisms as alone have the power to stir their torpid imaginations. Their hopes and fears are of the narrowest description. Their domestic affections are feeble, and they have no others. They think of any commerce with their species but as a means, never as an end, and as a means of the basest forms of personal advantage.'[1]

For Shelley, as for Cobbett, these people dominated the situation. He is obsessed with the sinister alliance; with the old masters of the land—King and Noble—using the new wealth to nurse the Army and the Church, their props and tools; with the wars; with the consent of both aristocracies in the exploitation of the poor; with the bane in the heart and mind of all classes: the unhappiness, the torpor, the vulgarity of the rich; the want, the drudgery, the savagery, the vice, the desperation of the poor.

## 2. THE THEORY OF ACQUIESCENCE

### (a) Burke

The two greatest of the intellectual powers of the age more or less resigned themselves to these conditions. Burke was an adversary with whom Shelley never came to close quarters. For, having no sense of the main truth which Burke proclaimed, he could find in his dominant authority only a sort of intangible

---

[1] *A Philosophical View of Reform*, ed. Rolleston, pp. 43–68. Cf. *Queen Mab*, v. 22–37, 79–93, 158–66, 237–48.

imprisonment, and fight with it only as one who beats the air. To make the case harder, there was the great man's past. He had been the High Priest of the liberal spirit in the gravest crises of our history, and but for him and a few like him, the cries of oppressed millions in India would have been, as he said, 'blown about over an unheeding ocean'. And if he withstood the Revolution it was in a sacred tenderness for 'the works of God established in order and beauty'. Nor would he blind himself to the suffering inherent in the societies he cherished. No leveller could have written of it more feelingly than he, when, in *A Vindication of Natural Society*, he forgot his parody and delivered the indictment of things as they are with no forced intensity. Yet no classical economist proclaimed these hardships irremovable with more conviction. The servile multitudes were by their servitude politically disabled. They were 'the children of the State', justly unenfranchised, free to cry in their trouble, but not to declare the cure. Nay, their unruliness and their wildness were a sort of Titanic menace to the fair order of the world. Woe to the rulers who were deaf to them; but woe indeed to those who in a hankering for ideal justice should lay rough hands on the organic State, and give no ear to the wisdom that alone can save it in the voice of the 'natural aristocracy'. For this is the sentence of Nature upon all peoples—that the many are to live powerless and to live hard. And how could one who loved so dearly the glory of the nations and the glory in the hearts of men subscribe the unchangeable doom? How could he bless and ban the stuff we are made of, and love and fear? If it is Nature that moulds the State (as he was among the first to see), does she then work to a model and limit her hand? Does she implant the desire of life in vain? And 'the glory of Europe', the arts and graces and codes of honour: is she always to beggar the many that with these she may gild the few, careful of the plumage and careless of the bird? These questions were hard to answer; but for 'beautiful idealisms' rushing in there were arrows in Burke's quiver keen enough.

### (b) Wordsworth

If Burke loomed upon Shelley from afar, Wordsworth's 'apostasy', so called, touched him. How completely the supposed leader was lost he learnt in 1814 from *The Excursion*, and addressed its author in lines of mingled reverence and reproof: Where was now the mind that had been like a 'lone star', like 'a rock-built refuge above the blind and battling multitude'? What now of the songs 'woven in honoured poverty' and 'consecrate to truth and liberty'?[1] Shelley had responded deeply to the discovery of 'the life of things', to the ballads of the sufferings of the poor, and to the poems of National Independence. It appeared a sad transition from the lines on Hofer or Toussaint to the deliverances in *The Excursion* of the Wanderer and the Priest. Yet the sentiment of the patriotic sonnets and the counsels of 1814 are by no means hard to weld in one.

On the day when Wordsworth and his sister walked into Grasmere to make it their home, the Vale and all its tenants seemed to conspire. The cottages from among the trees 'darted at each other cheerful looks'; the lake and the swans of the lake, hill and field and all that moved and rested on them rejoiced in the light and air; the universal soul 'circulated from link to link', and beat in Man. This was one of the days on which 'the deep power of Joy' leaves its mark upon us. But at a lower pulse on ordinary days the quickening stream flows on from things to thoughts, from thoughts to responsive things, and the rill from Grasmere pours itself into the great volume of being and doing that is marked off by the national bounds. Within the comity of mankind and the narrower comity of Europe these national entities constitute our life. In some historic system of love and labour abetted by the living earth the European whose rights are not denied him garners up his heart. Once a foreign invader shall be master of their land, in the hearts of all its children the Universal Soul will cease to circulate, and earth, air, and skies for them will fail:

> Never be it ours
> To see the sun how brightly it doth shine,
> And know that noble Feelings, manly Powers,
> Instead of gathering strength must droop and pine,
> And Earth with all her pleasant fruits and flowers
> Fade, and participate in Man's decline.

Internal liberty may wait for its fulfilment; that is a consummation in due time or manner wholly to be wished; and an ardent

---

[1] Sonnet: *To Wordsworth*, 1814.

patriotism will of itself induce it, in spirit if not in form. But of national independence the need is absolute.[1]

'Nay', was the answer, 'but the Rights of Man are primary; it is they that must not wait.' And Wordsworth is divided between the conservatism he had learnt from Burke and his own strong sense of the iniquities upon the poor. The literature of the time has no more powerful words than those of the Wanderer for the mutilation of human nature in the new towns,[2] and the Solitary follows with the drudgery and brutality of the field worker.[3] At this point enter two vigorous trout-fishing boys, one gentle and the other simple, both attendant at the village school, but free at other hours of hill and vale. They are an earnest of better times and a sample of the 'true equality'.[4] Fortune and class will part them in years to come, but in the essentials of happiness the poor man's son (given a tolerable livelihood) will not have fallen behind. The 'primal blessings'— duties and charities and saving influences—will be 'scattered like flowers' before them both in the fair field they inherit. Not all who labour on the land are taxed too hard, nor are they a few only whom hardship never unmanned. Teach all your people to read and write and think religiously; open to them the vast lands oversea; and you relieve their material distresses and their sick hearts, and if the townsman can never live as best conduces to his peace, you put all other classes in the things of supreme moment on the same level. Whatever shall accrue hereafter to the status of the common people, so it be not come by at the peril of the State, will make for good; and meanwhile count your mercies: your safety, your freedom, your time-tried Constitution and humanely minded Church.[5] These counsels are delivered, however, with a certain diffidence. The Pastor's wife doubts if the Wanderer be not too visionary,[6] and the Pastor lays the issue in conclusion on the grace of God.

[1] This is one of the main positions of the pamphlet on the Convention of Cintra (1809), where he is meeting the view that the Spaniards are governed by despots of their own, and the French will do them no more harm, but rather good. That the poet of *The Excursion* to the end of his life cherished a Fabian hope of liberty to the extent demanded by the Chartists is thoroughly well proved in the second chapter of Miss Edith Batho's *The Later Wordsworth*.

[2] viii. 82 ff.     [3] viii. 333 ff.     [4] ix. 237-49.
[5] vi. 1-73.       [6] ix. 459-73.

### 3. General Melancholy

Burke and Wordsworth thought of human nature nobly and gladly. But for the greater part of the first half of last century, the disillusion and the sufferance, so rife in other countries, ran, though in a thinner current, under our own skies. Michelet has described in rememberable chapters the brooding night in France after the first bright day of the Revolution: the grandiose pretences of the Empire; the hollow peace with the Church; Chateaubriand's literary Christianity; and the sense everywhere of an empty life. And what could come of the Holy Alliance but a far worse issue of broken hopes, spurious revivals, and spiritless acquiescences? 'But as yet struggles the eleventh hour of the Night: birds of prey are on the wing, spectres cry, the dead walk, the living dream'—so wrote Jean Paul Richter of that exhausted age. This was the world that Byron shook with his pain and longing, more accepted in other countries than his own. For over here there were motives to cheerfulness. The general mind of the nation made itself easy in Burke's great grip, and few of the old order saw farther than the Parsonage and the Park. The new industries were coming on, and with them a radical and forward-looking creed. Jane Austen was a contented, and Bentham an eager spirit, and, wide asunder as they were, both counted on the normal running of our nature. But under this complacency were bitter strains. There were disheartened idealists who had thrilled to the mighty pulsation of 1789, like Wordsworth's Solitary; and those who had seen in Napoleon the destined saviour and in heart fell with him. 'I was taught to think', wrote Hazlitt, who was one of these,

'and I was willing to believe that genius was not a bawd—that virtue was not a mask—that love had its seat in the human heart. Now I would care little if these words were struck out of the dictionary. . . . Instead of patriots and friends of freedom, I see nothing but the tyrant and the slave, the people linked with kings to rivet on the chains of despotism. . . . I see the insolent Tory, the blind Reformer, the coward Whig! If mankind had wished for what is right, they might have had it long ago.'[1]

And those who read Byron in his own spirit, and saw the banner of Freedom 'torn but flying', were inspired with a hate of their

---

[1] From the Essay 'On the Pleasure of Hating', written in 1823 and published in *The Plain Speaker*.

enemies not always differing from a scorn of their kind. More-over, in the pattern of contemporary thought there were colours yet more sombre. Michelet has written of Malthus as a type of the failing trust in Life; and the *Essay on Population* in 1797 laid the foundation of Ricardo's *Political Economy* in 1817. The inexorable books were a judgement. In the 'classical economy' presented in them, and supplements to them, the labourer might read, if he would or could, of 'Nature's mighty feast' where 'the tables are already full and unbidden guests are left to starve'; of diminishing Returns; of the Market of his Labour for ever uncontrolled; of Rent ever usurping on the national income; and pressing down his wages to a fixed and a minimal sum— so fixed, this Wage Fund, that if any of his class should ever earn more money, it must always be at the others' cost. With all these 'laws' and necessities descending and hemming him around, the man in Poe's tale of *The Pit and the Pendulum* was not unhappier; unless indeed 'Moral Restraint' might help, and the proletarians by a falling birth-rate and the rising price of labour might lead captivity captive once again, as when the medieval pestilences had done them so much good. Necessity, not setting free but killing: that way lay desperation; and the fear of a violent dissolution of society in the bitter years after the war punctuates Shelley's letters. 'The change', he writes in 1819, 'should commence among the higher orders, or anarchy will only be the last flash before despotism. I wonder and tremble.'[1] Finally—with regard to diminishing returns—in 1804, Grainville, a young apostate priest fallen upon obloquy and penury, published his now forgotten poem, *Le Dernier Homme*. The theme had dawned upon him in his youth as he watched the ocean by Le Havre laying bare the granite skeleton of the earth; and his grandiose Vision described the end of a man and a woman, the sole living creatures on a wasted globe. Science had already pointed in that direction with its prophecy of another glacial age. It was a good subject, too good for the poets and novelists to let fall; and here in England from Coleridge to Beddoes it ran its course, chiefly rememberable for Byron's ghastly *Darkness*.[2] Shelley too was among the infected.

[1] To Peacock, 22 Aug. (?).
[2] *Darkness* was written in 1816, when Shelley and Byron were together, and published in that year in the volume containing *The Prisoner of Chillon*. See

In the summer of 1816 the Alpine fastnesses spoke to him of Ahriman enthroned and 'Buffon's sublime and gloomy theory that this globe will be changed into a mass of frost by the encroachments of the polar ice'.[1] And he wrote in the last and greatest of his poems of

> All those whose fame and infamy must grow
> Till the great Winter lay the form and name
> Of this green earth with them forever low.

In a phrase of Dr. Johnson's, no one ate a spoonful of pudding the less in the imagination of planetary Death. But it was a dark allurement, agreeable to the temper of the times.

### 4. HOPE

The poet, says Shelley, is a nightingale singing in the dark. The poetry of the Romantic Revival, or the greater strain of it, is intensely conscious of the cruelty of things and the dejection of the times, and from Grandeur and Beauty and Love proceeds to Faith and Hope. But the two masters who more directly than the rest perform the function of a prophet are of wholly different moulds. Shelley would scarcely quarrel with Wordsworth for political caution in particular and impending issues, for in those he was himself not without it.[2] What he charged him

introductory note in the edition of Byron's *Works* by E. H. Coleridge, who mentions *The Last Man or Omegarius and Sideria, a Romance in Futurity*, 1806. Campbell wrote a short stanzaic poem, *The Last Man*, first published in 1823, a pious effusion on the Mercy that shall end 'the tragedy of Time', while not permitting the soul of Man to die. He says in one of his letters of that year: 'Many years ago I had the idea of this Last Man in my head, and distinctly remember speaking of the subject to Lord Byron.' Coleridge in *Religious Musings* (1794) supposes the end of the world to come by the arrest of the sun, 'making the noon ghastly' (ii. 384 ff.). *Omegarius and Sideria* must have been based on Grainville's poem, where Sideria is the name of the Last Woman. And that is remarkable; for Michelet states in his fascinating chapter on Grainville that the publisher of his Vision could sell only four or five copies. In *Le Dernier Homme* there is very little of the frost, but much of darkness and sterility. See Michelet, *Révolution Française, du 18 Brumaire à Waterloo*, Bk. I, ch. x. In 1823 T. L. Beddoes began a drama on this subject, of which a few fragments remain. Mary Shelley's third novel, *The Last Man* (1826), varies the tradition. In this story the world is devastated by plague, and the hero, supposing himself the sole survivor, sails along the shores of the Mediterranean, and writes the story of Man on leaves of trees. Cf. *The Prelude*, v. 1–165.　　[1] To Peacock, 24 July.

　　[2] 'With respect to Universal Suffrage, I confess I consider its adoption in the present unprepared state of public knowledge and feeling a measure fraught with danger. I think that none but those who register their names as paying a certain small sum in *direct taxes* ought at present to send Members to Parliament.'—*A Proposal for putting Reform to the Vote*, 1817. The italics his.

with in *The Excursion* and after was a fixed horizon, a bounded hope, no insurgency, no fire, and all this leading him on to positive time-serving. Not that he thought lightly of his extra-ordinary power—he has defined it well[1]—or that, in view of the great sonnets, he would have echoed Landor's saying that Wordsworth's instrument 'has no trumpet-stop'. But one con-stant feature of that austere and reserved Muse he was sure to note, and note unkindly: Nature in *Peter Bell the Third* kisses Peter with a sisterly kiss, and wishes he could love like Burns.[2] And there lies the root or best example of their differences. For Wordsworth stands at gaze upon the object, absorbent, and yet aloof; *spectator haud particeps*, as Coleridge put it; 'never a moun-tain man, but always down below upon the road'. Shelley throws himself into the object and makes it his expression. In face of human suffering, therefore, Wordsworth's way was to scan it *ab extra*, and yet 'most feelingly',[3] till

> what we feel of sorrow and despair
> From ruin and from change, and all the grief
> The passing shows of being leave behind,
> Appears an idle dream;

while to Shelley it was an agony of his own, till in a mysterious access grace and melody washed his heart of it, and so away to glory. On the one hand the wisdom of the man; on the other 'the bright wisdom of youth's noon'. Further, the one rejoices in permanence at the heart of action; while for the other a purging of the world as by a West Wind is the favourite form of his prophecy. If the hope of a new urgency of the divine stress faltered at times in Shelley's later days, he stayed it again on the

---

[1]
> Yet his was individual mind,
>   And new created all he saw
> In a new manner, and refined
> Those new creations, and combined
>   Them, by a master-spirit's law.
>
> Thus—though unimaginative—
>   An apprehension clear, intense,
> Of his mind's work, had made alive
> The things it wrought on; I believe
>   Wakening a sort of thought in sense.

(*Peter Bell*, IV. ix, x.) 'Unimaginative' is shown by the context to mean 'undramatic'.

[2] Cf. the verses to Mary prefatory to *The Witch of Atlas*.

[3] *The Prelude*, viii. 648–50. Cf. vii. 382 ff., and especially viii. 503 ff. for the intenseness of these retired sympathies.

surest of all the signs. In 1821, in his *View of Reform,* he read the omens, making Wordsworth rich amends for his jibing at him, but not without rebate:

> 'The most unfailing herald or companion or follower of an universal employment of the sentiments of a nation to the production of a beneficial change is poetry. . . . The persons in whom this power makes its abode, may often, as far as regards many portions of their nature, have little correspondence with the spirit of good of which it is the minister. But though they may deny and abjure, they are yet compelled to serve that which is seated on the throne of their own soul. . . . It is impossible to read the productions of our most celebrated writers . . . without being startled by the electric life which there is in their words. They measure the circumference or sound the depths of human nature with a comprehensive and all-penetrating spirit at which they are themselves perhaps most sincerely astonished, for it is less their own spirit than the spirit of their age. They are the priests of an unapprehended inspiration; the mirrors of gigantic shadows which futurity casts upon the present; the words which express what they conceive not; the trumpet which sings to battle and feels not what it inspires; the influence which is moved not, but moves. Poets and philosophers are the unacknowledged legislators of the world.'

But in 1813 the evidences, apart from Wordsworth, were not so clear. Coleridge was 'flagging wearily through darkness and despair'; Byron had not yet proved himself 'the pilgrim of Eternity'; and seven years were to pass ere Shelley greeted in the author of *Hyperion* 'a rival who will far surpass me'. Only 'that which was seated on the throne of his own soul'—only, in other words, a religious instinct—could tell him that the world was in good and mighty hands. They alone could save it, and they would. A reasoned theology was, therefore, the first of his needs, and one, at the same time, to which his powers were in no way adequate.

# XIII

# GOD AND NATURE AND MAN

## 1. Shelley and Science

MUCH has been written of Shelley's aptitude for science and debt to scientists. Having regard to his intuitive grasp of the law of transformation, Professor Whitehead has declared even that, 'had he lived a hundred years later, the twentieth century might have seen a Newton among chemists', ranking him at the same time with Berkeley and Wordsworth as a vanquisher of the mechanical cosmology.[1] He is considered to have caught up ideas from Newton, Erasmus Darwin, Herschel, Davy, and others, and to have put them forward in his poems, more especially *Prometheus Unbound* and *The Witch of Atlas*, in symbolic imagery.[2] And by assuming that he read through, or read extensively, the works on natural philosophy mentioned in his letters and Notes, you can certainly put to his credit, by the time he was twenty-one, not much less than erudition. But, though estimates as uncontrollable as this of his scientific acquirements have a way of swelling, no one supposes he was more than a gleaner—an ardent gleaner—in any portion of the field. And his gleanings sufficed for their purpose. He went to Nature principally, as a poet, for her power and splendour, and, as a philosopher, to sustain his 'atheism' and to explode by her testimonies what he called 'the evil faith'. And the 'evil faith' was the Newtonian deism coupled with Christianity in its crudest acceptation.

[1] *Science and the Modern World*, pp. 104 ff.

[2] On Shelley's probable indebtedness to Adam Walker see above, pp. 9, 10, and footnote. This side of the subject has been illuminated for the first time in Professor Carl Grabo's four books: *A Newton among Poets*, 1930; *The Meaning of The Witch of Atlas*, 1935; *Prometheus Unbound, an Interpretation*, 1935; and *The Magic Plant*, 1936. He says that Shelley 'must have read at an early age', conjecturably in the Library at Field Place, Priestley on electricity, Darwin's *Botanic Garden*, and 'Newton's *Optics*, perhaps' (*A Newton among Poets*, p. 3). He says further (ibid., p. 86): 'Scientists mentioned in Shelley's letters and the scientific encyclopaedias of Nicholson and Rees, mentioned in the Notes to *Queen Mab*, are, of course, on the face of it, primary sources of his knowledge.' These scientists would be Laplace, Boyle, Cabanis, Bailly, and Herschel, as well as Newton. That is rather much for a young person with other interests equally urgent, unless the 'reading' were sparse and slight.

Shelley's almost life-long hatred of Christianity was not as yet in its fullest blaze. It was more evolved in *A Refutation of Deism*, published in 1814, and the later years when he 'dieted on Greek' inspired it a second time. Yet much of the verse of *Queen Mab* and five of the Notes add up to a lengthy polemic from the earlier point of view. Equally ridiculous as a chain of dogmas or a history of events—so his argument runs—Christianity had debased and fettered the human mind. Relying on brute authority and the fable of the Judgement, it had broken the real springs of goodness with the motives of cupidity and fear. For between the type of Torquemada and the type of Paley there was really no choice. Both had looked on orthodoxy as the basis of morals and called in, the one sooner and the other later, the sanction of fire. For the famous definition of virtue as 'the doing good to mankind in obedience to the will of God and for the sake of everlasting happiness' was only the Anglican mollification of a fearful threat. The divinity with the rods and recompenses, the exacter of the great sacrifice, the parent of untold wars and woes: how little did He accord with the pure life and luminous wisdom of Jesus himself, who had sought to deliver his countrymen from their superstitions and suffered the 'common lot' of men so minded. 'Jesus was sacrificed to the honour of that God with whom he was afterwards confounded.' Man had never recovered from what was incomparably his greatest Fall, and the release of his soul, the authenticity of his virtue waited for the overthrow of that *Infâme*. And in Shelley's view the idea of the Watcher and the Master hung by the theory of a Creator. That, then, is his butt in *Queen Mab*, as it had been in *The Necessity of Atheism*, and here especially his natural science is brought to bear.

Moreover, in the spring of 1812, while planning and writing his poem, he had made new contact with the Illumination, not 'cold and unimpassioned' this time, but eager and eloquent and overwhelming, in the *Système de la Nature*.[1] The book carried familiar burden; for Godwin had taken toll of it, and itself took plenteous toll of the *De Rerum Natura*, annexing the substance and inflaming the spirit. And throughout *Queen Mab* and the Notes Shelley takes over the main pillars of its argument: Nature's vastness and unswerving law, beyond the wit and above

[1] See p. 144.

the necessity of a Maker or a Manager. The stars that sang to Addison of the hand that made them sang to Holbach of no such thing. Whereas the great Mechanic was now and then put to it, according even to natural philosophers, to nudge the machine, Holbach saw it running determinately, by a law sufficient to it, and of itself. But it ran, he thought, or had started to run well, on the whole, for men. The uncreated molecules in their unoriginated motions for ever break and make; but so that the fairest flower and finest stuff of Nature, mind or reason, was thrusting more and more towards the light; science extending; theology, the arch-depraver, warder of ignorance, ally of misgovernment, no longer lording it; and mankind making at long last for the far-off goal of reasonable laws and virtuous magistracies and a life that has more in it of pleasure than of pain. Shelley was an optimist of a temper quite different from this; but Holbach had re-inspired him with the argument from the grasp of Necessity, and the stellar wildernesses, and the speed of light, and with a fierce impatience of the Christian priest, *le fabricateur de la divinité, le tyran des esprits, l'émule et le maître des rois.*

## 2. LUCRETIUS AND THE *ALMA VENUS*

Yet Shelley never thought of life in Holbach's way as a form of matter, though he might, on occasion, use the language of materialism without commitment.[1] In his most negative humour his 'stony principle in stones' or 'existing power of existence' is more than the body it appears in. He could never forget the vivid moment in his boyhood when a 'shadow' of the Presence in Nature's beauty and Man's love had 'fallen' on him; nor could he easily have dismissed the dualism of mind and matter that had floated for over a century in the air, or the vague immanentalism in Godwin, or the Platonic idealism of his ardent adventuring a few years before, or least of all the poetry of the divine interfusion by the great seers from the

---

[1] In his essay *On Life* (? 1815) Shelley states that the 'absurdities of the popular philosophy of mind and matter . . . had early conducted me to materialism'; but he was then discontented with it, for man is of a nature 'disclaiming alliance with transience and decay, incapable of imagining to himself annihilation, being not what he is, but what he has been and shall be'. This 'materialism' must mean the view of mind or soul as an 'appendage' of matter or body, not the view that it *is* body, which he seems never to have held.

classics down to Wordsworth. If, however, we are determining how his spiritual outlook came about, except as an integral element of his consciousness, we must reckon, at this early period, with the paramount influence of Lucretius, long since loved and laid to heart, and confessed on the title-page of *Queen Mab* by the verses in which the great Roman declares his will to tread untrodden ways, and discourse on high matters, and loose the minds of men from the strangleholds of faith. Here was not a purveyance of ideas merely, but an inspiration of power. Shelley, it is true, was to Lucretius as a feverish quest and a limitless yearning to a mind in sovereign calm; but he commanded like him, and nourished at his board the highest virtues of metaphysical poetry.

Many a casual phrase betrays the affinity: *daedala tellus, lucida 'tela diei, caeli cavernae, palantia sidera passim.*

Pinnacled dim in the intense inane

not only echoes Lucretius with his *magnum inane, profundum inane,* but looks up to infinity with his eyes. Nor is it only the deeps of space that move them. In the foundation of all Shelley's think-ing the concept of the soul's inviolable recess, the 'soul within the soul', the 'epipsychidion', is a conflation of a well-estab-lished tenet of religious mysticism with what he had found in Lucretius about the elements of the *animus* and the inmost of the four, which is the active substance and the source of all sensation:

> Nam penitus prorsum latet haec natura subestque,
> Nec magis hac infra quicquam est in corpore nostro
> Atque anima est animae proporro totius ipsa.[1]

And beside these deeps and splendours they both conceived of Nature as a single actor in a drama that, under the law of ages, knits together constancy with change, and beauty with terror,

---

[1] iii. 273–5. This is the section on the *animus* and the *anima*, iii, 94 ff. The passage in the Essay *On Love* which propounds the theory of the 'epipsychidion' is evidently reminiscent of Lucretius. The inmost soul, he says, using the language of materialism once in a way, is 'an assemblage of the minutest particles of which our nature is composed'; and that goes back to the lines on the superfine stuff of both *animus* and *anima*, and especially the nameless fourth substance of *animus*:
> Qua neque mobilius quicquam neque tenvius exstat,
> Nec magis e parvis et levibus est elementis.          (243–4.)
*Ex adyto tamquam cordis,* says Lucretius elsewhere, the 'unentered' part of the temple, the penetralia.

and good, as men call it, with evil. In that self-operating law and tremendous operation, that *rerum majestas*, was a refuge of their souls and the riddance from the primal burden of the master God:

> Quis regere immensi summam, quis habere profundi
> Indu manu validas potis est moderanter habenas?

All the materialists had said these things, but only Lucretius in so great a style. Moreover, if again and again he testifies that soul depends on body, and is body, and neither universally nor individually lives discarnate, he nevertheless puts back as a poet the divinity that his science put away. And no place, perhaps, in literature had more hold of Shelley than the magnificent Invocation of the *alma Venus genetrix*, Mother and Sustainer of power, joy, grace in and under the heavens, in the laughing harvests or the Muses' eternal charm, peacemaker also among men; yet bound inseparably to an enemy principle of war and waste, contending and in the last resort prevailing with it,

> quoniam rerum naturam sola gubernas.

From this point, however, the two minds draw apart, albeit in degree only, according to their characters and the pressure of their times. How Lucretian, with a difference, is the *Ode to Heaven*. There are suns beyond suns, so many, says the Roman, that this our firmament is to the others as a man's body to the whole earth. There are the *aeterni sidera mundi*,

> Ever-canopying dome
> Of acts and ages yet to come.

Yet the poet of the Ode concludes by denying to his stars their apparent abidingness, and seeing them, like bubbles in a river, 'tremble, gleam, and disappear'. For, though Lucretius is deeply sensible of the transformation of things and of the possibility that 'a single day shall render up the whole frame to ruin' (though of the substance nothing be lost, and new forms arise for the old), yet he apprehends oftener and more firmly than Shelley the *validae aevi leges* that stand for ever and the central peace subsisting at the heart of endless agitation.[1]

---

[1] One more item of the debt to Lucretius, if so it is. In *The Triumph of Life*, ii. 469, 543, the ghastly dancers throw off from their forms and faces images or shadows of themselves in incessant succession, so that the air is thick with them. They are, apparently, the ever-wasting states of men, the tissues of desire or will perpetually

## 3. A PURPOSIVE UNIVERSE

For Shelley's universe is like himself, passionate. Power, Life, Spirit, infinitely ranging, deepening, rejoicing, throbbing, from sun and star to worm and fly, in beauty, grandeur, good, in things accounted evil, above all in the love to one another of the sentient creatures and the fruits of the spirit of love in the life of man—so burns his sovereign principle.[1] In his earlier view at least it has to do with Matter: 'gets inside it', or 'fills up its interstices', as some philosophers thought, or, as Shelley once wrote, is 'a superior appendage' to it. But the fiery Power kneads it, as it were, to an animal body, and under the integument all things soever are 'living Spirit' and 'comprehend a world of loves and hates'.[2] But the Spirit 'o'er-informs its tenement', 'tortures' it, sweeps it from form to form in 'a storm of change', blowing away pyramids and empires like desert dust, and so transforming that in the aeonic process there is no atom but it once inhered in flesh and blood, nor any spot of earth but a city of men once rose over it.[3]

The fierce labour is ruled to its faintest motion by immutable law, and presses to a sure and certain end.[4] It moves not merely, as he once wrote, in a 'rotation of change', but in a spiral. For in the period represented by *Queen Mab* he builds on the theory of the ascent of being bequeathed by Aristotle to a long posterity. 'There is in all things', says Hooker, 'an appetite or desire whereby they incline to something which they may be, and when they are it, they shall be perfecter than now they are.' 'Life is infinite', writes Shelley, 'and as the soul which now inhabits this frame was once the vivifying principle of the infinitely lowest link in the chain of existence, so is it ultimately destined to attain the highest.'[5] Hence, for us men, personal

---

fading and being shed. This strange fancy may have been suggested by the long account in the *De Rerum Natura*, ii. 26 ff., of the *simulacra*, the filmy images discharged continually from the surface of things, floating in the air, and impinging on the senses, by which visions and perceptions may be accounted for.

[1] *Queen Mab*, i. 264–77; ii. 102–8; iii. 214–25; vi. 146 ff.

[2] 'Fills up its interstices' is a phrase of Erasmus Darwin's, quoted in *A Newton among Poets*, p. 42. Professor Grabo surmises that Shelley rummaged a good deal in Darwin's copious notes. See iv. 89–97, 140–6, and the letter to Elizabeth Hitchener, 24 Nov. 1811.

[3] ii. 211–43.

[4] vi. 146–219; supported by the Notes on Necessity (on vi. 171–3, 198).

[5] 2 Jan. 1812.

immortality may be counted on, as well before as after birth and death ('the creation of a soul at birth is a thing I do not like');[1] and Shelley was never so confident of it as at this time. Somewhere, apparently at the animal stage, in the process, as the interminable life passes upward from one embodiment to another, it is individuated, and the human self, here or elsewhere, is the same living entity, and this, as he supposes, in spite of the fact that memory may not be carried over from span to span. The soul will rise—and *ex hypothesi* cannot fall—to 'a different mode of terrestrial existence to which we have fitted ourselves in this mode'[2] or to some existence not terrestrial, 'losing all consciousness of having formerly lived elsewhere', and 'beginning life anew possibly under a shape of which we have no idea'.[3] And sometimes he thinks otherwise of the survival of memory, and dares to hope that in the hereafter friends and lovers will meet and know each other and share their lives again.[4]

To personal felicity, spiritual affluence, larger and larger, and to some great 'day', some turn of the historical drama and swift ending of the sins of Time the whole world yearns, and 'the restless wheels of being, instinct with infinite life, bicker and burn to gain their destined goal'. All the operation of the orbs bears upon this. All these ages past the immeasurable churn has churned for Man's felicity, and it will one day 'come'. Again the Universe is man-centred. When the Ptolemaic astronomy faded out, and Man exchanged his cosmic prerogative for his cosmic nonentity, he repaired his pride, it has been said, by 'interpreting his humiliation as a deliverance'. He was now no longer pent in a compound in his Master's eye; he was the measure of all things, and all things important only as they affected him. In *Queen Mab* he has ceased to be that masterly adventurer in a world not made for him; but the world is life of his life, instinct, like him, with an infinite desire, and rewarded in his conscious and progressive spirituality as with a 'glorious prize'.

[1] Cf. viii. 6–8; ix. 149–57.     [2] 24 Nov. 1811.     [3] 20 June 1811.
[4] Certainly, he lays as much value on the indefinite filling out of life by vivid sensibility, so that man may be 'immortal upon earth' (viii. 203–11, elaborated in the Note to this passage, with a quotation from Condorcet). And in x. 12–16 he says only that it was a prevision of the millennium that implanted our 'rooted hopes' of heaven. But in ix. 161–3, 171–84, he clearly expects both survival and reunion, and he says so more than once to Miss Hitchener, e.g. 23 and 24 Nov. 1811.

## 4. TRANSCENDENTALISM

But this divinity is not merely 'emergent' or in process of becoming. It is that and more. Nor does it, or any of it, always inhabit body. Shelley occasionally writes of the Spirit as living only in and by the world; 'it is the essence of the universe, the universe is the essence of it'.[1] But on the other hand he plentifully affirms that the Spirit transcends the stuff it works in, just as the soul of a man or the soul of a flower lives on when the body dies.[2] The souls are again and again re-embodied and cope with matter; but ultimately, it seems, they are gathered into transcendental being, 'a sempiternal heritage', 'a peace which in the end all life will share'.[3] Compared with that ulterior state, life and death and the manifested world are but 'phantasmal', but a prison chamber dimly lighted from without.[4] Conversely, from its transcendental being the Spirit lets down, as it were, a portion of itself into form and time, and manages the expedition, in unbroken oneness with it, from above. It becomes and it is; it goes to its own assistance, and 'revivifies' its fainting powers.[5] It is the 'eternal spring of all existence'[6] and all things visible are its 'temple'.[7] Immersed in the temporal and the sensible, it is 'blindly working will';[8] but from above it 'guides' the activities of Nature, 'apportioning its place to each spring of the machine', and nothing happens that it does not 'recognize' or 'foresee'.[9]

## 5. THE DIVINE COMBATANT AND THE PRINCIPLE OF EVIL

So then, as operative in the world, it seems to be Mind or Will. If not a person, it is something like one. It has purpose, desire, zeal, and perhaps patience. All our hopes depend on its power and desire to do great works for us and lead us out of Egypt with an outstretched arm. For somehow we are in the power of evil. Evil is a first principle; hate disputes with love (repulsion with attraction) the empire of the atom.[10] Or it is a

---

[1] 11 June 1811; it is 'as the vegetative power to vegetables and the stony to stones'.
[2] i. 148–56, on Ianthe's living soul and dying body; and the letter of 24 Nov. 1811, on the surviving soul of a flower.
[3] i. 149, 185.       [4] vi. 190–6.       [5] vi. 21–2, 51–7.       [6] vi. 190.
[7] i. 264–77.                    [8] ix. 5.                    [9] vi. 155–89.
[10] iv. 145, 146. The beginning of tyranny, which was the beginning of all mischief, is said to be 'selfishness' (iv. 30, 31) or vice. These are names for the original inexplicable power. In iv. 117–20 he denies the 'original sin' affirmed by 'priest-led

taint or hindrance from the body to the soul.[1] Does it inhere in
Man only, and not in Nature too? The poet of *Queen Mab* at
times thinks so. 'All things', he says, 'speak peace, harmony,
and love', except 'the outcast'.[2] 'Throughout these varied and
eternal worlds', he says, 'soul is the only element', the single
principle of life; and soul, except in Man, takes no stain from
what it animates, as light takes none from what it falls on. But
Man 'is of soul and body', on him alone body has power, as
servant or master, for good or ill.[3] Elsewhere in the poem,
however, this invidious difference is swept away; not only do
sinister passions rage almost universally in the human breast,
infecting even in the womb,[4] but Nature fails and sins as well.
For what of the *tanta culpa* that dispelled for Lucretius the theory
of a kind Creator: wastes, marshes, and vast seas, parching heat
and cold, niggard soils, and storm, and flood?[5] What of 'the
giant ages' that 'make and break', and the earth and all that it
inherits running down and crumbling, as Lucretius presages in
the sombre ending of his second Book? What of the menacing
era of darkness and cold?[6]

To all this cruelty of Nature, present and to come, to evil in
all its forms, he replies with a wager of faith. He had heard of
the talk among the astronomers of the obliquity of the earth's
axis to the ecliptic, and therewith the inclemencies of the sky,
being gradually mended,[7] and Herschel had made some stir

slaves', but goes on to say that 'Force and Falsehood' (wherever they come from)
hang over us in our cradles and cause our misdeeds. Again, in the Note on war
and soldiers (iv. 178, 179) he inserts a dialogue in verse between Vice and Falsehood as the two angels of a primal curse. The infection by evil begins in the
mother's womb (iv. 133–5).

  [1] iv. 154–65.

  [2] 192 ff. 'O Man, seek no further for the author of evil. Thou art he—There
is no evil but the evil you do or the evil you suffer, and both come from yourself.
Evil in general can only spring from disorder, and in the order of the world I find
a never failing system. Evil in particular cases exists only in the mind of those who
experience it; and this feeling is not the gift of Nature, but the work of Man
himself' (Rousseau's *Savoyard Vicar*, Everyman Edition, J. M. Dent & Sons, Ltd.).

  [3] iv. 139–67, an obscure passage which I cannot otherwise interpret.

  [4] iv. 104 ff.

  [5] *De Rerum Natura*, v. 198:

        Hoc tamen ex ipsis caeli rationibus ausim
        Confirmare, aliisque ex rebus reddere multis,
        Nequaquam nobis divinitus esse paratam
        Naturam rerum, tanta stat praedita culpa.

  [6] See footnote pp. 227, 228 on *The Last Man*.

  [7] The Note on vi. 45, 46, deals with this subject. 'There is no great extravagance

with his mare's nest of lunar volcanoes.[1] And it had been held of old time, and the tale had been told in *Paradise Lost*[2] how God brought in the axial obliquity, and harsh seasons, and malice and disease and death when Man had fallen and all earth shuddered to her bounds at the inflow of sin. Would not that which goes from end to end and 'lives along the line' demonstrate once more in the day of reclamation the 'perfect identity' of moral and physical being, and all things 'melodise with Man's blest nature', in undeclining springtime, and green fertility all lands over, and the moon made soft with heat and big with life?[3] Blessedness, pure joy, and 'the unbounded frame without a flaw': these must be the purposes of the Spirit. Or if not, if it shall continue that

> Worlds on worlds are rolling ever
> From creation to decay,

our faith can still assure us—'It does seem to me probable', says a modern writer on entropy,[4] 'that there will always be a created Universe which in places is the abode of conscious life. I do not claim that this opinion rests on any evidence. I only say that, though God may exist without a world, it is difficult to imagine any reason why He should choose to create a world

in presuming that the progress of the perpendicularity of the poles may be as rapid as the progress of intellect.' And he adds that astronomy teaches us that the movement goes forward, adducing Laplace, Cabanis, and Bailly in support, and arguing from the evidence of changing climates that 'some event of this sort has taken place already'. He seems to have lighted on this subject in Newton's *Return to Nature or Defence of the Vegetable Regimen*. On 19 Feb. 1813, he asked Thomas Hookham to get him information, and Hookham answered with a list of authorities.

[1] *A Newton among Poets*, p. 88.

[2] x. 648 ff.

[3] viii. 58 ff.; and *Prometheus Unbound*, Act iv. Shelley no doubt had in mind the eighth chapter of the Epistle to the Romans, about creation 'made subject to vanity' (or frustration) 'not willingly' (not for its own fault, but Man's), and God having inflicted the calamity 'in hope' (the hope of our redemption), with which expectation all Nature groans like a woman in travail. In this St. Paul rested partly on Genesis iii. 17–19: 'Cursed is the ground for thy sake. . . . Thorns also and thistles shall it bring forth to thee'; and partly on passages in Jewish writers like Ezra xiii and the Book of Enoch about the Renovation of Nature through the Messiah. And these apocalyptic writers drew in turn on O.T. sources, especially Isaiah lxv. 17–25. See the commentary on the Epistle, with an article on the Renovation, by Sanday and Headlam. There is evidence enough that Shelley knew and loved the relevant places in Hesiod and Vergil. Cf. the lines in Vergil's *Pollio, Alter erit tum Tiphys . . .* (34–6) with

A loftier Argo cleaves the main.

[4] W. R. Inge, *God and the Astronomers*, p. 29.

for a period only, and then destroy it.' For substantially the same reason Shelley will wager that, whatever happens, humanity will be provided in its indefinite future with habitations of some sort, 'regions of eternal hope',[1] and with bodies 'possibly under a form of which we have no idea'.

## 6. SPINOZA AND CONTRADICTION

So far the reader of *Queen Mab*, if he ignores a good deal of the poem and proceeds, as it were, in blinkers, can see his way. There, to a certain extent of what is propounded, and in the obvious meaning of the words, is a distinct theism that denies a Creator, but confesses a Mind or Will immanent and transcendent. There is the *ratio mersa et confusa*; there too the *deus absconditus*. But the theory all together, taking one affirmation with another, falls to pieces. For Shelley would have a God and do without one, or rather would have Him, and yet amerce Him of what He principally signifies as God to men.

In the spring of 1812, while planning or writing his poem, he came upon a philosophy that swept across that faith of his in a divinity with an end in view and a good hand upon us in the *Academical Questions* of Sir William Drummond. Drummond was a high personage in the diplomatic service, a wide-ranging scholar, and a philosopher not without his imperceptions, but with a clear and graceful pen and a dialectic the acutest, as Shelley considered, in that age.[2] The *Questions*, which came out uncompleted in one volume in 1805, aimed at combining a resolute deism with an entire acceptance of Hume's analytical premisses, taking in material from the main philosophies as far down as Kant, and in the fourth chapter from Spinoza. This chapter is a debate between a champion of providential deity and a Spinozist, who sets out the primary ideas of the *Ethics* and points out Spinoza's kinship with the Eleatic and the Stoic schools. Here in clear definition is the eternal, all-embracing, all-generating 'substance', 'incapable of more or less perfection than it always has or has had' in what it is or what it brings to birth, and unmoved by passion or desire, since 'passion is power limited by something else'. Here are the 'attributes' of

[1] ix. 163.

[2] 'The most acute metaphysical critic of the age'—to Leigh Hunt, 3 Nov. 1819 (on the trial of Richard Carlile).

mind and body that 'make one being', one world, but so that
the being (in Drummond's interpretation) is 'not mind, but a
principle superior to it', not mind, but 'that by which mind [as
well as matter] is'. It follows, in the system expounded, that
the soul of a man is 'a part or discerption of God', and yet only
to be so regarded when we think 'after a finite manner and
inadequately', God being really or ultimately without parts or
differences.   Here once more, in Drummond's chapter, is
infinite existence, not proceeding by laws imposed, but freely,
that is to say, by the necessity of its nature, by that necessity
which, as Coleridge puts it, 'takes away from history its acci-
dentality and from science its fatalism'.  Lastly from all
these premises a hard saying follows: that evil has no reality,
and we vainly sever it from good; since, though to us men
evil does subsist 'to the point of stinking', yet all that comes
forth and is conduces to 'a nature infinitely rich' and utterly
blessed.

These ideas, then, Shelley occasionally uses to his inevitable
confusion.  For there is no reconciling pantheism and the Will,
nor pantheism and divine compassion.  Nor, if Shelley accords
his God a will, is he ready to allow Him a love of souls.  From
place to place in his poem he interdicts whatever might savour
of a personal converse of Man and God, and traverses what
he has said already of the divine purpose.  Man, we are told,
obeys the Spirit 'unconsciously', and not even the illuminated
Ianthe ever prays to it.[1]  The great purgation is coming of
itself.  'The eternal change that renovates the world' in springtime has a long-term action and will cleanse us of unrighteous-
ness in the same unbidden way.  More particularly in a passage
in the sixth canto[2] one part of his metaphysic quarrels with the
other.  For his militant divinity will not go with that which

> Strengthens in health and poisons in disease

and looks 'impartially' on good and ill.  The Spirit burning to
save us, whose angel and intimate is our glowing champion
Mab, and to whom our felicity is a 'glorious prize', will not
tally with the Power which 'neither loves nor hates' nor feels
for human sorrow.  The necessity that shall loose our chains is

[1] She says, however, many things about it in the vocative case.
[2] vi. 197–219.

the same that bound them; and the world that never was wrong does not square with the world that never was right.

### 7. *A Refutation of Deism*, and an Abjuration of Atheism

Soon after finishing *Queen Mab*, Shelley would seem to have read, perhaps not for the first time, Hume's *Dialogues concerning Natural Religion*. Under the impact, as we may surmise, of that searching and sapping inquisition he increased and invigorated and braced together his hitherto disjected polemic on Paley's apology, couched it in a dialogue, and 'at the beginning of the year 1814'[1] published anonymously the most nervous of his early prose writings as *A Refutation of Deism*. In the first part of the treatise the Christian defences are set up only to be knocked down, and the history of the Jews, the narrative of the Gospels, and the faith or dogma of the Church, one or other, in one respect or another, are once more aspersed as unreasonable or unbelievable or ineffectual or immoral. The inquiry then passes to the idea of a Creator and (with Hume's assistance) to the testimony of a design. Is there a design? How much of the world disclaims one! How far too little we know of God (if God is) to compare him with a craftsman! And who designed the Designer? And why put on a cause of causes? Matter instinct with power and motion predeterminate: will not these account for most of what we know in the natural and the moral worlds? And that will save us from saying that harmonies and discords lie together in the plan of the Benefactor, or that good and evil divide the world between them. For good and evil, order and disorder, are not in things themselves, but in what we think of them, and this creature's meat is that one's poison. Finally, power is an attribute, and cannot be the parent of matter; and God is merely a designation of the whole world, present from eternity and going by itself.

So far the deist has used dissolvent reason on Christianity, and the Christian has turned it on deism. Are we then to follow Reason, which will have no God at all, or build on Revelation and save society? 'I am willing to promise', says the deist,

'that, if after mature deliberation the arguments which you have advanced in favour of Atheism should appear incontrovertible, I

[1] Hogg, ii. 484.

will endeavour to adopt so much of the Christian scheme as is consistent with my persuasion of the goodness, unity, and majesty of God.'

In neither of his interlocutors is Shelley impersonated. But he speaks authentically in much that is said of Christianity, and in much of the argument on a First Cause; and it is he, and not another, who, at the end of the treatise, abjures atheism. That is to say, he perceives and admits the dependence of his theism on what he at times calls 'feeling'.[1] And surely a *cri de cœur* is translated into each turn of his theology. The fiery insurgent, he wanted the divinity of the purging storm. Tired of discords, he desired one who fills all things with unvarying harmony.[2] Tired of life itself, he thought of a God above the battle, above the evil and the good, true and tranquil being, of which the best of our experience is a small whisper and a vain shadow.

[1] See pp. 192, 249.                    [2] vi. 203.

# XIV

# THE MAN AND THE POET

## 1. THE ONCOMING CRISIS

IN Shelley's professions—and they are many—of what he was or wished to be he is often the soldier of freedom, dauntless in suffering or defeat, or the lover of men whom, for the truth he told them, they branded and cast out. At other times he is a youth of noble nature and lofty aims consumed by a fever of the soul and bound for early death. The portrait is in the main just, and the two sorrows, from without and from within, are history. 'A man', wrote Carlyle, 'infinitely too weak for that solitary climbing of the Alps which he undertook in spite of all the world. A haggard existence, that of his.' But it was the trouble at the heart's core, and not the trouble in the world that made him the supreme lyrist of our tongue, for poetry begins at home. In the chapter of his life that occupies this book there are many signs that the long disease is hatching out, and we know from abundant evidences of what nature it was.

The Poet in *Alastor* leaves his cold and alienated home for the grandeurs of Nature and the ruins of antiquity in quest of secret truth. His heart is enclosed in that purpose, and maiden's love asks for his in vain. In a dream a veiled woman 'whose voice was like the voice of his own soul' is seated by him, talking of the sovereign things: truth, virtue, freedom, poetry. Suddenly the veil is swept away; she is a dream of no abstraction, but of the human lover, his own 'antitype', who waits for him somewhere in the wilderness he must needs travel. Through the wastes and wonders of life the visionary form flies before him till, mocked, spent, and comforted only by the beauty of the natural world, he dies.

Towards the end of 1817, two years after *Alastor*, Shelley started to enlarge the story by a new element. Prince Athanase is the Poet again, and what was intended to befall him we learn from Mary Shelley, who issued the fragment in 1824. The poem, she tells us, was originally named *Pandemos and Urania*, and in the design Athanase, seeking the One whom he might love, was to fall in with the vulgar Aphrodite, and by reason of her treachery pine away. 'On his death-bed the lady who can really reply to his soul comes and kisses his lips.' In 1821 *Epipsychidion*, his *Vita nuova*, as he called it, departed but inessentially from that tale. Here was love's first call, and as the lover sets out into 'the wintry forest of our life':

> One whose voice was venomed melody
> Sate by a well under blue nightshade bowers:
> The breath of her false mouth was like faint flowers,
> Her touch was an electric poison,—flame
> Out of her looks into my vitals came,
> And from her living cheeks and bosom flew
> A killing air, which pierced like honeydew
> Into the core of my green heart, and lay
> Upon its leaves; until, as hair grown gray
> O'er a young brow, they hid its unblown prime
> With ruins of unseasonable time.

From the horror of that presence the lover speeds on his way through love's vicissitudes, not to Death, as it happens, but to Emilia and the Aegean refuge. Yet the dying Athanase is better sped. In 1820, before he wrote the great rhapsody of love's sublunary fruition, Shelley had related his pilgrimage once more in a short allegory, first written in Italian prose as *Una Favola*. Again the youth, the lady of the dream, the wilderness, Love to lead, and a siren, here named Life, to lead astray. Life persuades Love to leave the youth, and then the female figures in her train, garlanded, sweet-voiced, amenable to his will, put aside their veils and discover their terrible forms. He flees from them to the cave of Life's sister Death, and becomes enamoured, but she will not love him till he shall cease to love her. And his desire changes into hate when he comes upon the lady of the quest. 'I await ye where ye needs must come,' says Death to them, 'for I dwell with Love and Eternity, with whom the souls whose love is everlasting must hold communion.' In passionate iteration the parable is taken up a fifth time in *The Triumph of Life*, when the sinister power is the ghastly Conqueror,[1] compelling the demented crowd. For though she

---

[1] The Conqueror, a female personage, is described twice, the second time under a coloured canopy, but at the outset under a dark one. Gloom and deformation are her marks. The charioteer on the beam of the chariot seems to stand for the keen and hard intelligence, the 'calculative faculty', which is said in *A Defence of Poetry* to stifle Imagination or the power unto goodness. The charioteer has four

stands for every form of fell desire, the form most prominent in the picture is the vile Aphrodite,

> that fierce Spirit whose unholy leisure
> Was soothed by mischief since the world begun,

tyrannous over youth and age.[1] As in the other versions of the theme the first draught of the holy love is followed by the assault or mastery of the evil. Rousseau has quaffed the lucent drink; the Car comes by and sweeps him with it; and the memory of childhood's gladness is blotted from his brain.[2] The high and infinite desire hastes blindly to be slaked. The infinite in the lusts of men make them fatal as they are. How the poem would have ended we may only guess. On the verge of the way to the side of the Triumph the 'Shape all light' that gave the fateful cup speeds obscurely to some divine event.

*Dirae facies inimicaque Trojae numina*: many are the angels of 'Life'. But of the plague of the poet's own heart we are not left in doubt either by him or what we know of him. It is Rousseau, the prey of sensibilities, by whom he chooses to be taught. We cannot say of the woman in the nightshade bower who she is among the actors in his history, as we can in the same poem of the Comet or the Moon. She is a 'power upon him when love is at a loss'. Soul confused by sense is the verdict he would seem to write on all his moth-like follies in the mighty Vision of the days before he died. But he surely saw in what he came to remember as the 'rash and heartless' commitment, and ultimately the 'loathsome communion', of the first marriage[3] the especial trophy of the enemy by the way. And yet, wrong as it had been to assume the bond, he had always to answer in his own court for sundering it. Even at the end there was enough affection in it to shake the whole frame of his mind when it came to the severance, and 'the feeling for Harriet's death', says Peacock, 'grew into a deep and abiding sorrow'. It gathered with other

---

faces looking, perhaps, to the four quarters of the world. The eyes are blindfolded, and are indeed no little blind; but their beams pierce through the folds to read the causes of things; like the eyes of a cold science.

[1] 138–69. The power of lust over old age is for Shelley one of the ghastlier facts.

[2] 402–12. On his brain the beautiful images were half erased, and after them came the sinister images, like the track of the wolf in the sand close on the track of the deer.

[3] See the remarkable letter to Hogg of 3 Sept. 1814, reprinted in *The Athenians*, pp. 27–9.

memories of 'error and suffering' into a load of melancholy, into a persecution under which the love of living not seldom left him and self-destruction seemed alone to promise rest:

> Thou wouldst forget thus vainly to deplore
> Ills which, if ills, can find no cure from thee,
> The thought of which no other sleep will quell,
> Nor other music blot from memory,
> So sweet and deep is the oblivious spell.

Not that he was always so dejected, or lost his bright resiliency. No one can so think of him who has read *The Boat on the Serchio* or *A Letter to Maria Gisborne*. What blitheness in these verses! What delight in mountain and river and the Italian fields, and friendships and little joys! Peacock supposed that Shelley, had he lived on, would have been a weary spectator of the world about him, desiring, like Volney, to have written on his tombstone his name, the dates of his birth and death, and the single word DÉSILLUSIONNÉ. But what of the beating heart with which he looked on the rekindled Revolution in Spain and Naples and Greece? What of his declaration on one of his serener days in the last year of his life: 'My mind is at peace respecting nothing so much as the constitution and mysteries of the great system of things'?[1] His gladness and his disquietude were contending tides. There would have been a crisis; the buoyancy would have had it out with the heaviness, to an issue of which we can be sure only that it would have been sensitive and intense. And in this event the head and the heart would have laboured in concert as before. What were the terms of his problem as he ultimately faced it, and what had become by then of the ideas he had faggoted in the earliest chapter of his exploration?

## 2. PLATONISM

The answer to the last question has been in part anticipated. As time goes on, the cause of political justice takes its place in an outer circle of the vast conflict of good and evil, life and death, of which for him the centre is his own soul. And there, in the long ordeal by the phantom of Love, the divinity of his proposition changes to the divinity of his prayer, if that word may be applied to a felt dependency and a pressing desire. The passion of Prometheus as Asia draws near to him—'Life of Life,

[1] 22 August 1821, to Medwin.

thy lips enkindle'[1]—is beyond his disposition in the period of
*Queen Mab*. But as early as 1814, in a page or two of *The
Assassins*, he has conceived that the moral life of man—or say
rather all man's life—is an aspiration to the source of good.
And if the hero of *Alastor*, written in the following year, subsists,
as it were, on the indefinite solace of great landscapes and
the starry heavens, the poems and fragmentary essays of 1816
resume the positive way, and these, taken together, complete
the orientation in which the greater lights are the sayings of
Christ and the writings of Plato. In the *Essay on Christianity*, as
in the *Hymn to Intellectual Beauty*, the good heart answers to
divine 'visitations'; and in the essay *On Love*, the 'soul within
the soul' is an incandescence of the Universal in every one of
us. There is an end, then, of the divinity which aims at our
happiness in the gross, but deals not severally with us, and of
that other also which, caring for us not at all, will accomplish
our salvation absent-mindedly. The Power that Shelley acknow-
ledges in his riper age, and Plato in his later dialogues, not only
'wields the world with never-wearied love'[2] but puts a value
on each and all of its members. As day dawned on the valley
of the Serchio one summer morning of 1821,

> All rose to do the task He set to each,
> Who shaped us for His ends and not our own.[3]

'Disdain thee?' says the Seer to the Tyrant in *Hellas*:

> Disdain thee?—not the worm beneath thy feet!
> The Fathomless has care for meaner things
> Than thou canst dream.[4]

These assurances are of the heart, as Asia remarks to Demogorgon in their metaphysical colloquy, and of such high truths,
she adds, 'each to itself must be the oracle'.[5] But the dogma,
taken on faith and confirmed by Christian gospel and Platonic
dialogue, goes farther than to furnish God with loving providence; it renounces, at least at moments, much of the earlier
theology. As if to suffer no subtraction from divinity, Demogorgon, in the discourse just referred to, abandons the long
contention for an unoriginated Universe.[6] And to conceive of

---

[1] *Prometheus Unbound*, II. v. 48 ff. The MS. B proves that these words are spoken by
the Titan.

[2] *Adonais*, 377.                                    [3] *The Boat on the Serchio*, 30–1.

[4] *Hellas*, 762–4.          [5] *Prometheus Unbound*, II. iv. 121–3.          [6] Ibid., 9 ff.

God possessing all things through and through, and of Man disclaiming alliance with 'transience and decay', the essay *On Life* gives up the dualism of Mind and Matter, and the *Ode to Mont Blanc* takes the affrighted sense of the great world itself as spiritual and ideal. Moreover, the warmer theology engages deeper in the problem of infinite and finite and Plato's wrestle with it. And here the signs of temperament in the Master of all idealists touched an echoing chord. In the *Symposium* this fair earth and the fair things in it are an image and earnest of the eternal beauty 'laid up in some heavenly place'. In the *Phaedo* the soul 'is dragged down by the body into the region of the changeable . . . and the world spins round her, and she is like a drunkard when she touches change'. In the *Symposium*, 'drawing towards the vast sea of beauty', the well-formed nature will get itself noble thoughts and the love of wisdom. In the *Phaedo* the soul, herself invisible, departs to the invisible world, to the divine and immortal and rational, and is there released from error and folly, and dwells for ever with the gods. In the *Timaeus* 'the Father and Creator, who is past finding out . . . made the world after the eternal pattern, the fairest of creatures, and he the best of causes'. But he worked on foreign elements he could not wholly 'persuade', and his best was 'the best attainable'. He is even said in a passage in the *Laws* to share his empire in primal enmity with an Evil Spirit.[1] But though his work be all his own, and all instinct with mind and soul, a double blemish still impairs it. As 'becoming' it is but a shadow of 'being', neither true nor wholly false, and it is infected for ever with the irrational or the brute in the matter it has to inform. There are times when Plato barely escapes from pessimism:

> 'Evils can never pass away; for there must always remain something at variance with good. Of necessity they hover round the mortal nature and this earthly sphere. Wherefore we ought to fly away from earth to heaven as quickly as we can.'

But even here he does escape:

> 'And to fly away is to become like God as far as this is possible, to become, that is, holy, and just, and wise.'[2]

What may be marked as the last phase of Shelley's evolution

[1] 896.    [2] See *Theaetetus*, 176.

begins with a poem in which the sense of this evil and this glory and
this 'eclipse of birth' are vividly, though cryptically, expressed.

### 3. *The Witch of Atlas* and the Pains of Finitude

In August of the year 1820 Shelley started from the Baths of
St. Julian under the Pisan hills for a short tour to the summit
of Monte San Pellegrino. In a deep trance of inspiration following his return home he wrote the 670 lines of *The Witch of Atlas*
in three days. A month earlier he had translated into lively
verse the Homeric *Hymn to Hermes*, and was still infected
with its blitheness. The Witch is, again, a Platonic 'Daemon',
a divinity whose dwelling is with men, our friend and
genius. She lives on Atlas, the dome of the world, the place
between heaven and earth, and her father is the Sun. The
tale tells of her cave, and how all the demons and creatures of
earth were attracted to her, and how she tempered her beauty
to mortal eyes by a veil of cloud and light. At first she lived
alone, sending out her thoughts through all the Universe; and
when the beings of earth desired to live with her, she refused
them, saying that there could be no equal love between mortal
and immortal, but wept when they went away. Then she
tempered fire and snow together in the medium of Love, and
made from them a shape of great beauty, a Hermaphrodite
with no defect of either sex and with all the grace of both, and
in this company sported in her magic boat along the rivers.
She would fare to the Antarctic Ocean and live there in a misty
tent, where her ministers would bring news of mankind, at
which she would grow pale, or laugh, or cry. Or she would
pass by night among the cities on the Nile to watch the slum-
berers, rejoicing in the sight of fair and happy life, and not
dismayed by the sight of evil, for her spirit could plunge at any
time to the deeps of calm beneath the welter of mundane things.
She would cause the spirits of the good to mingle with her own,
or give them panaceas, or turn their deaths into dreamy sleeps.
In the slaves of Custom she would raise dreams that mocked
the purposes of their lives, and bring together bashful lovers and
estranged friends. Such were the tricks she played, and thereby
she did not feel that longing for a reciprocal love which in after
days is said to have vexed her soul.[1]

[1] lxviii.

This thing is of the attar of his poetry: a riot of fancy, a gambol in earth and sky, a throng of echoes, and truth in a kind of dream. The Witch has come of Spenser's Phaedria as well as the Maia and the Aphrodite of the Homeric Hymns, and there are echoes of Southey and even of M. G. Lewis.[1] And in Shelley's way the things imagined in the old Hymn pass into a spiritual world and 'put on incorruption': Maia stores her vasty cavern with 'nectar and glad ambrosia and gold and silver and glistering raiment', but the Witch rejoices in boxes and phials of visions and thought-stirring odours and elixirs the death of death. Similarly, Aphrodite is transformed. In the fragmentary Hymn she comes with her train of wild beasts mastered by her influence to the dwelling of Anchises and mourns her unhappy love:

> 'If, being as thou art in beauty and form, thou couldst live on and be called my lord, then this grief would not overshadow my heart. But it may not be, for swiftly will pitiless old age come upon thee. Deep and sore hath been my folly, and distraught have I been, who carry a child beneath my girdle, the child of a mortal man.'[2]

The Lady of Atlas, if she will have a companion born of perishing elements, must mould one of her own device, one subject neither to the mortality nor to the desire of the flesh, one in whom, in Shelley's own words, 'the detestable distinction of man and woman is done away'. She loves the fierce beasts under her spell; she loves the good and the happy among men, and mocks and fools the evil; but the earthly and homely love she must needs forgo, not without tears. She has, therefore, a double aspect. She stands for all Shelleyan lovers, who come to know that they cannot have in time 'the likeness of that which is eternal', and console themselves, not all in vain, with ideal beauty rendered in sound or form.[3] These are lovers in the

---

[1] See above, pp. 88, 89. There are one or two apparent 'sources' in Lewis's tale of *Amorassan, or the Spirit of the Frozen Ocean*.

[2] Excerpted from the *Hymn to Aphrodite*, 240–55, Andrew Lang's translation (Allen & Unwin, Ltd.). Shelley translated the first 57 lines of this Hymn in heroic couplets in 1818.

[3] The subject asks for too much room; but it may be added that the boat (xxx f.) which could not contain the fires of Venus, and so was bought by Apollo or, as others feign, grew from a seed planted and tended by Cupid in his Mother's star, should mean the art which is inspired by sexual passion, but will not do instead; and the River looks like the stream down which Asia will sail in union with Pro-

widest sense, friends of their kind, 'daemons of the world' which is not their hearts' home. But, on the other hand, and in the next moment, the Lady stands for the Power she lives by, the Good itself, whose presence is felt from end to end and its beauty phenomenally veiled. For Divinity, no less than its scintillation in Man, suffers a state of sorrow and a kind of Fall in its 'vesture of decay', be it a body or a world.

*The Witch of Atlas* is Shelley's first long descant of the exiled soul. The disparagement of the temporal world as less than perfect beauty and real being, as a place of detention or eclipse had alighted here and there in his poetry before this, but not to stay and brood. It is thrown into the miscellany of *Queen Mab*,[1] which at one point takes over the famous image in Plato's *Republic* of the Prisoners in the Cave. The prisoners, or the mass of humanity, are so chained that they see only the fire-cast shadows on the wall before them, or the notions or 'opinions' they live upon, not true, nor a copy of the true, as sound knowledge is, but a copy of the copy thrown by a wavering light. And what Plato has written of those who are not philosophers Shelley here applies to men altogether and the mortal state. Again, in the epic of Islam, after the multitudes at the Golden City have breathed the air of freedom, the force of tyranny rolls back upon them, and Laon and Cythna escape from 'life's envenomed dream' to the Valhalla where the light of love or good shines full and for ever. But the Serpent, the good genius, so lacerated by the Eagle, its eternal foe, nestles in the Woman's breast to gather strength for the next encounter and at last the victory: the victory of Prometheus and Asia, when there will not be much to choose between earth and heaven. *The Witch of Atlas* in 1820 contains and makes addition to the argument of *Alastor*. Love's want or 'hidden want', our immedicable unquiet, our homeless finitude is salved by beauty and by good, the pledges of Eternity. But after this *fantasia* of playful joy and delicate sorrow the music darkens in *Adonais* and in the phantasmal *Triumph* with the stains of Time on the 'white radiance' that is after death. Death, in his earlier poetry, is oftenest a stroke that hovers over life, sad and over-shadowing,

---

metheus (II. v. 72 ff.), that is, the River of Life, with its perilous crags and whirlpools. Shelley hardly ever writes of a river without ulterior meaning.

[1] vi. 190–6.

though on the principle of Love or Beauty it has no power. Later, and in *Adonais* especially, it is a kind or sphere of being. It is the Eternity which will fulfil our values and from which our values flow. It 'lends what life must borrow', and if Death were not, Love were not either.[1] More than once, in 1820 and after, Shelley resumed the prophecy of humanity reclaimed and earth imparadised, but never before had he faltered in mid-flight, as in the hymn of the coming age at the close of *Hellas*, where the thought of the old world's ways strangled the gladness and stopped the 'luminous wings'.

### 4. *A Defence of Poetry* and the Value of the Sensible World

But his faith and his theory continually fluctuate. *A Defence of Poetry* in 1821, or the larger part of it, abandons the other-worldliness for the field and function of Imagination, the organ of the moral life; and here not the *Phaedo* but the *Symposium* sets his course. For Imagination is Love 'drawing to the vast sea of beauty'; 'a going out of our own nature', says the *Defence*, 'and an identification of ourselves with the beautiful which exists in thought, action, or person not our own'; an enlarger of the heart and purifier of the will. It 'strips the veil' of commonness from the face of things, and discovers that 'ideal perfection and energy' that we desire or conjure in all we admire or would become. And the mark of that perfection, as the *Symposium* tells us, is an order, or harmony, or rhythm, which composes all difference. Nor is this fair agreement accomplished or attempted in the finer arts alone, but wherever beauty is an end or aim, in the craft of Athene or Hephaestus, in the rule of Zeus over gods and men, in the graces of a temperate soul. Here were precious clues, if Shelley could have held them firmer. Here he might have laid to heart that all life thrives by tension and the reply to it, and that by stooping to the conditions given him, the matter or the circumstance, and only by stooping, the artist or the moral man may conquer. Of these truths he is at times aware. What of the ugly or terrible in the paths of our experience? Shall the artist put them in or put them by? The effect of tragedy, we are told, is 'the exalted calm' that assuages terror and sorrow, and stills our censoriousness,

---

[1] Lines entitled *Death*, written in 1820.

while it raises our self-respect, 'in awe of the unfathomable agencies of Nature'. Nor is it in the ideal only that the imaginative power subdues to beauty. The author of *Prometheus Unbound* can sometimes see, like Burke, that 'the restraints on men are among their liberties', and in the *Ode to Liberty* and the *Ode to Naples* give effect to 'the poetry of institutions' and of national careers. Roman law, we are told, was a poem, and in *Hellas* an unfolding revelation goes forward in the rise and fall of creeds. Nay, where our limitations and necessities wear the aspect of positive evil, the evil also may be represented as of God and his economy. So in *Prometheus*, where evil can stand only when wedded to good and, so wedded, begets its own undoing.[1] So in the *Prologue to Hellas* after the prologue to the Book of Job. The wild West Wind is sister to the azure spring, and in the rhythm of falling and uprising the tired soul will be refreshed, and the rejected thoughts 'scattered as from an unextinguished hearth among mankind'. The writer of that great ode was no truant to the void.

Yet now and then even *A Defence of Poetry* devalues the world of us all. At the back of Shelley's mind harmony is good, but transcendence better, and insurgency the manner of all things. In his imagination the vernal buds 'leap from their detested trance', while the green lizard and the golden snake are 'unimprisoned flames'. Earth and sky abound in creatures that have broken free or cloven barriers or put on tameless speed: winds and rivers, the antelope and 'beamlike ephemeris', tiger, basilisk, ounce, shark. Dikes and confines are there only to be spurned. The gladdest beings are they that wander uncontrollably in endless caves and forests, or, better, like the winds of heaven,

> Voyaging cloudless and unpent
> In the boundless element.

Imaginations like Browning's may rejoice in massive and resis-

---

[1] In the old myth Prometheus has a fatal secret concerning Zeus which he will not disclose, namely, that if Zeus marry Thetis he shall beget a son who will overthrow him. At last he reveals the secret, and is unbound, and Thetis is given to Peleus. Shelley's Titan will not disclose, and Jupiter, married to Thetis, the 'bright image of Eternity', engenders Demogorgon, his child whom he does not know. That is to say: tyranny can hold on only if it cherishes the fruitful things—if, say, it founds Universities and forwards the arts—but in that way it will let in liberal ideas eventually fatal to it.

tive things, in mountains like 'the teeth in an old lion's jaw'.
How Shelley abhors the resistance, sees the towers of Venice
wavering in a strange light, or 'dissolves' the hills in the 'last
red agony of the day'! So in the soul of Man. The wave or
breath of Universal Power carries it for a time to the height
of its being and its ken, 'clear of the nets of wrong and right'
and of all but intuitive knowing. In the *Symposium* 'Love, who
is a poet', climbs upward from visible beauty to invisible; but
in *A Defence* the poet sets out from blind intimations of 'the
eternal, the infinite and the one', which he will interpret to
others, but never so that the mystery of our being shall be
plumbed:

> The many rose to toil, and One to teach
> What none e'er knew, and never can be known.

In the perfect organ of the 'soul within the soul' this sense of the
Intellectual Beauty is minted into 'idealisms of passion and
power', the 'unchangeable forms' or the 'eternal truth' of
patriotism, say, or any high endeavour; and these the poet
represents in concordant order and music to the inward eye
and ear. And Homer, he thinks, when he put in the vices of
Achilles, may have known and grieved that, as was expedient,
if not inevitable to his art, he veiled the 'unchangeable' loveliness of his conception in the moral fashion of his age, and
'tempered his planetary music to mortal ears'. Nay, the poet
in beginning to compose has lost altitude, and 'his inspiration
is already on the wane'. And so, generally, the spirit chafes in
its embodiment, the will would be borne away beyond obedience and beyond endeavour, love would be free, and code and
creed and custom are toils around our feet.

## 5. THE CHEAPENING OF THE INDIVIDUAL

With his speculative infirmities upon him he could not have
ascended to the first rank in poetry. His early theism streng-
thened and mellowed in the Platonic sunlight; and the fallacies
taken in from the air about him were crossed and tempered by
second thoughts; but the main line of his thinking ran con-
tinuously. In *Queen Mab* all things are and shall be and have
been what they ought in the being of the all-inclusive God, and,
again, all things are mixed with evil, but the Winnower is

coming, and his fan is in his hand. And these incompatibles
are still the answer to his problem in the latter days and the
darker mood. If the sons of Hellas shall fail in their glorious
strife, where are evil, failure, time, the event, or Nature or
Man but in the bosom of the Absolute, where all is one and all
is well and nothing to fear?[1] And what of the Shape or Spirit
in *The Triumph of Life* that glides by the dance of the fallen
souls, each of them given to the captor by tasting of her cup,
the desire or longing that may degrade and alone delivers?
She must have acted more or less nearly as in *The Mask of
Anarchy* Hope had done: Hope that stands up before the riders,
and steed and rider are fled and thrown, and the trampled
victims saved.[2] Again the wondrous change and taking over
and levelling up of souls. True, it is a dream; but it implies a
frame of mind. Is the evil in us an accident or incrustation that
the saving hand smites off? Is it a disease merely, not punishable, not our doing? Or are we our worser, as well as our better
selves, aspiring to the 'true poem', as Milton puts it, in which
these odds are evened? There are passages in Shelley's text that
make against the prophecy of the moral conflict overpast and
man as good as deified; but more in which fancy is one with
hope, and the visitant divinity takes us by force and carries
us. In the great Vision some have achieved their freedom
by the conquest of themselves—Christ and Socrates and the
'sacred few', who,

> When they had touched the world with living flame,
> Flew back like eagles to their native home.

Such are not to be found in Life's triumph, nor anywhere, we
may take it, in 'the valley of perpetual dream'. 'To be holy and
just and wise is to fly away.' These are a stronger breed,
vicarious prevailers, 'intercessors', who for the common run of
men 'plead before God's throne'. But as for the rest, as for the

---

[1] *Hellas*, 762 ff.: Ahasuerus to Mahmud.

[2] That the Spirit was to come in again at the end of the tale we may infer from
the source. The poem rests on Petrarch's *Trionfi*, a series of six poems in *terza rima*
describing in turn the triumph of Love over Man, of Chastity over Love, of Death
over all mortality, of Fame over Death, of Time over Fame, of Divinity over Time.
Shelley drew, in the main, from the first; his Spirit is, of course, the divine conqueror
at the end. See 'Notes on Shelley's Triumph of Life' by A. C. Bradley in the
*Modern Language Review* for Oct. 1914. In Shelley's poem, ll. 412–33, the fair
Spirit is compared with Lucifer, fading in the dawn, returning at night.

mob around the chariot, how much personality have any of
them, driven like leaves as they are in the wind of evil or the
wind of good? The sacred few are the Teiresias of Homer's
nether world, where 'he only inhales the breath of life, but the
rest are flitting shades'.

Once more the two abstractions. Godwin supposes us bur-
dened with evil like an oppressive skin, casting it as snakes do,
and leaping to our proper and perfect selves; each provided,
as a moral agent, with an unfailing light, which, though the
lights of others may be thrown in with it, is all his own. But
put the case as Shelley put it, the dejected Shelley who took
turns with the joyful and the brave; let reason shine upon us,
like the moon, with intermittent splendour; let 'the breath of
universal being' falter and leave us desolate; let the infamy
of our nature weigh us down; or suppose the obscuration to
fall on peoples and for a long time: then the Godwinian may
well lose faith in his sweeping premisses and tall hopes, as
Shelley sometimes did. Godwin's hopes were tall indeed, but
his individualism leads as easily to dismay. Let the believer
ever call in doubt the power of the individual of himself to
help himself, then in his misgiving eyes the scheme will one
day crash, and goodness fail, and poetry, 'like Astraea's parting
footsteps', die away:

> O write no more the tale of Troy,
> If earth death's scroll must be.

Then, if he be Shelley, he flees to the Absolute, or cries for
a swift divinity to penetrate and possess us, to turn us into
pensioners by a vast gratuity, or unmake all 'identities' in its
own. For ever and again his desire of oneness bears down
everything in its way: the desire that in the warmest moments
of his vision confounds the landscape in a single glory,

> Be it love, light, harmony,
> Odour or the soul of all,

and how much more the souls and wills of men.

### 6. Possibilities

By all the signs a struggle or crisis was at hand that might
have composed in a measure what he somewhere calls 'this
chaos, me'. It has been the argument of this book that he hovers

between the great abstractions ascendant in his age and conspicuous in Rousseau. He runs between the One alone and the
Many by themselves. He stands for the free individual with a
dash of fierce Jacobinism in his heart. He is ethically antinomian,
but steeped as few men are in the moral sense. Such in general
was the 'chaos', and his 'haggard existence' the consequence
or the cause. To follow at once his personal life and the course
of his thinking is to see him all together and to ask the answer-
less question if he had it in him to become happier, to be less
distracted in his heart and less divided in his mind, and reconcile his opposing impulses. He would then have loved not
'being' less, but 'becoming' more. He would have underlined
what he had written of all things working together, and looked
accordingly on the historical process. He would have seen
constantly, instead of now and then, that the general sense of
right and the conscience of the individual flourish or fade on
the same stem and things are not perverted because they are
ordained. He would have amended the notion of a God who
takes his kingdom by force and in whose love the wills of men
dissolve. He would have worshipped one who 'penetrates and
clasps and fills the world', 'who made us for his ends and not
our own', and without whose aid we cannot help ourselves.
But he would have trusted more firmly that this informing
Power lives and lets live, so that the soul shall not suffer, here
or hereafter, the deprivation of its selfhood by the death of the
body or whatever else may come.[1] And, with regard to the
self he would have seen, as at times he does already, in moral
evil and its penalties not an alien infusion or an appended
weight, but a passion of the soul under stress of which she may
acquire salvation, or not at all. By all this gain and growth we
should have lost not a little, it may be, of the lyrical Shelley
whom we know, but there would be no such gulf as now divides
even his greater critics: Charles Lamb, for example, to whom

[1] Shelley's incessant hopes and doubts as to a future life speak their last word in
the Note to the chorus in *Hellas*, 'Worlds on worlds are rolling ever', ll. 197 ff.,
where the balance is still swaying. 'As it is the province of the poet to attach himself
to those ideas which exalt and ennoble humanity, let him be permitted to have
conjectured the futurity towards which we are all impelled by an inextinguishable
thirst for immortality. Until better arguments can be produced than sophisms
which disgrace the cause, this desire itself must remain the strongest and the only
presumption that eternity is the inheritance of every thinking being', or, as he
again puts it, 'every distinct intelligence'.

his poetry 'rings of its own emptiness', and Robert Browning, who selected him among all the moderns as having 'thrown swifter, subtler, and more numerous films between Power and Love in the absolute and Beauty and Good in the concrete than any other artificer'.

How he would have continued on the formal side of his art is a question no less tempting. His many artistic powers were coming on and gathering, and his course was one of restless experiment in almost all the kinds and forms. Apart from lyric, he does best, one instance excepted, in elegy, rhapsody, and the allegorical 'vision'; but tries oftenest at drama of one or another sort, and produces the finest example of the tragedy of criminal passion in the tall Elizabethan manner since Ford relinquished it. What would he have made with his grasp of subtle and masterful emotion and the majestic will? Almost certainly new ventures like *The Cenci*, one, perhaps, upon the life of Tasso, as we know he designed. But no less surely the trend of his genius committed him to the metaphysical poetry represented by the masters of his art whom he loved best and read oftenest: Aeschylus, Dante, Milton, Calderon. It has been suggested that he would have given us a religious drama on the model of Calderon, and he is known to have purposed a tragedy built on the Book of Job. But drama, much as he leaned to it, would not have afforded easy room for the whole array of his capabilities, and in particular his sensibility alike to familiar and sublime, the spirit that breathes in the first scene of *Prometheus Unbound* and that which indited *A Letter to Maria Gisborne* or *The Boat on the Serchio* or the poems to Jane. Byron, he writes from Ravenna in August 1821,

> 'has read to me one of the unpublished cantos of *Don Juan* [the third] which is astonishingly fine. It sets him not only above, but far above all the poets of the day. . . . I despair of rivalling Lord Byron, and there is no other with whom it is worth contending . . . It [the canto] fulfils in a certain degree what I have long preached of producing—something wholly new, and relative· to the age, and yet surpassingly beautiful.'

But, whatever their form, the poems he did not live to write would have attested a philosophy and appealed to us in a degree depending on its serviceableness. A philosophy, or any piece of one conveyed in a poem must be an assurance of the heart's

desires, and as such we give it hospitality while we have the
occasion to and if we can. So far as we cannot take it home for
the time being in acceptation and content, so far as it does not
fortify, the end of poetry, which is pleasure or a crown of pleasure, will be missed or marred. And so it is in Shelley in the
degree in which he has written in an outworn phase of thought
and lays us, while we read him, under a sense of its dubitable
element. Nor is it on the intellectual plane only that he falls
below the best that has been done in the poetry of ideas. None
of the greatest writers of that order comes to us but with affirmations that set the seal on joy or peace. But Shelley died a
troubled spirit, in the midst of upheaval, in a defiant faith and
wild and pining hopes, and who can say with confidence that
he would have lived to assuage his disquiet and to exceed his
date?

Is he therefore 'ineffectual'? Poetry lives on passion or
thought that is one with passion. If a coherent philosophy may
be the roof and crown of a poet's work, beauty can be born also
of unordered intuitions. If at the highest height poetry is sure
and glad, it may be 'sweet with saddest thought'. For the most
part Shelley's is so. The mental strife, the wild desire, the
drooping and the soaring flight: it is just these that carry him
to his star in the heaven in which the glories differ. If to us who
come after him the investing ideas jar in a measure with the
sense of truth, or he for his own part is less than a master in the
speculative field, a case arises like that of the Homeric vices
considered in *A Defence of Poetry*. 'Every epoch', he writes, 'has
deified its errors', and in these the poet dresses his conceptions;
but the dress will 'cover, but cannot conceal the eternal pro-
portions of their beauty'. If the marble lamp is here and there
discoloured, the interior fire is lucent even in the stain. And
what of the strange essence of that light? The 'workmanship
of style' that as Wordsworth once declared 'made him one of
the best artists of us all'; the subtle and vivid senses; the gift of
ecstasy and the joy in power: these are among the elements,
and with them the foretelling and divining mind that, by his
own account, is the breath of great poetry. He dreams a young
man's dream. And in an age awaking to intimations of a spiritual immanence alike in Man and Nature he is among the
writers most conscious of it. Nothing in English poetry is quite

like the little lyrics that distil his melancholy each in a handful
of notes and blend him with the life of things, or his repossession
of the fancy—or more than fancy—that made the primal myths
and bore the seed of all idealisms. The denizens of his earth
and heaven are a host of Shelleys. Sometimes they seem to be
burning in his eyes into 'one annihilation' in the joy of life;
sometimes passioning as he did over the surd of evil and redemption long upon the way:

> Rough wind, that moanest loud
>   Grief too sad for song;
> Wild wind, when sullen cloud
>   Knells all the night long;
> Sad storm, whose tears are vain,
> Bare woods, whose branches strain,
> Deep caves and dreary main,
>   Wail, for the world's wrong!

And it was in unrehearsed, but not unconscious symbolism that
in the last office his friends could do him they compounded his
body with earth and air and sea and fire.

# APPENDIX

## THE PSYCHO-ANALYSIS OF SHELLEY

In *The Psychology of the Poet Shelley*, 1925, the main argument is put in the second part (pp. 55–125) by Mr. George Barnefield, and handled in anticipation in the first part by Edward Carpenter, who does not, however, at all points subscribe to it.

Mr. Barnefield argues as follows. Shelley had the bi-sexual or 'intermediate' nature that is often found in artists, as, for instance, in Leonardo, in Michelangelo, in Tchaikovski. His face and gait, the way he writes of the ecstasy of love, his interest in androgynous types, like Prince Athanase or Laon, and his ideal figure of the Hermaphrodite in *The Witch of Atlas* show how strong in him was the feminine element, and how innate the duality. The fascination laid upon him by the theme of a marital union between brother and sister came of this particular temperament. His heroines and heroes were dual types, and by creating Laon and Cythna to be brother and sister he 'emphasised their similarity', and 'achieved a more complete fusion of the two natures'.

As bi-sexual, he was also homo-sexual; of which there were many indications. He was 'not very susceptible to the *physical* charms of real women'; hardly at all attracted in that way to Harriet West-brook, whom he married for quixotic reasons; and not sufficiently to Mary Godwin, though her masculinity 'roused in him a genuine romantic passion', for erotically his life with her was not contented. His stronger and steadier attachments were to men, especially at the time of his first marriage, to Hogg, and later to Peacock and Tre-lawny, with both of whom he was 'more naïve and feminine than normally', for 'like all bi-sexual people he automatically altered his polarity in accordance with his company'. The record of his school-boy devotions—notably to Dr. Lind—point to the same temperament, and it lurks in his notes on Greek sculptures in Italy, and in his fondness for writers in whom it may be felt—Theocritus, Moschus, Plato, and for Shakespeare's sonnets. He was lavishly generous to his friends; a devoted nurse to sick people (especially on one occasion to Tom Medwin); and did not understand the sentiment of jealousy, on the husband's part or on the wife's; and for the psycho-analyst all these are signs.

But that he had the homo-sexual disposition he never knew; and he shared to the full the aversion of society to all its manifestations, as may be seen in his fragment *On the Arts and Manners of the Athenians*, and in his avoidances in the translation of the *Symposium*. The very avoidances, however, betray the temperament, and evidently towards his life's end 'the repressed impulses were forcing themselves up into consciousness'. His tragedy was that they were never quite conscious; that he inevitably idealized women, and found them wanting, and wondered why; that he was melancholy and solitary, and afflicted with the visions and illusions incident to his case. 'Had he lived a few more years, he would have been driven either into some final and serious neurosis, or else into some form of conscious recognition and expression of the repressed component of his nature.' As it was, the continual conflict impeded and kept back those abnormal powers of divination and intuition that would in time have placed him among the greater mystics, had he seen the causes of his trouble and in some way put it by. If it be asked in what way, the answer is, it seems, by being content to 'experience love as an ardent and exalted comradeship towards those of his own sex'.

This is a valuable inquiry, and throws light on much that is else obscure. Mr. Barnefield has put in, as it seems to one reader, a good deal of dubious evidence; but his hypothesis does work out into many of the strange phenomena of the case. At the same time it seems likely that too much is made of it; that the abnormal was and would have been a minor, and not a main component, and permanently weaker than the more regular condition. If Shelley's epithalamian poetry goes for anything, he was a passionate lover in the ordinary sense, and if daring aggression and masterful purpose are masculine attributes, he had them plenteously. Clearly the feminine strain was there; but that suggests how rich and various his love might be, and that an ideal marriage, had it ever come about, would have harmonized the elements. And this conclusion is much the same as Edward Carpenter's, who believes that Shelley 'in the majority of his love affairs was quite normal', meaning evidently that in any of the affairs the normal strain predominated, if the other came in now and then. 'How are we to reconcile these varying attitudes and moods—or is it necessary to reconcile them? Perhaps this last suggestion is the best. It is this very variability which gave him his wide sympathy with and understanding of different and almost opposing types of humanity. If he had had a longer and more effective experience, it might have been possible for him to bring into line these two sides of his nature' (pp. 12, 13, abridged).

# BIBLIOGRAPHICAL NOTE

THE chief biographies cited in the text and notes, as a rule by the author's names, are:

*The Life of P. B. S.*, by Thomas Jefferson Hogg, 2 vols., London, 1858.

*The Life of P. B. S.*, by Thomas Medwin, new and extended edition edited by H. Buxton Forman, Oxford University Press, 1913.

*Shelley's Early Life*, by Denis Florence MacCarthy, London, n.d.

*The Life of P. B. S.*, by Edward Dowden, 2 vols., London, 1886.

*Shelley in England*, by Roger Ingpen, London, 1917.

*Shelley, his Life and Work*, by W. E. Peck, 2 vols., London, 1927.

*Shelley*, by Newman Ivy White, 2 vols., New York, 1940.

For citations from the Works and Letters I have used *The Complete Works of Shelley*, Julian Edition, edited by R. Ingpen and W. E. Peck, 10 vols. (the Letters in vols. viii–x), London and New York, 1926–9.

Peacock's *Memoirs* and Trelawny's *Recollections* are combined with Hogg's *Life* in *The Life of P. B. S.*, ed. Humbert Wolfe, 2 vols., London, 1933.

In quoting from the poetry I have not consistently followed one edition, but have used, as a rule, the text given by Thomas Hutchinson in the Oxford Shelley, 1904.

# INDEX

Aeschylus, text purchased by S., 172, 260.
Albertus Magnus, 25.
Aurelius, Marcus: copy of *Works*, bought by S. in 1812, 172.

Beddoes, T. L., 227, 228 n.
Berkeley, George, 122; works bought by S. in 1812, 172.
Bethell, George, 13, 15.
Bible, 225, 260.
Blasphemy, law of, 77 n., 148.
Blunden, Edmund: *On Shelley*, 69 n.
Bradley, A. C., 257 n.
Brooks, John, 189 and n.
Brougham, Lord, 171.
Brown, Ford K.: *Life of William Godwin*, 123 n., 157, 162.
Browning, Robert, 20, 30, 255, 256, 260.
Buffon, 228.
Burdett, Sir Francis, 30 n., 155.
Burke, Edmund, 222–3, 226, 255.
Bury, Lady Charlotte, 53 n.
Byrne, Mrs., alias Rosa Matilda, or Charlotte Dacre, her *Zofloya*, 31, 35.
Byron, Lord, 226, 227 and n., 228 n.; *Don Juan*, 260.

Cabanis, text purchased by S. in 1812, 172.
Calderon, 260.
Calvert, R., 119.
Calvert, William, 119, 127.
Campbell, Thomas, 184, 228 n.
Carlile, Richard, 188 n., 189 and n.
Carlyle, Thomas, 90 and n.
Castlereagh, Lord, 173.
Chatterton, Thomas, 23.
Chichester, Earl of, 141.
Christ, 60 and n., 152, 232, 249, 257.
Christianity, *see under* Shelley, Percy Bysshe.
Clairmont, Jane (or Claire), 163.
Clark, William (pirate of *Queen Mab*), 188.
Cobbett, William, 120, 221, 222.
Coleridge, Samuel Taylor, 11, 119, 131, 227, 228 n.; *The Ancient Mariner*, 37 n.; works bought by S. in 1812, 172.
Condorcet, 25 and n., 28, 54.
Copleston, Edward, 69 and n., 73.
Cowley, Abraham, 172.
Croft, Margaret L., 178.
Curran, John Philpott, 130.
Cwm Elan, 95, 96, 97–100, 146.

Dante, 260.
Darwin, Erasmus, 172, 236 n.
De Quincey, Thomas, 47 n., 121, 123.
Diderot, text bought by S. in 1812, 172.
Dobell, Bertram, 86 n.
Dowden, Edward, 5 n., 9 n., 22, 27 n., 40 n., 58 n., 70 n., 72 n., 89 n., 97, 119 and n., 153 n., 184.
Drake, Henry, Town Clerk of Barnstaple, 154.
Drummond, Sir William, 241–3.

Eaton, Daniel Isaac, 146–50.
*Edinburgh Literary Journal*, 30 n.
*Edinburgh Review*, 22 n.
Edwards, Evan, 10, 24.
Ellenborough, Lord, 146, 147, 149, 170.
Emmet, Robert, 129, 130, 183.
*Empire of the Nairs*: *see* Lawrence, J. H.
Epicurus: text purchased by S. in 1812, 172.
Esdaile Manuscript, 37 n., 126 and n., 174, 183.
Eton College, conditions and manners, 12–17, 27; curriculum, 22–4.
Euripides, 23, 172.
*Examiner*, character of the, 170–1.

Faber, George Stanley, 85.
Ferguson, Sir Ronald Crawford, 189 n.
Field Place, 1, 2, 6–8.
Finnerty, Peter, 51 and n., 53 n.
Forman, Buxton, *Shelley Library*, 53 n., 188 n.
Franklin, Benjamin, 25 and n.
*Fraser's Magazine*, 30.
Freeling, Francis, Secretary to the Post Office, 140, 141, 154.

Garnett, Richard, 27 n., 44 n., 56 n., 177 n.
*Gebir*, 53.
George, Prince Regent, 87, 88, 170, 171 and n.
Gibbon, Edward: his *History* bought by S. in 1812, 173, 192.
Gibbs, Vicary, Attorney General, 148–9, 171.
Godwin, Fanny, 123, 156, 163, 168, 182.
Godwin, Mary Jane, 123, 162, 163.
Godwin, William, 54; career and character, 122–5; first contact with S., 124, 125; reproves S. for Irish Association, 139, 140; futile visit to

# INDEX

and force, 203; his affinities to S.,
206; S.'s admiration for, 207; and
pity and regret for, 207; on the function of women in society, 208, 209;
*Confessions*, 206, 207; *Émile*, 67 n.,
208; *La Nouvelle Héloïse*, 207, 208;
Letter to Malesherbes, 207.
Rowley, George, 50, 72 n.

Schubart: *Der Ewige Jude*, 36 n.
Scott, Sir Walter, 23, 184.
Scott, Walter Sidney: in *Harriet and
Mary*, 44 n., 60 n.; *The Athenians*,
71 n., 94, 247 n.
Seneca: text bought by S. in 1812, 172.
Shakespeare, William, 23, 172, 219 n.
Sharpe, C. Kirkpatrick, 53 n., 68.
Shelley, Sir Bysshe, 1–3, 5, 109, 111.
Shelley, Elizabeth, *née* Pilfold (mother),
2, 5, 6, 57, 83, 85, 93, 110, 181.
Shelley, Elizabeth (sister), 2, 51, 57, 59,
61, 62, 79, 84, 86 n., 92–5, 101, 110.
Shelley, Harriet (*née* Westbrook): at
school on Clapham Common, 81;
personal appearance, 81, 104; meets
S., 82, 86 n., 99–100; in trouble at
home, sees Shelley, July 1811, 97;
elopement and marriage, 100–2; as
S.'s wife, 103–6; doings in Edinburgh, 108; attempt by Hogg to
seduce her, 111–15; receives yearly
income from her father, 118; S.'s
affection for, 126; in Dublin, 134,
136, 137, 142; *To Harriet*, 143, 144;
the Hitchener scheme, 145; charges
against Miss Hitchener, 160; in London with S., October to November
1812, 161, 163, 166–7; return to and
dislike of Tremadoc, 169; describes
outrage at Tanyrallt, 175–9; in Ireland again, 179–82; arrives in London, 180; her relations with S. in early
1813, 181, 182.
Shelley, Hellen, 2, 9, 18, 19 n., 81, 82,
86 n., 116.
Shelley, Percy Bysshe: birth, 2; childhood, 4–8; early relations with
father, 4, 5; and with mother, 6, 7;
at Sion House, 9–12; at Eton, 1804–
10, 12–17; necromancy, 15; 'The
Atheist', 15; an early friendship, 19;
publishes *Zastrozzi* and *St. Irvyne*,
29; writes *Wandering Jew*, 29; apocalyptic moments (Intellectual Beauty),
38–42; in love with Harriet Grove,
51, 58; reviews Hogg's *Prince Alexy*,
44; enters University College, Oxford,
and meets Hogg, 47; habit of life at
Oxford, 47–51; letter to Leigh Hunt
on his future plans, 51; *Original Poetry*

by *Victor and Cazire*, 51; literary enterprise at Oxford, 54; conversation, 54–
5; sees Stockdale in Pall Mall, December 1810, 56; persecuted at home
as a deist, 56–7; rejected by Harriet
Grove, 59–62; design to engage Hogg
to Elizabeth, 62, 92–5, 98; publishes
*Necessity of Atheism*, 66; expelled his
college, 68–73; in London, March
26–May 15, 1811, in company with
Hogg (until April 16), and in dispute
with his father, 74–84; dinner at
Miller's Hotel, 75–7; question of his
profession, medical studies, 77, 78;
proposes to resign entail of his
estates, 78; wishes to borrow Rowland Hill's pulpit, 80; meets Harriet
Westbrook, 82; progress of courtship,
82–4; comes to terms with his father
and returns to Field Place, 84; at
home, May 15–July ? 5, 1811, 84–96;
letters to Elizabeth Hitchener, 86–8;
schemes secret visit of Hogg to Field
Place, 95; in London, July 1811, 96–
7; departs to Cwm Elan, 96–100;
begins *Essays, Moral and Metaphysical*,
98; distress of mind over Elizabeth
Shelley, 92–100; deliberates marriage
with Harriet, 99–101; leaves Cym
Elan for London, 100; visits Field
Place, 101; flight to Edinburgh and
marriage, 101–2; review of his first
marriage, 103–6; invites Elizabeth
Hitchener to share his household,
105; embroilment with Field Place
over his marriage, 106–11; joined by
Hogg in Edinburgh, 107; translates a
treatise by Buffon, 108; appeals to his
father for money, 108–9; takes lodgings at York, 109; visit to Cuckfield
and Field Place, 109–11; returns to
York, 111; estrangement from Hogg,
November 1811, 111–15; at Keswick,
November 1811–February 1812, 113–
27; renewed appeals to his father, supported by Duke of Norfolk, 115–16;
attempts secret correspondence with
sister Hellen, 117; refuses to entail his
estate, 117, 118; receives £200 a year
from his father unconditionally, 118;
assaulted at Keswick, 118; meets
Southey, 120–2; makes contact with
Godwin, January 1812, 124–5; literary
projects, end of 1811, 125–7; attitude
to Elizabeth Hitchener, 126–7; plans
association for Reform, 127; arrives in
Dublin, February 1812, 127; attitude
to Irish parties, 128–30, 132; Irish
writings, 131–4; writings in hands of
Government, 140–1; proceedings in

Dublin, 134–40; at Nantgwillt, 142–6; tranquil mind and the lines *To Harriet*, 143–4; at Cwm Elan again, 146; *Letter to Lord Ellenborough*, 147, 150–2; at Lynmouth, 152; happiness and literary activity, 153; propaganda by sea and air, 153–5; the arrest of Healey and flight from Lynmouth, 154–5; at Tremadoc, 157–61; and the Embankment, 159, 160; annoyances at Tremadoc, 160–1; quarrel with Miss Hitchener, 160, 161, 167; visits London and meets Godwin, Newton, Hogg, Peacock, October–November, 1812, 161–8; becomes a vegetarian, 164–5; at the dismissal of Miss Hitchener, 168; at Tremadoc again, and tired of it, 168–9; sends money for the Hunts in prison, 170–1; feloniously assaulted at Tremadoc, 175–9; in Dublin and Killarney, 179–80; in London, 180; relations with his family and Harriet, 181–2.

Characteristics: appearance, voice, dress, 15–17, 47, 48; element of disorder, 47–9; moral duality, 20, 55, 247–8; phantasy or imagination, 5, 7, 10, 18, 20, 21; histrionic bent, 9, 16, 17; temperamental instability, 12, 15, 80, 113, 176–9; independence and strength of will, 15, 55; impatience and bitterness, 60, 80, 143; love of books, 10, 17, 24, 25, 50, 80; love of children, 18; as a lover, 18, 19, 20, 21, 60–6, 102, 126–7, 245–7; aristocratic preferences, 54; caution in theology, confidence in politics, 54–5; charity and charm, 4, 16, 18, 55–6, 164, 169–70.

Intellectual history: *see further sub* Berkeley, Bible, Christ, Condorcet, Godwin, Holbach, Hume, Kant, Locke, Lucretius, Paley, Plato, Pliny, Rousseau, Southey, Spinoza, Wordsworth.

Classical studies at Eton, 22, 23, and at Oxford, 50; no divinity at Eton, 23, 24; Gothic romance, 11, 29–38; early addiction to natural science, 9, 10, 25, and eventual attainment, 231–3; influence of James Lind, 26–9; first studies in philosophy, 25, 28, 50, 54; discovers *Political Justice*, 25 and n., 28, and is inspired, 38; the Intellectual Beauty, 38–42; political libertarianism, 51, 53; deism, 64; deism rejected in *Necessity of Atheism*, 66; exasperation of prejudice after the dismissal from Oxford, 80, 87–8; influences from Paine and

Godwin in Irish pamphlets, 131–4; at odds with Godwin on collective action, 139–40; his theories disturbed by social misery in Dublin, 137–9; inspired by *Système de la Nature*, 144, 153, 194, 232–3; *Letter to Lord Ellenborough* and zeal for liberty of the Press, 146–52; persuaded by Godwin to read history, 173; turning-point of intellectual evolution in essays and poems in or near 1816, and supervenient authority of Plato, 249; on the teaching of Christ, 248–50; diagnosis of political situation in England, 221–2; fear of a revolution, 227; priority of women's rights, 209–11; problem of sexual relations set by Godwin, 202–3, by Rousseau, 206–9, by Mary Wollstonecraft, 211–13, in Lawrence's *Empire of the Nairs*, 213–15; S.'s doctrine of the nature of Woman and free love, 58, 86, 93, 94, 114, 202–3, 215–20; immediate measures to reclaim society, 219; ideal equality, 119, 134, 195–6, 221 and n., 222; Burke in the atmosphere, 222–3; the 'apostasy' of Wordsworth and the two dissimilar minds, 222–5, 228, 229 and n., 230; God the only hope, 230; idea of a Divine Comedy taken from Southey, 88–90; the great advance foreshadowed in contemporary poetry, 230.

The animated, uncreated, ever-changing Universe, 68, 232–3, 236; the purposive 'ascent of being', 236, 237; spirit 'appended' to matter, 64, 233, 236 and n.; support given by Lucretius to S.'s cosmic scale and *anima mundi*, 233–4; fluctuation between Spinozistic pantheism and belief in the Will, 236–43; later conception of God as approachable, as the Creator, and as a lover of souls, 248, 249; Evil, 238 and n., 239, 240, 255, 257, 259, 262; decline of Nature and the 'Last Man', 227 and n., 228, 241; 'renovation of Nature', 239, 240 and n.; One and Many, Infinite and Finite, and the principle of individuation, 238, 250–8; immortality, 3, 41–2, 64, 95, 113, 119, 236–8, 240–1, 253–4, 259 n.; Christianity, 42, 57, 80, 121, 232–3; evolution of religion, 90–2, 152, 255; feeling the criterion of religious truth, 192, 243–4, 249; influence of Godwin on S.'s ethics, 196, 200, 204–5; a two-storied morality and moral endeavour, 197–201, 256; the pains of conscience an